Discourses on the Meaning of History

American University Studies

Series V
Philosophy

Vol. 23

PETER LANG
New York · Bern · Frankfurt am Main · Paris

William Kluback

Discourses on the Meaning of History

PETER LANG
New York · Bern · Frankfurt am Main · Paris

Library of Congress Cataloging-in-Publication Data

Kluback, William.
Discourses on the meaning of history/William Kluback.

p. cm.—(American university studies. Series V,
Philosophy
; vol. 23)
1. History—Philosophy. I. Title. II. Series: American
university studies. Series V, Philosophy; v. 23.
D16.8.K54   1988
901—dc19
ISBN 0-8204-0387-3   88-743
ISSN 0739-6392   CIP

CIP-Titelaufnahme der Deutschen Bibliothek

Kluback, William:
Discourses on the meaning of history / William
Kluback. – New York; Bern; Frankfurt am Main;
Paris: Lang, 1988.
  (American University Studies: Ser. 5,
  Philosophy; Vol. 23)
  ISBN 0-8204-0387-3

NE: Kluback, William: [Sammlung] ; American
University Studies / 05

© Peter Lang Publishing, Inc., New York 1988

Printed by Weihert-Druck GmbH, Darmstadt, West Germany

These Studies Are Dedicated
to

Marcel Régnier, S.J.

Xavier Tilliette, S.J.

Michel Sales, S.J.

Contents

Introduction *ix*

Introduction

A book grows from questions which, over the years, have interested us and which we have posed to ourselves in various forms. It is only when we begin to write that we understand the import of the questions that we thought were meaningful and significant. Dimensions of thought are opened and explored, contradictions arise and confuse, unexpected insights are revealed. We are engaged in realms of possibilities never envisioned at the beginnings of our endeavors. To write is a monumental act, a new world is brought into existence, the unexpected is encountered when least expected, and awareness is heightened and deepened. The thinking man knows that the exploration of any serious intellectual problem is a journey into the unknown. This occurs with problems of history. There are questions which linger and find no solution. The first signs of comprehension arise when we face the fact that solutions are not offered for every problem. Some must be lived and struggled with; we must seek accommodation. My concern has been the meaning of history. How do we come to know the past? Is there a past which can be known without the present and its peculiar existence? Does not our search into the past become preparatory for a future in which we have lodged our hopes for a better world, a more humane and reasonable life. We need the future as an object of belief; we must know that what is developing and changing will have a dimension for growth, a security for perpetuity. Yet, we are aware that the meaning of history depends on situation, that we are in a given place, at a given time, and are absorbed by the problems of our milieu. We are fallible beings, never to be in control of totality -- this we have left to God -- but we have the capacity to interpret, to comprehend our indigency, to grasp the contradictions which plague us. We think them because they are embraced in reason. In reason they are understood as contradictions. Thought doesn't remove them, but it does make it possible for us to speak about them. We also know that history is not only a study of the object, but of the subject. We want to know ourselves. We want to know why we study history, and what significance it has for our lives. "Being what I am in the situation I find myself, I address myself to history in order to form myself *for myself*."[1]

The following six essays grew from my attempt to comprehend the subject and object of history. I chose six thinkers and dialogued with them through their real and supposed contact with Kant's philosophy. I imagined Kant speaking to them, i.e., reacting to their thought as they had reacted to his. I proposed no systematic approach. I didn't attempt to create a piece of classical sculpture. The movements of thought have varied paths and we don't necessarily accept as virtuous the fact that the shortest distance between two points is the straight line. The sideroads are, at times, the most colorful. They are the sources of variation which lend the curves and tones to the otherwise sparse and Spartan quality of logical thought. Kant is at the center, because I consider him the father of the philosophy of history. In the teleological judgment, he raised that fundamental question of meaning to which I believe all serious thought must remain loyal. My purpose has been to comprehend and discuss. Each essay is such a discussion and comprehension. This is the way we enter into the philosophical discourse which we discover in thinking, because we know that we didn't invent it. Similarly, we didn't determine the world in which we developed, nor the language we speak, the history we inherit. We didn't find consistency. How could we, then, avoid contradiction? In fact, we find it valuable for the continuity of thinking. What we are sure of is that without discourse, the violence from which it is born becomes ever present and threatening.

Many times certain works stimulate the questions which continually motivate and nag us. One such influence was the article of Eric Weil, "The Interest We Take in History." Published in 1935, it can be called a very early piece, realizing that Weil died in 1977 at the age of seventy-three. The questions raised in this article were for me fundamental. They were concerned with the meaning of history. I will not outline the article in this short introduction, but two statements from it are important. "The world which man occupies is man's world, and who is concerned with it, is the man of this world. There is no man without world, and no world without him. There is only man who has a world. The animal has only a milieu, *Umwelt*. For him there is no reasonable knowledge of existence because he poses no questions."[2] Everything depends upon the questions we put to the world and to ourselves, to the few who were and are philosophers, and to those other thoughtful human beings, people who seek meaning because they want to act, who comprehend the intercourse of subject and object, that mutual dependency which gives meaning to both. Here we discover the discourse of reason. The second thought which was significant to me refers to the nature of reason. Reason liberates "man from the contingency of perspective, not because it suppresses particularity, but because it comprehends it. Reason redeems man from isolation. Man has a language which is entirely his by belonging to all. He can speak with others, he is always with others. He possesses a tradition, i.e., a history.''[3] The fact that we are not only individuals, but live in communities which have histories, forces us to comprehend ourselves not only from ourselves, but from the community in and through whom we grasp our values, traditions, and purpose.

The influence of Hermann Cohen and the School of Marburg made it imperative to see history in terms of purpose. Cohen's greatest and perhaps lasting book, *The Religion of Reason*, offers a vast panorama of historical, theological, and philosophical insights into man's attempt to comprehend history from a particular religious tradition, and yet realize this comprehension in reasonable and rational terms. The reader may shy away from the religious beliefs which permeated Cohen; but his deep and powerful search for the relationship between reason and belief is rewarding even for the most skeptical reader.

Discussions with Herder, Hume, von Ranke, and von Humboldt continue the perennial search of reason through question, discussion, and ongoing discourse. The realization that when the pen is put down thought has already gone beyond what has been said, is a cause for sadness, but also joy. There is space for new discourse and a deeper and more fruitful grasp of reason. If reason is always being discovered, if discourse is always being negated in order to be discourse, then we know that no solution is final and that we, indigent men, must learn to accommodate to our condition. Should we not say that in the finiteness of our condition we find our nobility? Are we not free in our failure to be all-knowing?

We can't escape our interest in history. This does not mean that we are necessarily interested in history *per se*. The history of our people, the nation, the history of problems and ideas, the history of immediate concerns like family and traditions continually affect us. We are never free of some interest in meaning and purpose. We might go so far as to say that history defines us. Caught between past and future we feel intimately caught up in time. We need to comprehend, we need not fear the loss of answers, the realization that every conclusion is a new question, that nothing is repeatable, and that every period of our lives brings new insights. It is good to know that when we read what we wrote at an earlier period it does, at times, make sense, but not *all* sense, and that what we will now say has similar limitations. We are free because we choose in defined situations; we are free because within limitations we make decisions. We read history from the perspective of our needs, with the desire to become more aware of ourselves. Is this not the necessary, if not the sufficient, reason to read history?

The final six chapters grew from the interpretations which emerged in the philosophical essays. They embody these interpretations but are motivated by other concerns. The theme that determines their content is the struggle between Paganism and Judaism and finally between Paganism and Christianity which embodies the earlier struggle and gives it a universal dimension. The Jesuit scholar, Gaston Fessard, with amazing intellectual and moral sensitivity has created a new vision of this eternal conflict between Paganism and Christianity. His work is revolutionary and in these chapters the attempt is made to explore the magnitude of his work. In becoming acquainted with Fessard's studies of history and dialectic we venture into that Hegelian Marxian world of conflict from which emerged the great struggle of the twentieth century. The attempt was made to understand the place of Nazism and Leninism within this conflict between the Pagan and the Jew and the Christian. No longer is the religious problem divorced from the political or the political from the philosophical. Fessard's capacity to weave them into a coherent whole is an original philosophical achievement. Since the battle against Paganism is hardly over, we must again attempt to comprehend the nature of our contemporary situation. The problem affects the values and purposes of Western civilization. These final chapters show the dangers and the perversities which lie within our traditions when what we believe is the philosophical discourse becomes the ideology of racism, class struggle and any other form of thought in which knowledge is controlled by a fixed and determined form of history in which experience is limited and what is contrary to it is declared heretical.

The work of Fessard is a profound and unique contribution to man's unending search for purpose. For the first time, theology and philosophy are united in that singular enterprise of comprehending the meaning of Israel and the Church, their inseparability and mutual dependence. The Idea of one includes the other. The pagan defiance of their human and divine reality forces them to understand each other as members of that universal community of faith that refuses to deify human knowledge and its perverse consequences.

PART I

Philosophical Discourses

1

The Meaning of History:
Wilhelm von Humboldt and Immanuel Kant

No subject has intrigued the imagination more than the self-imposed question of the meaning of history. The question is self-imposed because it doesn't have to be asked, and it is not asked unless there is a problem which arises from a concern for the meaning of history and from a reflection on the study of history. The meaning of history confronts those thoughtful and reflective individuals who take seriously the cause of events, for whom there is an intimate and decisive interrelationship between past, present, and future and for whom the idea is not a mere abstraction, but a hermeneutical and efficacious reality having the force to mold and structure reality. If we think, and we know that we do not necessarily have to think, then the study of events forces us to turn back to their cause or causes and we are engaged in that interminable search for meaning. If, for example, we turn to a study of late-nineteenth-century diplomatic history by George F. Kennan and we read the Introduction, we are faced with the problem of how we are to comprehend Russian Communism, German Nazism, the Second World War if we don't grasp the nature of that "first great Holocaust of 1914-1918 . . . the event which more than any other, excepting only, perhaps, the discovery of nuclear weaponry and the development of the population-environmental crisis, lay at the heart of the failure and decline of this Western civilization."[1] We cannot work with the events of human history unless we are willing not merely to record or chronicle but to interpret, forge problems, speak of goals; in other words, we study the course of human events because we are concerned with the destiny of humanity, because we are committed to the identification of history and morality. Nowhere do we see this point of view more clearly expressed than in the work of Wilhelm von Humboldt 1767-1835 and Immanuel Kant, and no one before these two thinkers posed more clearly and distinctly the question of the meaning of history.[2]

In 1821 von Humboldt wrote an essay, "On the Historian's Task,"[3] in which he links the search and cultivation of those qualities within himself which make it possible for him to increase and deepen his sympathy and comprehension of the humanity to which he belongs and with which he communicates. "The more profoundly the historian understands mankind and its actions through intuition and study, the more humane his disposition is by nature and circumstances, and the more freely he gives rein to humanity, the more completely will he solve the problems of his profession."[4] Preceding his remark von Humboldt makes a significant hermeneutical observation by pointing to the need for a similarity between the searching force of the intellect and the object of its search,[5] a similarity, but not an identity. This intimacy between the mind and the object of its search reveals a *pathos* which joins the object to the subject, avoids the logical formula which states that object is subject and subject is object, but embraces that warmth of feeling which this *pathos* embodies as the mind moves to penetrate the object, to transform its sensual reality into a spiritual one. This transformation and transfiguration delineate von Humboldt's principle of individuality. Whether or not we call it a metaphysic of love, encompassing individuality with its graspable and ungraspable peculiarity and distinctness, it becomes the source of that intellectual and sensual force which refuses any denial of individuality and refines and sharpens that peculiar and unique feeling for individuality. The vision of man's fate as it is reflected in the history of humanity is never separated from an immersion in the narrative of human events. There can be no escape from the knowledge of events, no hiding in the veil of ideas, no imposition of ideas which deny to them their peculiarity and distinctness; there can be only an hermeneutical relationship between the idea and the event; the idea can be a point of understanding, not an all-absorbing universal within which the individual loses its peculiarity.

Von Humboldt rejects the idea that the knowledge of history provides us with special practical wisdom allowing us to become men of affairs, knowing which political decisions to make and which to avoid because we are in the possession of a multitude of historical facts. "History's true and immeasurable usefulness lies rather in its power to enliven and refine our sense of acting on reality, and this occurs more through the form attached to events than through the events themselves. It prevents the sense of reality from slipping into the realm of pure ideas, and yet subjects it to ideas."[6] If history does not tell us what to do and what to avoid because it cannot bring forth universal patterns of behavior and because we cannot deduce from the universal to the particular with certainty and regularity, then it can achieve a higher purpose: it can create a susceptibility both for the concreteness of reality and power of the idea. It can do this in a way which allows neither the deification of the material nor the absoluteness of the idea. History creates a sense of mediation between the two; it brings forth, in Aristotle's sense, the equitable which must always rectify the absoluteness of either the material or the idea.[7] This principle of Aristotle is fundamental for any comprehension of the education which history can give to the thinker, for whom history is a problem, and it is a source of that sympathy which links us to the nature and destiny of mankind. Here we learn that mediation between the real and the ideal goes beyond the logical and is comparable to that sense of *phronesis* which Aristotle deeply valued, because it provides that insight into the particular and different which is always denied to the theoretical in its abstractness and universality. This refined sense is cultivated in the realm of action. There the subsumption of the particular in the universal does not necessarily absorb the character of the particular. It is a perspective from which it can be comprehended and spoken of reasonably as the basis for that humane attitude to difference, which is disdained and rejected where the exclusive concern for abstract truth dominates all research. History was for von Humboldt an educating process, a deeper and deeper sense of that interplay between ideas and the event, sacrificing neither idea nor concreteness, but comprehending their inner relationship and mutual dependence.

Nothing is more distracting and destructive for the thinker who searches for meaning and is committed to that discourse of reason than the accidental. The problem is not the accidental as the irreconcilable and incomprehensible which slips away from thinking, but the realization that it is thinking which makes possible the irreconcilable and incomprehensible. The accidental is a category of reason. Von Humboldt states that "an historical presentation, like an artistic presentation, is an imitation of nature. The basis of both is the recognition of the true form, the discovery of the necessary, the elimination of the accidental. We must, therefore, not disdain to apply the more readily recognizable method of the artist to an understanding of the more dubious method employed by the historian."[8] When we speak of the *Absonderung des Zufälligen*, the holding apart of the accidental, the word "elimination" seems too strong for the dialectical sense of the argument. The accidental belongs to the whole from which it is understood as the accidental. Von Humboldt makes it clear that the historian thinks from the predominant movement of ideas back into the particular and must neither become lost in the medley of the particular nor fade away in the predominance of ideas. Ideas are constantly being actualized in history. The goal is the perennial confrontation of the finite and the idea, their dialectical relationship, which is not imposed upon them, but which is original to them as moments of reason, i.e., the constituent moments of the realization of reason. This interrelationship has an aesthetic dimension which appears when we become conscious of the interplay between the understanding and the empirical. The feeling which this interplay arouses cultivates that capacity in us to perpetuate the understanding as the realization of our humaneness. The interplay is constant and structures that challenge between the understanding as lawgiving and empirical reality as receptivity; receptive not only in terms of its limitedness, but also in terms of its usefulness, its goal-oriented possibility. There is a distinction and yet a mutual dependence between what is characteristic of empirical reality and the usefulness which it achieves through the end to which it is oriented.[9] The historian is like the artist because he not only imitates reality, but constructs it. The artist comprehends the force and meaning of the productive imagination.

Von Humboldt constantly returns to the notion that the mind can grasp only what it is attuned to, what it has developed the capacity to receive. A moral problem is meaningful only to the person for whom the moral is a concern, a commitment and an action. Aristotle made this abundantly clear: "But the mass of mankind, instead of doing virtuous acts, have recourse to discussing virtue, and fancy that they are pursuing philosophy and that this will make them good men. In so doing they act like the invalids who often listen carefully to what the doctor says but entirely neglect to carry out his prescriptions."[10] History is not a theoretical exercise of the intellect, a meaningless gathering of events, the preparation of detailed chronologies, nor the heaping forth of incomprehensible statistics to prove whatever thesis is the mode of the moment; rather, it is a delineation of the ideas in which and through which we think a more humane conception of humanity. "The ideas are not borrowed by history like an alien addition, a mistake so easily made by so-called philosophical history."[11] Similarly, the dialectical relationship between the finite and the idea is not forced upon reality, but is the very constituent of reality which the mind discovers in historical awareness of itself as the realization of reason. The awareness is historical, not logical; what can be stated logically has validity in the historical process, for otherwise the logical statement would be void of meaning. The logical and the historical dimensions of reality belong together, each clarifying the other in mutual dependency. Fatal has been the separation between the logical and the historical. The comprehension of history, in any age, belongs to the ability of the mind to formulate the problem; without this capacity reason as history makes no progress in self-awareness.

At this point von Humboldt is prepared to clearly formulate the underlying assumption of his conception of the possibility of historical knowledge. "All understanding presupposes in the person who understands, as a condition of its possibility, an analogue of that which will actually be understood later: an original antecedent congruity between subject and object. Understanding is not merely an extension of the subject, nor is it merely a borrowing from the object; it is rather both simultaneously. . . . When two beings are completely separated by a chasm, there is no bridge of communication between them; and in order to understand each other, they must, in some other sense, have already understood each other."[12] History is the consequence of the mind which attempts to comprehend it. Historical truth is in the comprehending mind; it is not outside it in an amorphous transcendent conception, but in the immediacy of the relationship between subject and object, truth is in time. The assumption of "eine vonrhergängige ursprüngliche Übereinstimmung zwischen dem Subject und Object" makes us aware of that intimate and profound grasp of reason which permeates von Humboldt's conception of history. "This original and thus antecedent congruity between subject and object" becomes an hermeneutical principle making it possible to understand that this congruity can be formulated logically because it is the ground of reason but that its actualization, its historical realization is always inadequate and partial. The subject is never adequate to the object, nor is the object adequate to the subject. The course of human history is a meditation upon this lack of congruity between subject and object, the violence which is born in this lack; the periods of progress and regression reflect the success and failure of reason to comprehend man's sensuous existence, the failure to overcome his violence and to make it a meaningful part of his existence. Reason is not a natural expression of man; it is acquired through struggle and sacrifice, and its success has no necessity. Von Humboldt reflects upon that original nature of reason and reflects in that circular way of all profound thought, knowing that the end is the beginning and the beginning the end. "The more deeply, therefore, the soul of a nation feels everything human, the more tenderly, purely and diversely it is moved by this, the greater will be its chance to produce historians in the true sense of the word."[13] Von Humboldt never allowed the peculiarity of individuality to submerge the cosmopolitanism which impregnates his devotion to reason. In this respect he remains close to both Kant and Hegel, conceiving the history of mankind as the true object of the historian's concern in which the nation-state has a role but one that is always subordinate to the higher goal of a more reasonable existence.[14] Whatever forces and whatever forms history brings forth, the ultimate significance of these belongs to that wider and deeper struggle between the universal and the particular, the realization of the idea in the finite. The universality of the moral remains the hermeneutical guide for whatever form the empirical may embody. Although we speak of the universality of the moral, we can equally speak of the uniqueness of its individuality. Universality in the depth of its reality is experienced in the intimacy of individuality. "For the individual cannot be thus split up, analyzed and judged according to experiences which, having been derived from its multitude, are supposed to be applicable to the multitude."[15] The individual and the universal are both moments of reason through which the discourse of reason overcomes the violence which is at the ground of its being and threatens it at every moment. Von Humboldt is correct in viewing individuality as a unique force necessary for a comprehension of the history of humanity. He is even more correct in grasping this force as a constituent moment of that cosmopolitanism upon which the development of mankind depends.

Von Humboldt was deeply aware that the capacity to think reality has its source in our being able to stand apart from it; to create and experience the highest intellectual and moral values depended upon our being other to the reality in which our empirical existence was circumscribed. "However one proceeds, the realm of appearances can only be understood from a point outside it, and the circumspect stepping outside of it is as free from danger as error is certain, if one blindly locks oneself up in it. Universal history cannot be understood without world governance."[16] Deeply ingrained in von Humboldt's thought is the realization that man's development depends upon a condition of freedom and the co-existence of variety among human beings. We can suppose that "breakthroughs" in ideas occur in those societies where the confrontation of ideas is sharpest and deepest, where the challenge of existence, both physical and intellectual, arouses the need for meaningful and purposeful response. In an earlier fundamental text, *The Limits of State Action* (1792), von Humboldt enunciated this idea: "And is it not exactly this which so inexpressibly captivates us in contemplating the age of Greece and Rome, and which in general captivates any age in contemplating a remote one? Is it not that these men had a harder struggle with fate to endure, and harder struggles with their fellow-men? That greater and more original energy and individuality constantly encountered each other, and created wonderful new forms of life."[17] Again and again von Humboldt stresses his fundamental commitment to freedom and the efficacious effects of reciprocity on all levels of existence. Deeper and more fundamental

than ideologies and nationalistic creeds, von Humboldt expresses an abiding belief, i.e., that philosophical belief fundamental for true philosophical discourse,
in the freedom of ideas which develops in confrontation, in that dialectic of reality in which the power of negation is the driving force of genuine intellectual
life. It is this description of intellectual life which is the task of the historian to
formulate and develop; the secret of human history is its comprehension of freedom as the dimension in which the true discourse of reason is realized.

If the secret of human history, of a more humane existence among men is
the degree of freedom which society makes possible and the consequent mutual
effects which it brings forth, then freedom and responsibility become the ultimate goal of mankind. Von Humboldt was convinced "that men are not uniting
themselves in order to forgo any portion of their individuality, but only to lessen
the exclusiveness of their isolation; it is not the object of such a union to transform one being into another, but to open communication between them. . . .
Hence the principle of the true art of social intercourse consists in a ceaseless
endeavor to grasp the innermost individuality of another, to avail oneself of it,
and, with the deepest respect for it as the individuality of another, to act upon
it."[18] It is remarkable to find that the principle of freedom is no mere abstraction, but one that belongs to the realization of the individual as a unique and inviolable being whose idea is rooted in the nature of existence, or to be more precise, is the condition of all legitimate societal existence. Rarely has the principle
of individuality and freedom been so intimately joined to societal life and made
dependent upon each. Nowhere among his contemporaries were these ideas so
deeply rooted in a societal existence. Only in Kant's notion of *sensus communis*
and *sensus privatus* can we find similar ideas. Society exists to foster communication, to end isolation, to realize the potentiality of each in comparison and
contrast with every other. Communication is the source of meaningful and reasonable life, to be left as free and unhindered as possible for growth and development. The object of all communal life is the protection of this dimension of
freedom. "For every restrictive institution comes into collision with the free and
natural development of energy, and gives rise to an infinite multiplicity of new
circumstances. . . . Anyone who has an opportunity of occupying himself with
the higher departments of state administration, must certainly feel conscious
from experience how few political measures have really an immediate and absolute necessity. . . ."[19] There is no glorification of the state and its divine necessity and purpose, its spiritual place in a divinely ordained order, but the
deeper realization that freedom and individuality are the highest and most sacred

values which can give meaning to human history. If we can speak of the historian's task, if we want to ponder the meaning of history, if from the study of history there are questions which we must pose and answers which we must seek, then we realize that the possibility to be constantly open to history and its values depends upon freedom, upon a society which makes such freedom possible, where the mind is not forced to do obedience to an already formulated and dictated social, economic, or political ideology that molds the historical development to some arbitrary purpose. Freedom and individuality by their very nature make it possible to be open to the new and changing, to the belief that every stage of man's development brings forth a possibility of reason which in and through itself becomes the source of its negation to rise again to a different and changed perspective. The discourse of reason, the dialectic of freedom is the never-ceasing confrontation of universal and individual, the communication of the reasonable revealing in its freedom the potentiality of reason at every stage of the development. "The goal of history can only be the actualization of the idea which is to be realized by mankind in every way and in all shapes in which the finite form may enter into a union with the idea. The course of events can end only at the point where both are no longer capable of further mutual integration" ("nicht mehr zu durchdringen im Stande sind").[20] If we throw open again the question of the historian's task, we find that, although von Humboldt found it different from the philosopher's, it attempts to reveal the struggle of an idea for realization, i.e., to have effect on the course of events, to have the force to clarify and formulate the spirit of the age. Both philosopher and historian have the same task; neither must impose arbitrarily upon reality nor force reality to be molded by preconceived ideas. The philosopher as well as the historian should be possessed of that freedom and susceptibility which make it possible to grasp the interrelationship between the idea and the concrete in a way that does violence to neither one nor the other. The dialectic is not mechanical; its subtlety comprehends its negation in all its extensive dimensions, realizing through it the scope of historical variety and individuality; its demise lies in the purity of abstraction.

The moral remained fundamental to von Humboldt's cosmopolitanism and sense of individuality. "The feeling of the inadequacy of human strength to the full performance of the moral law, the profound consciousness that the most virtuous man is he who feels most inwardly conscious of how unattainably high the law is exalted above him, inspires awe -- a sensation which seems to be no more shrouded in a corporeal veil than is necessary not to dazzle mortal eyes by the full splendour. Now, when the moral law obliges us to regard every man as an end in himself, it becomes fused with that feeling for the beautiful which loves to animate the merest clay . . . and embraces man all the more completely and beautifully in that it is independent of intellectual concepts. . . ."[21] This moral and aesthetic universe, open to the universal and the individual, its profound insight into man's struggle with his inadequacy for both the moral and aesthetic that is at the same time the source of his grandeur and nobility, founds the sense of history and the historian's task. History in its noblest meaning is philosophy, and philosophy in the comprehension of itself as reason, is history. From the realm of reason, its cosmopolitanism, its sense of variety, and its concept of development as the interrelationship between the finite and idea, von Humboldt makes it possible for us to pose that question concerning the meaning of history and to continue with him its perennial discourse which each age takes up again, rethinks, and continues. The reading of von Humboldt reminds us again and again of his closeness to Kant. We must now ask how fundamental was the intimacy of ideas and problems.

To begin with a lapidary statement, we could say that Kant was not interested in history as such; he was not concerned with the historical development of societal institutions, but he was deeply concerned with history when he was involved with moral questions. What fundamentally interests Kant is the moral dimension of mankind.[22] What he comprehends as the ground of this interest is that moral belief in an article in the *Berlinische Monatschrift* (1793): "And however uncertain I may be and may remain as to whether we can hope for anything better for mankind, this uncertainty cannot distract from the maxim I have adopted, or from the necessity of assuming for practical purposes that progress is possible."[23] Belief in moral progress is an obligation; we have no empirical evidence either to confirm or to deny that the course of events show purpose or reveal the possibility of moral progress, yet the moral, forces us to wager on the moral purpose of man and history. We can judge little from the short span of our individual life; we must assume that the meaning of events belongs to a future which cannot be determined, but only believed in. The meaning of what we accomplish in our lives belongs to those who come after us; what we know is that in the space and time given to us our obligation is to realize our freedom as reasonable and reflective beings, aware that this obligation is not universal and is not necessarily assumed by those beings for whom the reasonable and the reflective are not moral needs, i.e., for which there is no sympathy. Where this moral is a responsibility, there history has meaning as the realm in which the moral finds its actualization and ultimate realization. History and the moral belong together where there is a commitment to the future, to that moral hope which makes real the struggle which moral reason assumes with the indifference of human action and behavior to purpose and the idea.

From the point of view of the moral, time and space are not just "sources of knowledge, pure forms of sensible intuitions," the indifferent possibility of the being or nonbeing of objects, but "sacred" dimensions in which the majesty of the moral law and the worth of man take on a unique and an all-embracing significance. Emil Lask saw the greatness of Kant in the fact that he was able to go beyond "die ertötete Sinnlichkeit," that he produced a *Critique of Practical Reason,* or *Metaphysics of Morals* and a transcendental logic.[24] Not a series of rules of conduct, nor wise sayings and thoughts, but serious reflections on the nature of the moral, which I believe is a radical revision of the forms of time and space, a separation of the moral from the arbitrary and indifferent, that profound separation of the realm of value, i.e., of ideas, from the profane realm of empirical existence. If we conceive of time and space within these two realms we have the history of two "vessels," we have a "sacred and a profane history," we have that radical dualism which is the fundamental mark of Kantian thought. The dualism is fundamental in its interrelationship. The dualism sets aside every superficial monism because it recognizes that serious and meaningful moral thinking is dependent upon contradiction, confrontation, and challenge. We now ask, can there be a meaningful moral life without radical evil? "A temporal, unknowable, ungraspable fact in itself, fact and act before every fact and act, radical evil is the condition of the possibility of a moral life and its recognition is a grasp of life insofar as it is moral."[25] Man was not given an evil character; he is the author of it. If given such a character, man's freedom and responsibility would be meaningless. On the other hand, the good or evil which man does precedes his choice for the one or for the other; the good and the evil are in him antecedent to every experiential free choice. Good and evil are not revealed in and dependent upon experience; if experience is changed, good and evil are not affected. Good and evil constitute the very being of man before man as moral awareness comes to know that free choice is his responsibility, and the dimensions of the choice are the eternal constituents of his being. The history of man's moral life begins with evil; the struggle for the good we can term "sacred history." The neglect and rejection of the moral problem we can term "profane history." The terms are hermeneutical ones used to increase the understanding of the conflict inherent in moral life.

Kant clarified the issue in his famous treatise *Religion within the Limits of Reason Alone.* There he said that the proposition "Man is evil, can only mean he is conscious of the moral law, but has nevertheless adopted into his maxim the occasional deviation therefrom. He is evil by nature means but this, that evil can be predicated of man as a species; not that such a quality can be inferred from the concept of the species."[26] Man does not have to do evil. He is free, conscious of the moral law, but he is insufficient and inadequate for the good. As a moral being the awareness of his insufficiency constitutes the quality of his moral life. Man's moral history is the delineation of this struggle; the wager that moral man places in the future, as sacred time. What remains unfulfilled now will find its realization because the source of moral faith is the revolutionary content of history.

Kant speaks of radical evil because he wants to understand a reason that is moral, a reason that comprehends itself in and through its negation, in the violence which is sin, in the realization that the privation of reason lies at the ground of reason, as evil lies at the ground of the good. The moral history of man is the struggle with the ever-present reality of sin both within him and in the world. The challenge of the profane to the sacred is not one that comes from without, but one that lives and corrupts within the sacred itself. The anguish and anxiety that are man's, the needy and dependent being, are the soil in which the moral grows in conflict and contradiction. Without knowledge, without assurance that the good will be victorious, man can bring forth the noblest of attitudes; he can believe, he can hope, he can accept the challenge of the moral in an amoral world. But this same man knows himself to be insincere, selfish, weak, and capable of doing harm; he knows that evil on its most sophisticated level is not the foul deed or the repulsive action, but is a subtle and polished sort of deception which lies in the good, is covered with the good, works through the good, and accomplishes the destruction and violence for which we are unprepared and unaware. If we speak then of moral history and compare it with profane history, we must be aware that the two lines of development are not simply and arbitrarily divided from each other, but that their interrelationship and intercourse are intimate and interwoven. At times we can see clearly their outlines, but this belongs more easily to the past than to the present, leaving aside the unknown of the future. The separation of good and evil remains an enigma both for the observer of the self as well as for the observer of the external world. Knowing that evil is rooted in the good, that morality demands the realization of its negation, Kant recognizes the unredeemable separation of good and evil, finite and infinite. As long as we speak of man we must insist upon this dualism with all its tensions and stress, because in the reconciliation of good and evil, man's moral life is transcended and man as a being of needs, whose insufficiency and inadequacy are the source of his concern, is transfigured into a divinity. The great conflict of human history has no final victory, but a ceaseless challenge and confrontation without which mankind has no life or meaning. Satisfaction and salvation remain embedded in struggle and striving.[27] The monisms of the romantics and Hegel find no function for evil, and in this sense Kantian dualism is reduced to either Novalis' doctrine of love or Hegel's absolute. Kant is more at home with the unending striving of Faust.

Emphasizing the question of radical evil in this discussion of the meaning of history is significant because the perspective is focused upon the need which man has to humanize, to make more humane, his individual and societal life.[28] If we take seriously the problem of the meaning of history we cannot look aside when we face a discussion of man's nature, for it seems impossible that any sense can be made of history if we do not at first make some sense of man, his capacities, and his limitations. Goodness has and needs no history; again and again Kant repeats the basic fact that history begins with evil; without this fundamental notion it would be difficult to comprehend our concern and need for self-awareness, civilization as preparatory ground for moral life. "Because we know the enemy within us, our inability to resist temptation, the perversion of our intentions, we take seriously the good principle in us, the demand that we work to strengthen and enhance its capacity to resist perversion; we see Jesus as the moral revolutionary, the teacher of morality, the source of our strength and hope. His revolutionary stature is in the moral victory over evil; but this does not take place in His divinity, but in His humanity."[29] The moral victory lies in the power of such revolutionaries, for the struggle is man's and belongs to this world where assurances of success are few and far between. These revolutionaries bear witness to what Kant would call "a revolution in man's disposition," but we can ask about the origin of this cause and find ourselves facing two types of origins: "Es kann entweder, als Vernunft -- oder als Zeitursprung in Betrachtung gezogen werden."[30] This division between origin in time and origin in reason is basic for an understanding of history which begins in freedom, in reason and the history of causation in time. The origin in reason puts aside the contingent nature of man, rejects the attempt, as a contradiction, to see the origin of man's moral character in time. The temporal linkage of events to each other, in which man is caught with his personal and interpersonal relationships and dependencies, denying uniqueness to any event affirms that the pattern has appeared before and will appear again, a repetition, an *anakuplosis,* an eternal return. It is in the origin of reason that the true history of freedom begins, the breakthrough into profane temporality, as the revolution of intention, as the revolutionary moral person. Man does not create reason but is created by it; we discover in ourselves -- in our noumenal reality -- that there is an "idea of duty" by which and through which we break into the indifference of action, the arbitrariness of life and history; we rupture the circle of repetition and resignation; we are aroused by the "majesty of the moral law"; we become aware of the meaning which is incited in us of the "sublimity of our moral destiny." We discover what is already there, awakened either by nature or the revolutionaries -- the moral law -- who belong to history and who stand in defiance of the world about them. These are the men in whom the ideas of freedom, immortality, and God become efficacious, men who philosophically believe in the moral law and whose choice expresses "a confidence of attaining a purpose the furtherance of which is a duty, but whose achievement is a thing of which we are unable to perceive the possibility. . . . Faith as *habitus,* not as *actus,* is the moral attitude of reason in its assurance of the truth of what is beyond the reach of theoretical knowledge."[31] The realization of our moral destiny raises us above and beyond the world of our empirical existence, but it doesn't raise us out of it, leaving it to be condemned as a perverse and sinful world; we rise above it to return to it, to think it and to act in it, knowing that we are not angelic souls, never free of our needs and dependence and forever responsible in this world, i.e., responsible for its moral progress, for a more humane societal life, for perpetual peace, for all those ideas the realization of which we have no assurance, but only our faith and hope. Through reason we gain our moral perspective both toward ourselves and toward the world outside us. "The majesty of the moral law (as of the law of Sinai) instills awe (not dread which repels, nor yet charm which invites familiarity); and in this instance, since the ruler resides within us, this *respect,* as of a subject toward his ruler, awakens a *sense of sublimity* of our own destiny which enraptures us more than any beauty."[32] These two worlds are estranged from each other, but they do not exclude each other; there exists a dependence which reflects a moral command making us responsible as moral beings in a world that is indifferent and inadequate and in which the realization of moral civilization makes us optimists one day and pessimists the next. Kant was fully aware of how our moods change as we become involved in human affairs. There is no logical bridge between these worlds; there is only responsible action and striving; there is that search for the reasonable discourse which men have sought for and enhanced through the generations, but which they know to be fragile and can be lost at any time. Kant's view rises above a simple and steady progress of reason realizing at every stage a higher and profounder moment of itself; it is more than the becoming of the subject of philosophy that has found its path and moves forward with an unshakable steadiness.33

Whatever meaning the world comes to have depends upon the ability of man to make choices, and this aptitude of a being to choose in freedom determines the moral quality of his world. On the other hand, we can also say that the world has meaning which is not merely dependent upon us and our capacity to impose, for if what is imposed has no capacity to be received, it would be futile. The world *can be* moral; *man can be* moral. Stained with evil, man has the opportunity to bring forth a world that is more humane and just; from this perspective history has meaning. Kant recognized the self-imposed tutelage of man which flowed not only from external forces, but from internal ones as well; he knew clearly the difference between the claim that we live in an enlightened age and an Enlightenment. No, the age is not an enlightened one, but there is an Enlightenment, there is belief that in a reasonable world, in a critical philosophy and a philosophically imbued religion, we can help lift the burden of historical intolerance and dogma. "Enlightenment is man's emergence from his self-incurred immaturity. Immaturity is the inability to use one's own understanding without the guidance of another. The immaturity is self-incurred if its cause is not lack of understanding. The motto of the enlightenment is therefore: Sapere aude! Have the courage to use your own understanding."34 We can hardly imagine the possibility of using our critical faculties unless we are free, unless we can give reasonable purposes to our lives, unless we have the capacity and power to set goals, to ask teleological questions, to understand that intimate and vital relationship which exists between the history of man's freedom and his "self-incurred immaturity" and the reality of radical evil. Eric Weil puts the issue clearly: "For us the good takes shape on the base of evil; the function of evil is precisely to allow the good to appear, appearing to us such as we are: finite and reasonable beings, reasonable in our finitude, good and bad, but good in our badness and capable of making progress once we have recognized the enemy within."35 The more we are able to come to terms with this struggle of good and evil, the more we can recognize that in the depths of Kant's thought lies the worth of the individual who achieves an awareness of this worth and dignity not from divine legislation or fiat, but from a slow and even deeper comprehension of the meaning of freedom as critique and as philosophical faith. The fundamental categorical imperative is expressed in the *Metaphysics of Morals,* no longer as a noble sentiment to which we can all give proper lip service or take pleasure in the beauty and sublimity of the expression, but stands in contradiction to our basic inclinations and motives: "every man for himself: God for us all." The categorical imperative is practical, and for this reason its weight and its responsibility overcome and dazzle most men. Kant states: "But how can it be required, as a duty, that we go beyond benevolence in our wishes regarding others (which cost us nothing) and make this benevolence practical, so that everyone who has the means should be beneficent to the needy? Benevolence is satisfaction in another's happiness (well-being); but beneficence is the maxim of making another's happiness one's end, and the duty of beneficence is the necessitation that reason exercises on the agent to adopt this maxim as universal law."[36] It would be hard to understand the meaning and import of this imperative unless we first grasped Kant's reflections on radical evil as a basic and constituent dimension of his moral philosophy and his consequent interest in the meaning of the moral history of man. In Kant's last reflections on man's moral future the tone is pessimistic. Whatever be the improvements in man, societal life, a lessening of violence, the creation of a more cosmopolitan society, even the possibility of better personal relationship, do not add up to a greater moral capacity. "Such developments do not mean, however, that the basic moral capacity of mankind will increase in the slightest, for this would require a kind of new creation, or supernatural influence. For we must not expect too much of human beings in their progressive improvements or else we shall merit the scorn of those politicians who would gladly treat man's hopes of progress as the fantasies of an overheated mind."[37] Do we dismiss these remarks as those of a tired, saddened, and now brooding old man witnessing the bloodletting of the French Revolution, the chaos of European politics, or do we find a consistency in a thinker who was never naive about man's nature and who never failed to come to terms with the daemonic reality of human life, who did not fail to speak of radical evil and made us aware, as few before him, that the question of man's moral development needs not only the structure of the practical reason, to lay the *foundations* of the metaphysics of morals, but man's nature, sin and the daemonic. If Kant made it possible for us to think about the meaning of history, he made it so only because he confronted the problem of evil and found that it alone made possible our capacity to think about the good, to comprehend the need for philosophical faith, and to affirm the courage to hope. We should make a clear distinction in Kantian thought between his concern with the structure and foundation of the moral and his meditations on man, who with his needs, dependencies, inadequacies, strives to function in a morally indifferent world with a consciousness of morality, who attempts to comprehend what the past has been and what the future may hold both for the individual, the community of nations, which are not yet a community, and for men who still function in self-imposed ignorance and tutelage. We may ask if the moral law has meaning even in the formulation of its most practical application? We can hearken back to Aristotle and say that it moves not as an object of love, but as a loved object. With this love the moral law realizes its efficacy in reality; it is the history of this efficacy, its revolutionary nature and effect, which gives us insight into that great struggle of human history which puts the moral law against that maxim which puts the moral law against that maxim which declares "every man for himself."

We have considered some aspects of the historical and moral reflections of Wilhelm von Humboldt and Kant. We speak of philosophers not to draw conclusions from them and be satisfied with the neatness of our results, but to think with them in all their complexities, inconsistencies, and insights. For the philosopher the dialogue is perennial and circular, every new moment of the dialogue returns us to its beginning from which we again begin to think. History is the series of reflections that take up again the discourse of reason in all its dimensions and rethinks the discourse. With Kant and von Humboldt we have attempted to think again the meaning of philosophical history and its intimate tie to the moral, to philosophical faith, and to the metaphysical ideas which move and determine the discourse of reason. Both men were concerned about that delicate interrelationship between finiteness and the idea; both realized that the purity of either would be its demise, that both live only in confrontation with each other. The deeper the contradiction, the deeper the challenge; the sense of the dialectics of life pulsates where confrontation and contradiction heighten the meaning and the comprehension of that interplay between the good and the evil.

2

Hume and Kant:
The Nature of the Historical Object

We can legitimately ask why we can understand, but not explain history. We can come to terms with the question if we put forth some preliminary remarks indicating that there is a difference between understanding and explaining, between the idea and the concept, between what cannot be postulated, but only imputed. We could say that history can be understood because it has "no existence of its own,"[1] because it is only within ourselves that we confront history. With an interpretation of history we do not postulate universal consent necessitated by the clarity of conceptual deduction, but we can, through reasonable discussion, impute agreement which is subject to continual refinement and clarification. Thinking about history forces us to an awareness that the idea as a principle of understanding cannot and should not be confused with a principle of explication which is grounded in conceptual clarity and causal relationship. "We seek understanding of human affairs but approach this endeavor not as 'master of facts,' but as the source of meaning; we are necessitated to continuous discoveries, developments, and realization."[2] Explication forces us to move from cause to effect, from past to present, to indulge our hope that we could find that undeniable linkage which would explain history as a science. With moderation and prudence we turn to the understanding which allows us to proceed from the present to the past, subordinating the need to explain to the search, in and through the understanding for that changing but perennial discourse of the reasonable, the discourse of meaning. We put aside the explanation for the understanding because we know that we cannot reduce historical reality to scientific fact; we cannot reduce interpretation, with its infinite detail and possibility, the source of imagination and wonder, to the temporal and spatial indifference of the conceptual and the theoretical. When the philosopher speaks of philosophical history, he speaks of his discourse with the past from his values in the present. He proposes to show how he understands the past; he does not aim to explain it. The object of history is similar to a judgment of taste; at best we can as-

sume the concurrence of reasonable beings, i.e., we can assume that their understanding makes it possible for them to grasp the probabilities of interpretation,
to grasp the idea that the world has multiple meaning and value, because man
comprehends his action in the world as one who only imputes meaning both to
his inner and outer life.

The meaning of history is an essential part of Kant's philosophy at that
moment when he poses the significance of the teleological question, i.e., when
the questions of purpose and meaning become fundamental. We go to history in
an attempt to comprehend the institutions men have brought forth making it possible for them to live with each other in a reasonable manner, control their passions, and make possible the expansion of the arts and sciences. Man reflecting
on himself reflects upon history. The awareness of the inseparability between a
philosophical anthropology and a philosophical history belongs to the Scottish
philosopher David Hume. His capacity to realize the the study of history is *the*
essential philosophical occupation made it possible for him to comprehend the
fundamental dialectic of thought and development, the need to know events of
societal progress, and to comprehend the gap which lies between moral sentiment and political behavior. Hume explored the history of institutions in England, Greece, Rome, and Europe to derive an understanding of the interaction
of private and public morality. "But a republic can and free government would
be an obvious absurdity, if the particular checks and controls, provided by the
constitution, had really no influence, and made it not the interest even of bad
men, to act for the public good."[3] The study of history reveals a relationship
between morality and civic institutions indicating that if men act as a consequence of interest, and not from the abstract formulations of reason, i.e., if
morality is not a consequence of theory, but an analysis of action, then, Hume
believed, the "natural depravity of mankind" is not an abstract theory needed to
prove some theological doctrine necessitating a cosmic drama of sin and redemption, but has meaning to the degree that this depravity is realized or di-
minished by the societal condition in which man functions.

> Political writers have established it as a maxim, that, in contriving any
> system of government, and fixing the several checks and controls of the
> constitution, every man ought to be considered a *knave* and to have no
> other end, in all his actions, than private interest. By this interest, we
> must govern him, and by means of it, make him, notwithstanding his
> insatiable avarice and ambition, cooperate to public good.[4]

If we speak of progress in human affairs and if history allows us to confirm this possibility, then we comprehend this progress as the search for moderation both among men and in the structure of political institutions. The study of history is undertaken because we are concerned about the advancement of those human qualities which refine our feelings and moderate our passions. The truth, the evident, the intelligible we can affirm with a coolness and tranquility; they satisfy the speculative curiosity and fulfill our desires for research; but those moral attitudes which correspond to honor, generosity, and nobility permeate our public and private relationship and create that sympathy and interest in humanity which belong to our existence in ever wider and deeper circumstances and outlooks. In fact, the cultivation of moral sentiments forces us to seek that communicability which makes possible reasonable agreements among men. We should be aware that agreement is not to be achieved through theoretical speculation or deductive reasoning; we are necessitated to appeal to the interest of the moment, to what strikes the mind with a clarity and preciseness and causes us to give immediate adherence. What we realize is the fact that human behavior and action do not proceed from theory and speculation, but from those interests which motivate action. We are compelled to convince, to be reasonable, and to comprehend the interest of the people we are speaking to and attempting to motivate. Hume believes that if we want to motivate the actions of men we must comprehend that the situation in which they exist determines their attitudes and characteristics. There is no abstract man, there is man in situation and in society, and this society has a history, a possible progressive development. A philosophical history is an attempt to grasp this relationship between situation, fortune, and character.

Hume writes philosophical history; he asks the question of meaning; he structures the history of society from the point of view of the interrelationship between morality and political institutions.[5] In other words, the study of history presupposes that the thinker begins with certain assumptions with which and from which he organizes the past; there is no abstract thinker. The past is created from the values of the present. If we can speak of history as the expression of human freedom, as an act of the imagination, it is because history is the embodiment of that discourse of the reasonable through which we attempt to give meaning to both internal and external reality. Hume begins his *Enquiry Concerning the Principles of Morals* with some reflections on man's nature which make it possible for us to grasp the nature of human possibilities when not distorted by manners and habits destructive to moderation and reasonableness. Hume says:

> Disputes with men pertinaciously obstinate in their principles are of all others the most irksome; except, perhaps, those with persons entirely disingenuous, who really do not believe the opinions they defend, but engage in controversy from affectation, from a spirit of opposition, or from a desire of showing wit and ingenuity superior to the rest of mankind. . . . And as reasoning is not the source whence either disputant derives his tenets, it is in vain to expect that any logic, which speaks not to the affectations will ever engage him to embrace sounder principles.[6]

The problem of political and historical understanding necessitates a philosophical anthropology making it possible to avoid rash and meaningless generalities about man's assumed rational nature, his inherited goodness, and his predisposition for knowledge. Hume was convinced that the term "man" was indiscriminate; in its abstract form it was meaningless.

> The difficulties which nature has placed between one man and another is so wide, and this difference is still so much further widened by education, example and habit, that where the opposite extremes come at once under apprehension, there is no scepticism so scrupulous and scarce any assurance so determined, as absolutely to deny all distinction between them.[7]

Hume had little hope that reason could convert men to moderate behavior or action; left to themselves, he believes it hardly possible for them to move toward common sense and reason. The awareness of these profound differences among men forces us to treat the problems no longer with generalities, but requires a comprehension of the habits and manners with which each group of men function and derive institutions. Assuming that there are still "images of Right and Wrong," the problem is to develop those habits and manners which make it possible for us to avoid the wrong and seek the good. In other words, not through moral speculations, but through habit and action is moral behavior made possible. "Extinguish all the warm feelings and prepossessions in favour of virtue, and all disgust or aversion to vice; render men totally indifferent towards these distinctions, and morality is no longer a practical study, nor has any tendency to regulate our lives and actions.''[8] The self-imposed and incurred tutelage of man denies him awareness of the distinctions of moral behavior and the responsibility for actions; but there is a broader dimension to consider: the moral state of man viewed from the study of history.

Hume wrote *The History of England, from the Invasion of Julius Caesar to the Revolution of 1688* (1754-62). It should be noted that the first volume dealt with the reign of the first two Stuarts, James I and Charles (1603-49) and appeared in 1754, and the second volume, dealing with the commonwealth and the reign of Charles II and James II (1649-88), was published in 1756. Whatever the arrangement or the order of appearance, our concern is with the attitude towards history and its relationship to politics and morality. Fundamental is the fact that history and value judgments are inseparable. History, we must repeat, is similar to a judgment of taste: its meaning cannot be derived from conceptual deduction, its meaning presupposes a group of assumptions and interests whose reasonableness should elicit sympathetic understanding and discussion from cultivated men, its purpose is to refine our moral attitudes. We can speak of an *ought* to elicit; we assume the comprehension of other men; we assume communicability and a common sense, and from these we solicit agreement and comprehension. We know that in offering ideas we are appealing to the understanding and not to cognition; we seek perspectives and not definite concepts; we are involved in the indeterminate and have avoided the determinate. A philosophical history is not a scientific one, if such a one is at all possible. Philosophic history deals with materials for which ideas are only possibilities; they embrace and circumscribe indeterminately; they are neither inductive nor deductive; they are stimuli for the imagination, they embody values, they seek out agreement, they prepare the way for the continuous dialogue of discourse of meaning, they shun ideological captivity.

Hume fills his narratives with philosophical reflection, and the few illustrations that I offer I believe indicate that history can be read meaningfully only if we begin with moral assumptions and read the past in terms of the present and the future. Coming to the period of Edward V and Richard III, having surveyed periods of earlier barbarism, Hume speaks now of the dawn of civility and science:

> The view of human manners, in all their variety of appearances, is both
> profitable and agreeable; and if the aspect in some periods seems horrid

and deformed, we may thence learn to cherish with greater anxiety that science and civility which has so close a connection with virtue and humanity, and which, as it is a sovereign antidote against superstition, is also the most effectual remedy against vice and disorders of every kind.[9]

History gives insights, but these insights complement in a very significant way those which we achieve through speculation, analysis, and generalizations. The uniqueness of Hume's study of English history lies in the fact that although in his *Treatise* and *Enquiries* he developed theories of knowledge and morality, he found it necessary to turn to the study of political and institutional history and realized an interpretation and comprehension of human events inseparable from the narrative of historical development. In the same chapter Hume puts forth a thesis which is basic to his understanding of societal progress and his philosophy of history: "The use, progress, perfection and decline of arts and science, are curious objects of contemplation, and intimately connected with a narration of civil transactions. The events of no particular period can be fully accounted for, but by considering the degrees of advancement which men have reached in those particulars."[10] Hume was convinced that there is a closely linked relationship between the advance of the fine arts and the levels of sociability and communicability. It is at this point that Hume develops a clear and precise attitude towards the meaning of history, the center of which is the increasing sociability and communicability of men through the advance and realization of an enriched science and a cultivated leisure serving the arts.

In a remarkable essay, "Of Refinements in the Arts," Hume puts forth two notions: "first, that the ages of refinement are both the happiest and most virtuous, secondly, that wherever luxury ceases to be innocent, it also ceases to be beneficial; when carried a degree too far, is a quality pernicious, though perhaps not the most pernicious to political society."[11] The cultivation of the mind and moral feelings enhances our appreciation of beauty and science, encourages benevolence and beneficence, refines the sense of taste through moderation, encourages an avoidance of extremes, discourages the violence of ideologies which belong to the "pertinaciously obstinate" and those insensitive beings for whom moral distinctions have no reality and who practice disputation merely to show opposition and false ingenuity.

> The Spirit of the age affects all the arts, and the minds of men being once roused from their lethargy and put into fermentation, turn themselves on all sides and carry improvements into every art and science. Profound ignorance is totally banished and men enjoy the privilege of rational creatures, to think as well as to act, to cultivate the pleasures of the mind as well as those of the body.[12]

The realization that the cultivation of the arts and sciences belongs to the development of civility, that sociability, humanity, and the feeling of sympathy are tied to the arts and sciences, makes it possible for Hume to grasp the meaning of history as that advancement of society. In it he believed that politics, the arts, and the sciences interact upon each other; and that the free play of attitudes, the force of the productive imagination, the need for political moderation influence and condition each other in such a way that politics and the arts are no longer to be held apart or function in separate realms. It is to the esteem of Hume's historical thinking that he saw these connections, making it possible to determine every aspect of human existence as part, as a dialectical moment, of the larger fabric designated as reality. Within the political all aspects of human creativity function and ultimately find their justification and purpose.

> The more these refined arts advance, the more sociable men become: nor is it possible, that, when enriched with science and possessed of a fund of conversation, they should be contented to remain in solitude, or live with their fellow-citizen in that distant manner, which is peculiar to ignorance and barbarous nations. They flock into cities; love to receive and communicate knowledge; to show their wit or their breeding; their taste in conversation or living in clothes and furniture.[13]

Culture is an expression of communicability and communication, the development of a public sense and responsibility, and the rejection of that private sense which keeps man from his fellow-being; this need of communication, discussion, and mutual dependency is the source of civility and that societal responsibility which is at the ground of the arts and the sciences. Hume more than any of his contemporaries was able to grasp the fact that it is from and within the political that all human creativity begins and ends; although we can legitimately assume that the arts and sciences are moments beyond the political, we can never affirm that they proceed from sources that are indifferent to the political, comprehending the political as the source through which and by which men find that space and time in which their mutual dependencies enrich their individualities and contribute to the formation of those relationships and societal groupings which make all creative work possible. "Thus *industry, knowledge* and *humanity,* are linked together, by an indissoluble chain, and are found, from experience as well as reason, to be peculiar to the more polished, and, what are commonly denominated, the more luxurious ages."[14] This interrelationship between industry, knowledge, and humanity is to be understood not in terms of individual advantage, but more properly from a more highly developed political sense making possible that moderation of institutions and attitudes which calms the passions and contribute to human contentment and reasonableness.

There is a relationship between the cultivation of pleasure and happiness and the moderation of outlook and action. "In a nation where there is no demand for superfluities, men sink into indolence, lose all enjoyment of life, and are useless to the public, which cannot maintain or support its fleets and armies from the industry of such slothful members."[15] Contentment and the enjoyment of life are not only private concerns; they are political, involving a comprehension of history as the arena for moral advancement or retrogression. Hume was aware that no political system could function where there is discontent and austerity. To advance these qualities of critique and reasonableness, men must have the proper degree of leisure and luxury which provides the enjoyment and relaxation from which and in which the political is discussed and acted upon with tranquility and moderateness so fundamental for civilized life.

Ignorance and prejudice, scientific backwardness, and moral corruption, all contribute to government through violence and ideology.

Can we expect that a government will be well modelled by a people, who know not how to make a spinning wheel, or to employ a loom to advantage? Not to mention, that all ignorant ages are infected with superstition, which throws the government off its bias, and disturbs men in the pursuit of their interest and happiness. Knowledge in the arts of government begets mildness and moderation by instructing men in the advantages of human maxims above rigor and severity, which drives subjects into rebellion, and make the return to submission impracticable, by cutting off all hopes of pardon.[16]

These lines delineate the guiding thought of Hume's political and moral attitude. Ignorance breeds superstition, and where this infection permeates society it destroys the development of those political institutions that are suitable to the reasonableness, curiosity, understanding, and moral sentiment of men for whom luxury and pleasure become synonymous with the cultivation of the arts and sciences. The refinement of man's obstinacy and knavishness, the lessening of his selfishness and violence, belong to the communication which the arts and sciences provide insofar as they require mutual dependency, moral and political cooperation, and that cultivation of sensitivity, grace, and a sense of nobility which ought to embellish every reasonable creature. Where roughness and sharpness of view and position are moderated, i.e., where man learns from reasoning and argumentation the art of sophisticated social intercourse, there political action and discourse are free of ideological and dogmatic tutelage. Wisely, Hume says, "I am convinced that, where men are most sure and arrogant, they are commonly most mistaken, and have there given reins to passion without that proper deliberation and suspense which can alone secure them from the grossest absurdities."[17] The wisdom of these lines reflects an immersion in the history of human events, and are not simply insightful observations of experiences. Whenever we read the sad history of the rein of Charles I, we are confronted with the clash of obstinate attitudes and misunderstanding, showing that the perspective of each position, that of parliament or the king, there is justification, while from the view of mutuality there is only blindness, self-interest, and suspicion. Every perspective depends on circumstance and habit, making it impervious to others. Speaking of Charles I, Hume says,

> Had he been born an absolute prince, his humanity and good sense had rendered his reign happy and memory precious. . . . Unhappily, his fate threw him into a period, when the precedents of many former reigns savoured strongly of arbitrary power, and the genius of the people ran violently towards liberty. . . . But it must be confessed that these events furnish us with another instruction, no less natural, and no less useful, concerning the madness of the people, the furies of fanaticism and the dangers of mercenary armies.[18]

These remarks from the *History* indicate how significant it was for Hume to speak of political problems from an historical perspective. Here arose the realization of the importance of time, place, character, passion, and habit in the evaluation of men and events. The ideas of development and change are vital in moral discussions which are tied to actions and attitudes, to the exceptional, to chance and the indeterminate. Here the eye must focus on the unique, the different, the peculiar; where the sense of value and freedom creates that intimacy for individuality which is so easily lost in the realm of concepts. History not only shows continuity of traits and attitudes, but it reveals that the uniqueness of situation, character, and time changes radically the course of events and nature of human relationships.

Returning again to the question of the advance of the arts, Hume makes it clear that he believes that there is a close and intimate relationship between political freedom and artistic advancement.

> If we consider the matter in a proper light, we shall find, that a progress in the arts is rather favorable to liberty, and has a natural tendency to preserve, if not produce a free government. In rude unpolished nations, where the arts are neglected, all labor is bestowed on the cultivation of the ground; and the whole society is divided into two classes, proprietors of land, and their vassels or tenants.[19]

Why, we ask, is there a relationship between progress in the arts and freedom? To this question Hume gives the significant and profound reply embodying the fundamental difference between what is an explanation and an understanding. The essential differences for Eric Weil's Kant interpretation were already revealed in Hume. Hume affirms that with an object of knowledge there must be a just and true opinion, but an aesthetic object can excite a thousand different sentiments "because no sentiment really represents what is really in the object."[20] To find agreement among men about aesthetic objects we can appeal only to taste, reasonableness, and the inclination to discourse; we can appeal to common sense. Where this common sense is highly developed and has the space and time to grow and advance, to become refined and sophisticated, the political consequences are enormous. They are conducive to that freedom of argumentation, to that prudence and moderation which make for balanced and equitable institutions. In current language, the open society is the *space* in which imagination, experimentation, responsibility, and civility find their most extensive expression; it is that *time* in which development and change introduce value and meaning freely and critically. From the point of view of the understanding, time and space become the dimensions of that reasonable discourse which through history attempts to impart and impute the freedom of development to all reality. This distinction between explanation and understanding is Hume's key to philosophical history.

On the other hand, the crudeness which permeates a society where this refinement and luxury are not conducive to freedom is clear. "Wherever luxury ceases to be innocent, it also ceases to be beneficial; and when carried to a degree further, begins to be a quality pernicious, though perhaps not the most pernicious, to political society."[21] Vicious luxury destroys a man's capacity for moderation and generosity, which are both moral and political attitudes and behaviors. Yet Hume recognized that vicious luxury even when excessive is preferable to sloth and indolence because they are more harmful to the public good. Whatever be the evaluation of the vices and their comparisons, what is important is their intimate relationship to the political, to the devlopment or harm which can be incurred by the public spirit from the spread of one and the avoidance of the other. Vices and virtues never exist in their purity or exist without each other; the problem is not the choice between vice and virtue, it is between vice and vice. Theoretically, the differentiation between vice and virtue is basic; from the perspective of society the differences are less clear and the choice less precise. The differences are choices dictated by the moment, not in exclusivities. At best, we must comprehend what Hume states when he affirms that "whatever conduct gains my approbation by touching my humanity procures also the applause of all mankind, by affecting the same principle in them; but what serves my avarice or ambition pleases these passions in me alone and affects not the avarice and ambition of the rest of mankind."[22] Hume's moral discussion, which permeates his history of England, draws the reader very close to that intimate interaction between character, circumstance, and action. We deal not with abstract men, but with beings involved in decisions, in passionate disputes with each other, with fanaticism and implacable oppositions, with varying interpretations of tradition and privileges; we deal with conditioned and habituated men. With profound sensitivity Hume illustrates this position in speaking of the fate of Charles I: "Exposed, without revenue, without arms, to the assault of furious, implacable, and bigoted factions, it was never permitted him, but with the most fatal consequences to commit the smallest mistake; a condition too rigorous to be imposed on the greatest human capacity."[23] We read these lines and ask ourselves about the meaning of history, and we cannot fail but to comprehend that if we go to history with moral seriousness, with commitment to understand the political, then we have given ourselves that philosophical task of seeking to comprehend the course of human events as that great struggle between reasonable, moderate discourse and the violence which imposes ideology, dogma, and tradition, which shows man's option to deny thought. The dialectical struggle for freedom which is rooted in the expansive dimension of reason and the reasonable leads through all those attempts to confound the objects of historical study with those of conceptual science where time and space are no longer the foundation for change, development, and ultimately for meaning, but belong simply to the cognition of the predicate.

In the "First Introduction to the Critique of Judgment" Kant clearly states that "an aesthetic judgment can thus be defined as that sort of judgment whose predicate can never be cognitive, i.e., a concept of an object, although it may contain the general subjective conditions for a cognition."[24] Although Kant relates the analysis of the aesthetic judgment to art, i.e., to the beautiful and the sublime, it seems that the real intent goes far beyond questions of beauty and sublimity. We have reached the realm of the historical object and with it the question of meaning. No longer is the focus on the *how* or causation, but we shift now to the *that* which we must attempt to understand, to study, and to think; the problem of meaning takes precedence over all other problems; the reflective judgment, subjective purposiveness, and contingency no longer contribute to the knowledge of the object, but make us aware of the powers of the mind which seek to reflect upon reality from the perspective of meaning, i.e., from purpose and comprehension. If we can consider the aesthetic object as the historical object, it is possible to read the critique of the power judgment as the critique of the historical object. Hume had made clear that geometrical propositions can be proved, "systems of physics may be controverted; but the harmony of verse, the tenderness of passion, the brilliancy of wit must give immediate pleasure."[25] He might have added that there is pleasure in historical insight, in the power to read the past with meaning, to show the causes of moral development or moral retrogression, to see patterns, to ask those vital questions which every age must do if it seriously thinks about its political and moral survival. The legitimate question of historical judgment belongs to that philosophical understanding and recognition which wants to think more than it wants to know. Here lies an assumption which makes it possible to go beyond knowledge, although without the realm of knowledge no just overcoming in the sense of preserving would be possible, to *think* the universal in relationship to the particular, the contingent, i.e., to provide the universal as a conception of the understanding for the particular in which the universal is already given, as the particular is in the universal. Yet, the understanding does not reduce contingency to a fixed unity in knowledge; it makes possible a reflective relationship between universal and particular. We speak of the vital difference between the regulative power of understanding and the constitutive constructions of knowledge. The consequences which are drawn from the former must be carefully separated from those drawn from the latter; they open two distinct realities and bring in question the true significance of philosophy as the realm of the understanding.

Kant speaks of the free play of the imagination and the understanding which seems to imply a communicability which is not determined by the logical rules of syllogistic deduction; the interplay between particular or contingent and universal opens a realm of possibility and probability which reveals the inadequacy and insufficiency of either the thought to fully encompass the object or the manifoldness and variety of the object to be subsumed in an idea. In fact, it is this inadequacy and insufficiency which enliven and enrich the imagination and open to it incalculable options never to be exhausted by a finite mind: this is the challenge of freedom, the confrontation of finite and the infinite.

As the subjective communicability of the mode of representation in a judgment of taste is to subsist apart from the presupposition of any definite concept, it can be nothing else than the mental state present in the free play of imagination and understanding; for we are conscious that this subjective relation suitable for a cognition that this subjective relation suitable for a cognition in general must be just as valid for everyone and consequently as universally communicable. . . .26

This communicability becomes for Kant the realization of the progressive development of man's awareness of his societal dependency and the necessity for the actualization of man's critical and imaginative powers. We could think of the progressive and regressive moments of that history as constituting the ebb and flow of reason confronting human tendencies or propensities which disregard and put aside the value and efficacy of reason. This communicability arises from that indefinite quantity of the object which makes a claim to subjective universality and which must therefore "impute," but not "postulate," the agreement of others. If the first moment of the judgment is quality and states that taste is not a cognitive judgment, but aesthetic, "which means that it is one whose determining ground cannot be other than subjective," then it "denotes nothing in the object, but is a feeling which the subject has of itself and of the manner in which it is affected by the representation."[27] Both quality and quantity in relation to the aesthetic object spell out the need for communicability and the realization that the aesthetic object cannot be deduced, but must be seduced for the agreement of our fellow men. If conviction comes through argumentation and appeal to the common sense, then it is no longer a question of logical thought, but of rhetoric in its classical sense, in its Aristotelian meaning. Thus it is not enough to know which can satisfy our private sense; we must find conviction, we must develop the capacity to persuade, in the public sense, those other reasonable beings who we are responsible to inform because what we call knowledge is not self-evident, but must find understanding among other reasonable beings. Knowledge thus carries with it moral and political responsibility. If proofs are possible in this manner, then

> it is evident that, to be able to grasp them, a man must be capable of logical reasoning, of studying characters and the virtues, and thirdly the emotions -- the nature and character of each, its origin and the manner in which it is produced. Thus it appears that Rhetoric is as it were an offshoot of Dialectic and the science of Ethics, which may be reasonably called Politics.[28]

Leaving aside the distortion of rhetoric as the art of ornamental speech and assuming its dependency upon dialectics, ethics, and politics, we can say that the rhetorical object in the Aristotelian sense is another way of speaking about the aesthetic object or the historical object. Kant in the four moments of the judgment of taste began a delineation of a critique of historical judgment. His analysis raises similarities with the oft-forgotten implications of Aristotle's *Rhetoric*, which were easily forgotten images welded to theology and later to the self-evidency of mathematical science. The clear and distinct idea, its explicative and constructivist claim, holds sway, with its ideal of a universal science, over the argumentative realm of values with its impreciseness and dualistic implications.

The third moment in the table of categories is relation, and here Kant speaks of the reflective relationship of an end as causation. The question in the judgment is the nature of the relationship of the cause to the objects. "So we may at least observe a finality of form and trace it in objects -- though by reflection only -- without resting it on an end."[29] The end is a principle of understanding, an idea which is needed in order to give meaning to reality. We could call it a susceptibility to structure and organization, the guiding string needed to make sense of the disarray of empirical data. "For the judgment of taste . . . does not deal with any concept of the nature or of the internal or external possibility, by this or that cause, of the object, but simply with the relative bearing of the representative powers as far as determined by a representation."[30] What becomes paramount here is no longer the logical or conceptual power of thought, but the representative power, that ability to think in ideas, analogies, metaphors, and symbols. The whole range of power inherent in the productive imagination comes into play where the organization of data depends upon the free employment of the imagination actualizing reason -- not only on its logical possibilities, but also in its representative powers. Thus the aesthetic judgment is a faculty that determines its representation in its relationship to the subject, who has a need to comprehend, to think, and to believe that when faced with contingency, action and decision he is rooted in pragmatic belief, the source of our behavior in the political and historical universe of value judgments, in unclear and non self-evident reality. Useless labor would be the attempt to find a universal criterion of task by definite concepts. Useless, but dogmatically and ideologically attractive, is the never-ceasing longing to discover a self-evident criterion of historical knowledge, knowing that with such a criterion man loses his humanity and replaces the gods. Following Eric Weil, who has so wisely stressed the fact that man is not master of the facts and therefore must struggle for meaning, we become aware that this struggle for meaning opens vast possibilities, in every age, to come anew to history and comprehend again the discourse of reason as the task and challenge of every thinking man and every period of civilization. The circular nature of thought is the confrontation with reason actualizing itself in its rethinking and perennial comprehension of reality as historical development. Kant hints at this when he speaks in the third moment of universal communicability apart from any concept but rooted, "deepseated and shared alike by all men, underlying their agreement in estimating the forms under which objects are given them."[31] Through the ages there has been an awareness of man's struggle to deal with the aesthetic and not only with the cognitive object; but these periods are fewer and less successful in their attempts to give validity to objects which cannot be reduced to clear and precise delineations. Man as a judging subject arises from the realization that he is in a world which can be understood, that is not chaos, but reveals reason which must be discovered, and which is for the man who needs to think, a structured world, the belief in which is the expression of the interest of reason.

Modality is the fourth moment of the judgment of taste, and it assumes agreement which cannot be imposed as a logical truth but must be proposed, and thus appeal is made to the reasonableness of man with the assumption that agreement *ought* to be forthcoming. "We are suitors for agreement from everyone else, because we are fortified with a ground common to all. Further we should be able to count on this agreement, provided we were always of the correct assumption of the case under that ground as the rule of approval."[32] Vital to the understanding of this fourth moment is the assumption of a common sense, for if we could not make such an assumption society would be impossible and political and historical life would be meaningless; there would be no shared heritage. Communicability measures the actualization of reason and the reasonable, it calls forth a public responsibility, reveals the dependency of knowledge upon communication and the conditional and contingent nature of interpretation and understanding, the realization that the political and the historical belong to the public arena as objects of argumentation and discussion. Although we assume that everyone *ought* to be in agreement with our judgment and we must represent our views *as if* they presuppose universal agreement, we must nevertheless acknowledge that this does not occur and that our judgment must be given that degree of persuasiveness and reasonableness which would allow it to reach possible agreement and concurrence.

> The assertion is not that everyone *will* fall in with our judgment, but rather that everyone *ought* to agree with it. Here I put forward my judgment of taste as an example of the judgment of common sense, and attribute to it on that account *exemplary* validity.[33]

In other words, in the field of political, historical, and artistic judgment the ability to find conclusive explanations and constructions is not possible for a being who poses the question of the meaning of life and world, who knows that the answers do not satisfy gods, who asks no questions for free, reasonable, and finite men, who know that answers belong to a given age and situation and measure the degree of intellectual and moral refinement which that age is capable of displaying. For the man who decides and acts within the limits of his finiteness, certainty and self-evidence are not the foundations of his attitude and intentions; he decides with belief in the coherency and structure of the world, in the reasonableness of societal life, and in the possibility and probability of future progress. Man turns to history because he believes that he can learn something from it,

that it can make us more prudent and moderate in our present and future decisions and actions, that it gives no clear and distinct prescriptions which will determine the course of events, yet through its study we gain in understanding, in
that awareness of the fluidity and contingency of human behavior, in the significance of situation and character and, above all, in the hypothetical nature of our
assumptions, and the need we have to put them forth in the public arena for discussion and argumentation.

The four moments of judgment -- quality, quantity, relation, and modality --
reveal aspects of the aesthetic object and make us deeply aware that its contingency is the serious challenge of the historical task in its attempt to explore the
indefiniteness of historical relationships and need of men to give meaning to
their historical lives. History becomes a philosophic problem for Kant, and once
discovered its significance became the means through and by which we read
anew his philosophical achievement in epistemology and morality. The first four
moments of the judgment of taste reveal a distinctly new philosophical-histori-
cal perspective, opening that realm of teleological questions which focus upon
the problem of meaning for the man who knows and is aware that his finiteness
and dependency have denied him the capacity to know with certainty and have
made it necessary to seek meaning and find in belief the source of reasonable
action. The belief of reason is the motor power of action and decision. Hume
made it clear that "to seek the real beauty, or real deformity, is as fruitless an
inquiry, as to pretend to ascertain the real sweet or real bitter."[34] Kant focuses
our attention on the imagination and "the incentive it receives to indulge in poetic fiction, i.e., in the peculiar fancies with which the mind entertains itself as it
is being continually stirred by the variety that strikes the eye."[35] If we move
slightly away from poetic objects like the "shapes of the fire" or "a rippling
brook" we face the dazzling complexity of human events and find ourselves
stirred to find meaning which we know we must propose through all the tools of
speech -- the metaphor, the symbol, the analogy, the synecdoche -- if we want to
satisfy our need to order reality. Yet both for Hume and Kant the tools serve a
more significant purpose: the clarification of that inseparability between history
and morality. For if there is a purpose to human history, it can be no other than
the realization "of the freedom of man subject to the moral law," the univer-
salization of the idea of the political as the framework for man's education in
freedom and his escape from his self-imposed and incurred tutelage. The idea of
universality belongs to the understanding; it is an aesthetic idea, always inadequate for what must be comprehended, but in this inadequacy and insufficiency

the understanding attains its mastery, being perennially challenged to surpass itself in that vital dialectic of reality in which negation is never suppressed or loses its dynamicism to negate any perspective or position which attempts to maintain itself as conclusive and final, i.e., become absolute in its particularity. The study of history is an awakening to the dimensions of the understanding and the imagination, to that incongruity between the course of human events and the moral sentiment, to that inner need to subject the confusion and violence which surround us to meaningful discourse, to the overcoming of that inclination to retreat into the absurdity of incomprehensible fact, that refusal of thought inherent in freedom. If in the *Critique of Pure Reason* the table of categories provided the perspectives for the comprehension of the possibility of the object of knowledge, then the four moments of the judgment of taste make us aware that the object of taste can't be *known* but only *recognized* within a framework of values which we impute to the reasonableness and common sense of educated men. The object of taste, the historical object, can't be demonstrated, it can be discussed, studied, and comprehended. The historical object is the creation of the productive imagination, the striving to realize reason in all its multiple possibilities, and the consequence of that refined insight into the struggle between the universal and the particular. The achievements of Hume and Kant are embedded in their conviction that objects of taste and objects of knowledge belong to different realms of the human experience. The longing to fuse, rather than dialectically relate the two realms, does violence to the one as well as to the other. Their separation preserves their distinction and peculiarity; in these qualities they realize their richness; they open to us experiences which are unique and distinct; in the realization of their separation they prepare the ground of their renewed relationship and rediscovery.

3

Leopold von Ranke:
Unknown Follower of Kant

If we ask ourselves about the importance of the facts we seek to understand, then we must ask if their importance lies in them, i.e., in their facticity, or does their meaning or unity presuppose a logically given and precedent value and unity. Eric Weil observes that "history is not a whole that is relative to another which encompasses and founds it, as cause founds effects: it is *the* whole. History is not *explicable* for it is in reference to its structure that questions are posed and are given explications. History is, nevertheless, *comprehensible* to the reason which it has produced, being one of the aspects of the whole, an aspect of that inclusive totality which is philosophy."[1] Reason is not born in reason, but in history, in the concrete experience of political and moral reality. Born in history, reason must consider the past its own history.[2] Whatever be the ideological conviction of the historian, whether he considers history a lesson for the present, the expression of immutable laws of nature, or the work of the imagination freely constructing relationships among past events, he knows that the seemingly accidental nature of events must be made to appear necessary, that causation creates these necessary links, and that this act of causation is possible because logically the meaning of history precedes the categories by which and through which meaning finds its embodiment. The study of history and the question of its meaning pose those problems which give rise to the possibility of philosophy. If history yielded meaning without our need to draw it forth anew at every age, to constantly rewrite it, then the possibility of philosophy would cease. Philosophy, i.e., the possibility of philosophy, exists because history does not reveal its meaning; it shows reason struggling to find expression as freedom; as that negativity which confirms the fact that everything can be negated except negation. In the eternity of negation lies the structure of both history and reason, its meaning and development, the essence of man's humanity as the realization of freedom. If reason is born in history and not from reason, then we are forced to rethink and rewrite the past as the preparation for the comprehension of the present and the projection of the future. Reason being historical makes it necessary for thinking to be rethinking, past being reconstructed for the ever-new present; the circular movement of thought perennially turning back upon itself, comprehending itself from an ever-renewed discourse of past and present making possible that advance of freedom which denies to any moment fixity and determinacy.

We read the past from the present and we do this because we believe that the past has meaning, that it is in the present that it reveals its meaning, and thus from every present the past is rethought and rewritten. George Kennan concluded that Bismarck's *status quo* -- a position and perspective from which he hoped to assure the stability of the new German Reich by preventing wars among Germany's neighbors, thus avoiding the possibility of war against Germany herself -- was destined to failure because it was based on the political and military isolation of France and the suppression of Polish independence.

> Both of these purposes were in conflict with the developing forces of the epoch. The concept further assumed the indefinite endurance of the multilingual Austro-Hungarian Empire in the face of all the romantic nationalism of the time. It envisaged a Russia in which the authority of the Tzars would suffice indefinitely to hold in check both the nationalistic and revolutionary tendencies of the age.[3]

We read this history of diplomatic rivalries, alliances, and attitudes with excitement and purpose because later events and their meaning are important to us. We ask ourselves if the purpose is to find out how it happened, what were the causal relationships, what role do we ascribe to the weakness and strengths of men's characters, their limitations and inadequacies. We are also aware that our own needs to bring forth a moral and reasonable political world, to control and dominate the violence which threatens our faith in the meaning of history and moral progress, is fundamental in our reading of history. Without violence we would have no history, there would be no reason; living in peace, there would be no need to have an understanding of our past; in fact, the thought about a past would not occur. The shock of World War I and its massive destruction, its later consequences, forced Kennan to study its diplomatic background. If history is born in violence and reason is born in history, then history, being the meeting of violence and reason, becomes the judge of itself. History overcoming itself as violence and reason becomes history judging itself from itself as history, the realization of itself as universal and particular, as universality in particularity and particularity as the realization of universality.

In terms of these general considerations and observations let us take up the thinking of Leopold von Ranke, who more than any other modern historian lay the foundation of modern historical research and exposition in the nineteenth century.[4] The understanding of history begins with the assumption that the study of history is meaningful because it is the realization of reason and its negative, the capacity to comprehend itself with a meaning which surpasses either aspect, a meaning which is expressed in the totality which is philosophy. Ranke's approach to history is rooted in the assumption that political history, the history of the relationship of states to each other, is the circumference in which the course of man's development must be understood; he was certain that this history brought together two realities, one which belongs to the assumption that there is freedom in human action, while the other implies the realization of necessity. The fact that we condition events is counterbalanced by the fact that the force with which we condition has been created by conditions. Ranke was aware that history was not only the tale of deeds and counterdeeds, but that action and reaction, freedom and necessity, move together in uncanny ways to give us an infinitely perplexed and varied picture of political development. His journals are filled with reflections on the meaning of history and become a haven for the proof of any attitude one would like to ascribe to him. Then he tells us: "The state is like the world, an eternal becoming"; with its eternal greatness the Kantian System is "gottlos und heillos," and where does the misfortune lie but in the fact that Kant was a *Verstandesmensch*. "No teaching converts the world but only a great personality," "genius is the absence of personal limitations," and our passionate outcries express the difficulty and pain which belong to the search for truth, "aber was ist Wahrheit . . . wie kann ich's erkennen?"[5] These aphoristic remarks belong to the Ranke of his early twenties, and it would be precipitous to venture judgments about his attitudes from them. What we can observe from them is an intellectual groping, attempts to come to terms with conflicting ideas, to find excitement in the multiformity of particularity, and yet to feel the pull of universality. Ranke, who was born in 1795, lived in that glorious age of German literature and philosophy: Kant, Fichte, Jacobi, Hegel, Schelling, Goethe, Schiller, Novalis, August, Schlegel, and Wilhelm von Humboldt, Herder and Niebuhr. Comprehending Ranke within this age makes it possible to grasp the scope of influence which entered his historical thinking, the longing to join spirit and matter like Goethe's "in form so that they presented an

absolute beauty. Like the artist who brings forth a form, *Gestalt,* through force
and with the idea fixes the seal of his own spirit, so did Goethe."[6] This bringing
together of spirit and matter in form made a deep impression on Ranke and remained a guiding principle of historical outlook.

In 1854 Ranke delivered a series of lectures entitled "On the Epochs of
Modern History" to King Maximilian of Bavaria. In the first lecture he made
the following observation: "But I assert: every epoch is immediate to God, and
its worth is not at all based on what it derives from it, but rests on its own existence in its own self. In this way the contemplation of history, that is to say individual life in history, acquires its own particular attraction, since now every
epoch must be seen as something valid in itself and appears highly worthy of
consideration."[7] Two ideas arise from these observations. The reasonable of the
particular is dependent upon the universal, i.e., the comprehension of particular
histories is possible only as aspects of universal history and the fact that the validity of every historical epoch is equal as an expression of universality; every
particular is the revelation of the universal, as every universal is revealed in the
particular. Seen from the universal, the particular is its expression and incarnation to be valued and grasped as that coming together of form and matter, finite
and infinite. Every epoch gives expression to the embodiment of the universal in
the particular and of the awareness of particularity as universality. Ranke was
deeply aware that there were two ways of "acquiring knowledge of human
affairs -- through the perception of the particular and through abstraction."[8] The
former he called the way of history, the latter the way of philosophy. The historian, he says, must have "a feeling for and a joy in the particular in and by
itself."[9] Yet the two ways are in fact one way. Ranke's genius lay in the realization that without "a general view research would become sterile; without exact research the general view would deteriorate into fantasy."[10] To think is to
relate particular to universal, but not simply to enunciate a logical formula
which does no justice to either the richness of the particular or the embracing
power of the universal. Both moments of thought surpass conceptualization and
in their infinite variety and possibility relate to each other in such a manner that
they reveal the essence of man's humanity to that freedom which unfolds as
negation negating attempts to fix either the particular or the universal in conceptual entities. Both moments of reality encompass the eternal comprehension
of thought moving through world history gathering the past in its totality and
forming that interrelationship between universal and particular which is the
essence of freedom. Ranke had that fine susceptibility for the interplay of con-

flicting and confronting moments of thought which denied him the possibility of embracing one to the exclusion of the other, knowing all the time that every perspective has within itself its negation and finds its reality only in its own surpassing or overcoming. "From the standpoint of the divine idea, I cannot think of the matter differently but that mankind harbors within itself an infinite multiplicity of developments which manifest themselves gradually according to laws which are unknown to us and are more mysterious and greater than one thinks."[11] Ranke was correct in seeing that the historian is limited to his time and situation, that the infinite multiplicity of events and developments depend for their realization and comprehension on the infinite course of thought thinking upon itself, relating its past and comprehending anew the thought which prepared the way again for thinking which attempts to grasp and encompass world history.

Ranke was of the opinion that history was politics and politics history. The assumption is that political action is rooted in history and that the comprehension of the political is historical, while historical comprehension is political. The realization of the reasonable state is the purpose of world history, for it is in and through the reasonable state that man brings forth his humanity in all the varied expressions of his freedom.[12] "I am of the opinion that the mastery of politics must be based on history; it must be founded in the study of the powerful states that have reached a high degree of inner development."[13] Reason, we have stated, is born in history, i.e., it is born in the political, in the realization of those reasonable institutions which make possible the domination of violence and the realization of freedom and those artistic, philosophical, and religious forms in which freedom finds incarnation. If violence is the motor force of history, then the political, the embodiment of reason, is that other force, born together with violence, constituting the dialectic of world history in its movement through the political development of great states. From the reasonable state, which remains the moral goal of history, both the individual with his rights and dignity, and humanity with its collective responsibility, find their purpose and perspective. There can be no valid discussion of the individual without the state as there is no legitimate state without the recognition of the rights and dignity of the individual on whatever level they may be manifested and recognized. Art, philosophy, and religion may surpass the state, but the source of their expression and realization belongs to the existence of the state as the embodiment of reason.

> Everything depends on the supreme idea. That is the meaning when we
> say that states, too, derive their origin from God. For the idea is of di-
> vine origin. Each independent state has its own original life, which may
> have different stages and may perish like all living matter. But when it
> lives it permeates and dominates its entire environment, identical only
> with itself.[14]

With a skeptical frown we can disdain Ranke's notion of the state deriving its
origin from God and being a divine idea, but we must realize that although
states have their beginnings in specific times and places, the thought of the state
as the realization of man's moral and political being, the center of conflict and
confrontation between the rational and the irrational, the arena of compromise
and moderation, transcends every historical manifestation as its source and reference. Ranke was profoundly aware that the political dimensions of reality embraced the arena of man's cultural achievement. Within this dimension he saw
the conflicts of the great states, their diplomatic maneuvers, and the concomitant
struggles for power. These struggles permeated and gave rise to the moral conscience and to moral consciousness; we are aware that in conflict morality is
born and were it not, morality would have no cause to be born. The world is
moral and from this moral nature the moral problems arise which dominate and
control our lives. The state is the moral dimension of thought; it is the ground of
our political and moral consciousness; it is the force that penetrates the inner
and outer life of every citizen; it is the thought which is the source of all thinking and acting.

Ranke believed that struggle against French hegemony, the "Wars of Liberation," had renewed the vital energies of the states, and if we can think of
them as "thoughts of God," then these conflicts have brought forth a realization
of their divine principles. If we move a little away from this form of divinity, we
are nevertheless struck by the conviction that the state is the source of all the
spiritual energies that are manifested in a people. The history of mankind is not
a vague expression of an idea or of a culture, but is the struggle of states for
power and ascendancy which is never separable from cultural advancement or
retrogression, power which must not be identified with brute force, but closely
linked to the development of a natural consciousness, to a feeling of purpose and
to the realization of institutions capable of advancing the education of the people
and the maturity of political and moral judgment. Ranke quotes with approval
the saying of Heraclitus that "War is the Father of things" because he was con-

vinced that struggle and confrontation created the great personalities of history who were more decisive for the direction of events than historical trends and movements. Struggle is the source of life and history, an elementary fact when we come to see that history is political history and that the conflicts of states give rise to man's creative forces on all levels.

> World history does not present such a chaotic tumult, warring, and planless succession of states and peoples as appear at first sight. Nor is the often dubious advancement of civilization its only significance. There are forces and indeed spiritual, life-giving, creative forces, nay life itself, and there are moral energies, whose devolopment we see. They cannot be defined or put in abstract terms, but one can behold them and observe them. One can develop a sympathy for their existence. They unfold, capture the world, appear in manifold expressions, dispute with and check and overpower one another. In their interaction and succession, in their life, in their decline or rejuvenation, which then encompasses an ever greater fullness, higher importance, and wider extent, lies the secret of world history.[15]

The secret of world history is in the perennial comprehension of political developments, but this comprehension, which reads history from the present to the past, goes beyond the comprehension of events to the comprehension of itself as comprehension. This is what Ranke implies when he speaks of forces lying behind forces and laws behind laws or when he uses such expressions as "thoughts of God," knowing that divinity can never adequately be grasped or comprehended, but is always being grasped and comprehended, forcing us to rethink and rediscover what ages, before and immediate, have thought and discovered. Thinking is always the rethinking of the reality which precedes and must be rethought to become the reality which it is and is forever becoming. The significance of Ranke's thought is its sense of the need for multiple development and interaction in all spheres of life. "No one spoke of a world literature at the time that French literature dominated Europe."[16] In contrast to domination there is life. "Decided, positive prevalence of one [state] would destroy the essence of each one. Out of separation and independent development will emerge true harmony."[17] The meaning of history had found in Heraclitus an insight which Ranke made his own; firmly convinced that the hegemony of a single state is destructive to all, he understood that conflict and competition were the elements of growth and achievement and that in reality the only undeniable life force is negation, i.e., freedom. "No, the union of all must rest upon the independence of each single one. Then they can stimulate one another in lively fashion and forever, without one dominating or injuring the others."18

Ranke believed that the historian must cultivate his ability to grasp the event --

> its unity and fullness. It should be possible to attain this goal. I know how far I have achieved it. One tries, one strives, but in the end one has not reached the goal. Only let no one become impatient about this failure! The main thing is always what we deal with: as Jacobi says, our subject is mankind as it is, explicable or inexplicable, the life of the individual, of generations, of the peoples, and at times the hand of God over them.19

Ranke is certain that the writing of history presupposes a faith in history, in the fact that meaning can be discovered because history is meaning, a fact which emerges the deeper the historian penetrates the advances and declines of states and reflects not on their causes, but attempts to comprehend each moment as an expression of reason bearing within itself the past, the present, and the future. Each moment, being "the thought of God," reveals the contradiction and reconciliation of the divine life; each moment is a microcosm of reality comprehending the past through the present and preparing for its overcoming into a future which becomes presence. History is an aesthetic object grasped by no concept; history can be comprehended and thought; it cannot be known; it is not a fact; it is continual evaluation. Although the historian is devoted to constant investigation of data and documentation, the organization and validity of his material do not reveal the nature of the material, but the categories by which and through which the historian attempts to give meaning to his material. In his "Preface to History of the Popes" Ranke shows the shifting position of the papacy within the political structure of the great powers. The papacy, he shows, belongs to that complex of political movements in which its power is increased or lessened depending upon the strength and intelligence of its ruler. "As the history of the world has varied; as one nation or another has gained the ascendancy; as the fabric of social life has been disturbed; so has the papal power been affected: its maxims, its objectives and its pretentions have undergone essential changes; and its influence, above all, has been subjected to the great variations.''[20] Ranke was deeply aware of the interplay of historical forces, the dependencies of power and influence, but he was hesitant to enter the realm of explanations, knowing that here we can find the necessary but rarely the sufficient conditions of reality, and to remain satisfied with the one without the other does violence to our comprehension of history as a reality to which no concept is adequate and which could only be attained at the end of time, divine knowledge happily denied to man. Ranke, who moved easily between particular and general, knew the inadequacies and insufficiencies of any specific approach to history. "I am convinced that a historical work may also derive its internal logic from the intentions of the author and the nature of the task."[21] The historian assumes his task when he is prepared to face the question of meaning, when he begins that discourse of history from which reason emerges as the expression of the moral and political life of an epoch.

Whatever we may say about the influence of nationalism of the Napoleonic and post-Napoleonic era in Ranke's attitude toward history, the ideal of cosmopolitanism and the *Humanitätsideal* never faded from his writings.

> When then an author undertakes to make the past life of a foreign nation the object of a comprehensive literary work, he will not think of writing its national history. This would be a contradiction in terms. In accordance with his natural vantage point he will direct his attention to those epochs which have had the effectual influence on the development of mankind. . . .[22]

Remaining loyal to the tradition of Herder, Kant, and von Humboldt, Ranke always envisioned the writing of history to be the revelation of the continuous moral and political experience which each nation embodies and which influences and determines the destinies of the others. The historian comes to comprehend that reasonable discourse which Weil stressed as the presupposition of all theories of history, state, and society. The idea of the state is not man's creation, but the dimension in which man thinks himself as a moral and political being; it is the dimension in which the political and moral become comprehensible and in which reasonable discourse takes place. This ancient Platonic and Aristotelian wisdom was not lost on Ranke and prevented his historical outlook from being encompassed by nationalism. He always understood that the state was the embodiment of the reasonable and concrete universal, lodged in an historical community whose role in world history he was determined to delineate in a universal dimension. "The Muse of history has the widest intellectual horizon and the full courage of her convictions; but in forming them she is thoroughly conscientious and, we might say, jealously bent on her duty. To introduce the interest of the present time into the work of the historian usually ends in restricting its free execution."[23] Ranke was aware that all metaphysical theories of history represented attempts to discover laws of human evolution and progress hoping to provide infallible programs for either political action or religious quietism. These snares which can entice the historian reduce history to attractive but vague generalities, inevitable schemes of movement, and finally reduce man's efforts and purposes to fixed and determined destinies. Beyond these schemes, which make men into marionettes, and the national histories attempting to satisfy the political moods of the moment, there lies world history which tries to relate those events, and movements which tie nation to nation and control their mutual development.

> The history of mankind manifests itself within the history of nations themselves. There is a general historical life that moves progressively from one nation or group of nations to another. In the conflict between the different national groups Universal History comes into being, and the nationalities become conscious of themselves, for nations are not entirely products of nature.[24]

Nothing appears more dominant in Ranke's approach to history than the realization that history is written within history, that particular moments are universal expressions, and that universality is comprehended only in particularity. Yet, the logical structure of thought in no way hinders that fine susceptibility to the significance of time and personality for political action and its success. "How much depends on the times in which even the best men are cast!" The thought complex which structures historical writing is not a mold for events. It is an hermeneutical perspective, which makes it possible to understand the interplay of ideas which are necessary, but never sufficient for an understanding of historical reality. This reality in its multiplicity and variety defies conceptualization and ideas which have little possibility of being embodied in reality, forcing it to lose its indeterminacy. Understanding makes it possible to grasp the limits of ideas, to leave free the interrelationships and interplays between ideas and their manifestations; but, above all, understanding denies to any moment of thought the demonic reality of becoming fixed and expressing itself as truth. Ranke moved from particular to universal because, being a great historian, he was permeated by that profound philosophic insight into the dialectical movement of thought which in universality and particularity incarnates the freedom of negation as the father of thought.[25] The admiration of Goethe, which remained throughout his life, was embedded in that refined grasp of the interplay between the individual and the whole, which gave life its riches and profundity; in hope and confidence he called to Goethe: "Oh that your spirit visit me with its wisdom of 70 years."[26] This was Ranke at twenty-two, but I believe it remained in Ranke at ninety-one. If our question is the meaning of history, then through Ranke we have come to comprehend that dialectic which revealed and reveals the reality that is grounded in the deepening realization that the further we penetrate the particular, the deeper we become aware of the universal in its concreteness; we become aware of freedom, of concrete freedom, i.e., of freedom becoming itself in the becoming of the reasonable on a world-historical level.

Whenever and wherever we turn in the writings of Kant and pose the question of the meaning of history, we are faced with a problem that is inseparable from it: the moral destiny of mankind. To conceive of world history, the political confrontation of states and periods of cultural history which Weil has called "breakdowns" and "breakthroughs,"[27] without a moral framework would have been an inconceivable to Kant as it was to Ranke. In the *Religion within the Limits of Reason Alone* Kant speaks of an ethical commonwealth and a people of God, but the hope for their realization is dependent upon God, for what other being could redeem man from that "brutish freedom and independence from coercive laws,"[28] which is his desire to perpetuate, than God? The reliance on God does not free man from his moral responsibility. "Rather, man must proceed as though everything depended upon him; only on this condition dare he hope that higher wisdom will grant the completion of his well-intentioned endeavors."[29] The success of the collective endeavor of mankind is in God's hands; the source of man's hope is God's existence; the vision of a better world, of an ethical commonwealth, is forged in moral belief, a belief which carries over into a conception of history which separates sacred space and time from the profane, and yet allows the sacred to enter the profane and pose the meaning of their interaction. No more vivid exemplification of this interaction is needed than the distinction Kant draws between the visible and invisible church. The invisible church, he says, is "a mere idea of the union of all the righteous under direct and moral divine government, an idea serving all as the archetype of what is to be established by men."[30] The visible church "exhibits the moral kingdom of God in earth so far as it can be brought to pass on earth."[31] When we think of this church, we also think of the noble and courageous Job, "a man who in the midst of his most serious doubts could say, 'Until the hour of my death, I will hold fast to my piety' (27, 5-6). With this resolution Job proved that he did not base his morality in his faith but his faith upon his morality."[32] Faith based upon morality, the visible church upon the invisible, makes us deeply aware that the "mere idea" which we inject into history, the morality and ideas which give us the faith to defy the opinions and self-righteousness of those about us, constitute the breakthroughs of those supersensual forces into the natural course of human events and radically change the direction and movement of our history. To this "mere idea" Kant analogously applied the categories: quantity becomes universality, quality purity, relation freedom, and modality the unchangeableness of its constitution. Now the categories express not the possibility of the knowledge of an object of experience, but the realization of an experience which raises man from a world of conflict, fanaticism, and whim into one of ideas, i.e., a world in which and through which man poses what should be and what he, like Job, must affirm and project upon reality: a faith in the moral, the moral which in its universality confronts reality and poses the question of its meaning and finality.

Kant made it clear that knowledge of an object only referred to our capacity and possibility of knowing. What it *is* remains unknown. Our capacity to know delineates three kinds of knowledgeable objects: matters of opinion, matters of fact, and matters of faith.[33] We can assume that matters of opinion are objects of empirical knowledge and are possible, while matters of fact find proof and verification in experience or pure reason. At this point Kant injects a surprising assumption and states that freedom belongs to the matters of fact. "Its reality is the reality of a particular kind of causality (the conception of which be transcendent if considered theoretically) and as a causality of that kind it admits of verification by means of practical laws of pure reason and in the actual actions that take place in obedience to them and consequently in experience."[34] Freedom is verifiable in experience and is a fact, i.e., it is the foundation from which action proceeds. We are not concerned with its nature, but with the consequences which follow from its existence.[35] One can say that freedom *is;* its being is the source of causation and movement, although it is itself not causation nor movement. Freedom is a fact which we comprehend from its consequences. If we say that man is free, we reveal nothing of his essence; we confirm the idea that freedom is not an integral part of the knowledge of the object, but the foundation of the knowledge of the object; in other words man is not only the source of theoretical knowledge, explanation through cause and effect, but of moral-practical reason, the source of finality.[36] Closely linked to freedom is the "interest of reason," and this implies the fact that reason needs to be architectonic; it needs not only logical perfection, but cosmic vision. "Philosophy is the science of the relation of all knowledge to the essential ends of human reason (teleologia rationis humanae) and the philosopher is not an artificer in the field of reason, but himself the lawgiver of human reason."[37] The freedom which Kant speaks of implies the power to formulate the cosmical concept, the *Weltbegriff* which is the deepest expression of the 'interest of reason," the interest which reflects that vocation of man to pose the question of meaning as the fundamental question of philosophy, the question which incites discussion of those ends which are necessary and essential to mankind. Here Kant raises again his belief that the mind has "a natural interest in morality," and it is this interest which makes any study of history inseparable from an interest in morality. The study of history reveals this natural interest which man takes in the moral progress of his species, in the attempt which he makes to avoid dogmatism and skepticism, to follow that critical path which above all makes possible that reasonable and coherent discourse of reason forming the meaning of humanity.

In addition to opinion and fact, Kant speaks of matters of faith:

> Faith as *habitus*, not as *actus*, is the moral attitude of reason in its assurance of the truth of what is beyond the reach of theoretical knowledge. It is the steadfast principle of the mind, therefore, according to which the truth of what must necessarily be presupposed as the condition of the supreme final end being possible is assumed as true in consideration of the fact that we are under an obligation to pursue that end. . . . It is something that has a foundation in reason (though only in relation to its practical employment) and *a foundation that satisfies the purpose of reason.*[38]

We speak of the faith of reason which is the ground of that architectonic interest which reason expresses in its search for finality, making clear those necessary and essential ends by which and through which we comprehend the idea of humanity. Faith is the import which we bring to the efficacy and promise of the moral law. This faith is the foundation of both history and morality. The commitment to both is the source of their comprehension, the grasp of their reality, the understanding that their significance does not lie in *what* they are, but *that* they are. Morality and history are ideas which precede their realization in time and place. Reason discovers in itself, in the course of its development, ideas which it freely approves of and which open to it new dimensions of its infinite reality, but these are ideas whose attainability is inseparable from them; these are the ideas that arise in freedom, in the negation of negation, that eternal principle of reality. These ideas cannot be commanded by "any law of reason, unless reason, though it be with uncertain voice, also promises its attainability. The very term *fides* expresses this."[39] This is moral faith, a realization of freedom, the source of that nonbeing that lies at the core of being and denies it the fixity and certainty by which it determines itself to be totality. Freedom is the indeterminacy which belongs to the determinate as the moment of its negation. Therefore, Kant can say that of the three ideas of pure reason -- God, freedom, and immortality -- "freedom is the one and only conception of the supersensible which (owing to the causality implied in it) proves its objective reality in nature by its possible effect there."[40] The fact that freedom is the eternal ground of reality in which the contingent, the condition, and the indeterminate make possible the conception of the necessary, the unconditioned, and the determinate shows that in it the finite is immediate to the infinite and the infinite to the finite. Freedom transcends the conceptualization of speculative philosophy and is to be grasped as the "root-conception of all unconditioned practical laws, can extend reason beyond the bounds to which every natural, or theoretical, conception must remain hopelessly restricted."[41] This idea of freedom is the foundation of history. If history and freedom were not mutual expressions, then the course of history could be fixed and determined, the knowledge of history assumed and learned, man reduced to a natural object and explained in a theory. Man's freedom makes history the perennial discourse of reason coming to comprehend itself through ongoing reflection upon itself. The more we know, the more we need to understand, i.e., the more we are forced to begin again that circular movement of thought in which and through which thought comprehends itself. Kant has shown us the way, and it is along this way that history becomes the essential philosophical problem.

This problem moves to the center of Kant's philosophy when the implications of the differences between a *Weltbegriff* and a *Schulbegriff der Philosophie* become clear. This occurs in the last critique. Weil has stated the problem clearly and decisively: "For Kant the problem was always to understand, as a philosopher, the meaning of human life, the fundamental interest of man and philosophy, a living and acting philosophy, not a scholastic one. What is new in the Critique of Judgment is that it no longer seeks to determine this meaning -- this given -- but to think it in its reality."[42] To think the meaning which is and to comprehend it as existing meaning is the philosophical problem; man does not create meaning, he finds it in reality just as reason does not come from reason but is discovered in history. The radical quality of the *Critique of Judgment* is the discovery that meaning *is* and must be thought in its reality. The course of human events, in the political dimension in which they occur, can be thought and comprehended only if there is someone who is prepared and equipped to think and comprehend. What is fundamental both for the philosopher and the historian is the realization that the capacity and desire to think make possible the receptivity of thought. "Meaningful for man and meaningful through him, but which is a meaningless aggregate to the man who does not rise to meaning, to the grasp of the meaning of the world and of meaning in the world."[43] This truth lies in the assumption that "what is does not refuse to give meaning to whoever seeks this meaning, because finite man is immediate to the infinite."[44] The assumption thus confirms the fact that reality is and is meaningful because we can begin to think and comprehend only within a meaningful whole. History is possible because philosophy has made us aware, from its beginning, that thinking and comprehending reveal the discourse of reason, that reality as a meaningful totality belongs to the eternal ground of thought and comprehension. In the last section of the *Critique of Pure Reason* Kant speaks of a history of pure reason which found its course threatened by dogmatism and skepticism (throughout the ages), but the critical path which he has not delineated offers the hope that human reason will continually explore and discover its limitations and its architectonic, its canon and its discipline, and in these it will find its "high road; namely to secure for human reason complete satisfaction in regard to that with which it has all along so eagerly occupied itself, though hitherto in vain."[45]

Every age is concerned with the future and is never free of the question whether we are progressing morally, i.e., is there the possibility that we can have a basis for hope in moral progress? We study, believing that it will make us more competent to deal with our own problems, and leave to posterity a more ordered political world. Kant reflected on this problem and asked the same question in his last work, *The Contest of Faculties* (1798).

If it were possible to credit human beings with even a limited will of innate and unvarying goodness, we could certainly predict a general improvement of mankind, for this would involve events which man could himself control. But if man's natural endowments consist of a mixture of good and evil in unknown proportions, no-one can tell what effect he should expect from his own actions.[46]

Kant was fully aware that moral improvement depended upon situation; he knew that morality was born in every age, for it was this morality which made us aware of the pure morality that was timeless. The confrontation of historical morality and pure morality reveals the struggle of every historical period to come to terms with itself as the embodiment of reason. It is in this confrontation that the Job example is so meaningful for Kant, "the sincere and undisguised confessions of one's doubt" and above all "the avoidance of feigned convictions." Moral faith born in "feigned convictions" is the ground of his attitude toward history which is for him the stage of that all-encompassing struggle between violence and reason, the struggle for meaning, its absence being a genuine alternative, the affirmation of honesty where hypocrisy is equally possible, and where the *ought to do* has only a feeble relationship to what will be done. The connections which man finds possible in his explanations of the natural object, he finds nowhere in his perceptions of free human actions; "he must do without such hints or guidance when dealing with free actions. . . ."[47] The misfortune which we face in our failure to be prophets, to predict the course of actions, and to foresee the plan of future events becomes our good fortune; it calls forth in us that moral faith which orients us toward those moral ideas which make it possible in an amoral world to remain committed to the moral, to think in terms of the universal in the particular, and to comprehend the universal as the particular. This faith, Kant believed, bore witness to man's character. The devotion to the universal reflected in the enthusiasm caused by the French Revolution seemed to Kant to show "a moral disposition within the human race." Even if the aims of the Revolution failed, the event itself was for Kant so momentous, "too intimately interwoven with the interests of humanity and too widespread in its influence upon all parts of the world for nations not to be reminded of it when favorable circumstances present themselves and to rise up and make renewed attempts of the same kind as before."[48] Yes, Kant understood that history and morality are inseparable and that the writing of history, the investigation of the vast details which make it possible, requires a point of view, the posing of the question of meaning, the commitment of the historian to a moral perspective, to a cosmopolitanism which embodies a sense of the particular and the individual, a comprehension of man's limits and needs, a realization of good and evil inclinations, and, at the same time, the Jobian qualities which are present in every human situation. Kant had no illusions about man's hopes for progress; he was sensitive to man's frailties, to the fortuitousness of circumstances and all projects which offered quick and immediate solutions -- e.g., he refused to believe that education made good citizens. "To expect that the education of young people in intellectual and moral culture, reinforced by the doctrine of religion . . . will eventually not only make them good citizens, but will also bring them up to practice a kind of goodness which can continually progress and maintain itself, is a plan which is scarcely likely to achieve the desired success."[49] Education belongs to the needs of human beings, it is rooted in the immediacy of the situation and is imbued and determined by the ideas and events of the moment; it does not exist in a timeless Platonic commonwealth, its moral and political problems and orientation are those of the moment. Kant was convinced that all our endeavors had to be complemented by "a higher wisdom" in whom we had to trust because from it came the strength to struggle for the moral where the consequences remained unknown and unpredictable, to develop that autocracy of the will, i.e., the power to master our doubts and frailties, to live *as if* we are the embodiment of that supersensible faculty called freedom, by which and through which we assign our lives that worth which we achieve by what we do.

If we recall the thought of Ranke, we are impressed by the spiritual optimism which dominates his work, his feeling for that cosmopolitanism in which the various national states develop and to which they contribute. He had that deep sense for that close, intimate, and refined relationship of the particular and the universal, a sensitivity for purposiveness and yet a refusal to settle for a given purpose; it was this "purposiveness with purpose," so Kantian in thought, which finds expression throughout his work. It was Kant's profound distinction between logical and aesthetic judgments that became the determining attitude and outlook of the historian for whom purposiveness was the serious object of search while purpose remained with the gods. Ranke was loyal to the Goethe of his youth whom he admired for outlook and profundity, whose feeling for change and movement was intricately woven with universality and the unchanging. For Kant the progress of mankind was always in doubt, the autocracy of the practical reason subject to man's frailties and inadequacies, but from these demonic realities there arose a moral faith, an interest of reason, and an intense belief in virtue, *des Glaube an die Tugend*. Ranke did not share the intense Kantian feeling for the demonic, and his historical outlook was more optimistic; he had a deep conviction in the advance of historical scholarship, in the enlightenment which it brought forth and will continually bring forth. History embodied the total experience of man; in it the finite confronted the infinite, the universal the particular. Ranke had confidence in that higher wisdom that guided the course of human events; he believed those final words of God in the "Prologue in Heaven":

> But you, who are the real sons of That Lord
> rejoice in beauty's live dominions.
> May the Becoming, which eternally moves and lives,
> Surround you with the friendly walls of love!
> To all that wavers you must minister,
> basing it firmly in enduring thoughts.[50]

Ranke was indeed in love with the details and documents from which he wrote his national and world histories; he had that feeling for the whole, in which and from which he wrote and thought. "I go further and accept a spiritual life in humanity generally, which manifests itself in national origins but becomes a whole through the unification of them so that the whole culture rests upon it."[51] Ranke sensed finality; he avoided the fixed purpose; he remained close to Kant's critique of taste, finality without goal, the teleological conception, but not the telos. Deeply unaware how close he was to the mood of the *Critique of Judgment*, he nevertheless was embodied in its perspective. If Goethe was his conscious image of veneration, it was Kant's philosophy which worked itself into his perspective and was the major impulse of his historical thinking.

4

Herder and Kant: Nature or Freedom

When we are confronted with the problem of meaning, two distinct but dependent objects appear in their opposition to each other. Objects of the understanding and the objects of reason provide different and opposing realms of reality. Objects of understanding belong to the temporal spatial dimension; they are knowable objects, but devoid of meaning. They simply exist, while the objects of reason unfold as ideas, by which and through which we guide and direct the course and development of our work. We find meaning for our questions and perspectives for our interests. We comprehend these objects in meaning, we provide the purposiveness that become the regulative principles and heuristic guides that lie at the base of our hope and belief that the objects of the understanding have form and reasonableness. The two realms are not exclusive, forcing an irreconcilable negativity, but their confrontation and distinction cause a heightened sense of their peculiar reality and, at the same time, the realization of their dependency. Both moments, reason and understanding belong to the reality of thinking, find within it their exclusivity and mutuality, forming the constituent moments of experience. The absence of either leaves us with facts without ideas and purposiveness, or with ideas without the concreteness necessary for their realization and actualization. Ideas without historical facts are illusions, mere fictions -- facts without ideas, the violence of thinking, the demonic fixity of given experience. The object of reason is undemonstrable, its efficacy depends upon the philosophical faith in which these ideas of freedom, moral progress, and the meaning of history find their passion and will. "And however uncertain I may be and may remain as to whether we can hope for anything better for mankind, this uncertainty cannot detract from the maxim I have adopted, or from the necessity of assuming for practical purposes that human progress is possible."[1] The realization that philosophical faith is a responsibility, that it has a moral foundation, that it makes possible a philosophy of history, that it reveals man not only as a being of immediate interests, of natural desires and fulfillments, but that it shows that his essence is freedom and negativity. He is not merely a being who negates this or that, but that negation is the eternal law of development, the source of the positive, the denial of immediacy, and the comprehension that in man's abandonment of the naturalness of desire he achieves reasonableness. He is raised to that moral level that makes possible the mutual dependency of universal and individual; these moments of thinking that realize man as the source and consequence of reason.[2] We can no longer deal with man as an isolated being with abstract rights and privileges or as the primal element to which we return for the realization of freedom. Man is the consequence of what he does, of the family in which he functions as a sentient being, of the society in which he finds an actualization of his intellectual and mechanical capacities, in which he becomes aware that he has the capacity to change reality and becomes conscious that he has a will, a will that is his and that is "the *thought* of the negation of every condition, the *thought* of my freedom, the *thought* that I can refuse every given."[3] The object of reason makes it possible for finite and dependent man to comprehend those undemonstrable but necessary ideas which link him to the universal and make his life reasonable, lifting it from its immediacy of desire and satisfaction, providing the necessary architectonic for the realization of that thinking in which individual and universal find their proper expression. Considering both the objects of the understanding and the objects of reason as separate realms of reality which bear within their separation the source of their mutuality, we turn to the historical thinking of J. G. Herder[4] and ask to what extent Herder comprehended the idea of history as a philosophical problem; to what degree he contributed to an understanding of this problem and where the divergencies arise that brought him into conflict with Kant.

Isaiah Berlin has given us some idea of the scope of Herder's interests and perspectives from which we can glimpse the varied interests that occupied his fertile but discursive intellect. "Herder's fame rests on the fact that he is the father of the related notions of nationalism, historicism and the *Volkgeist,* one of the leaders of the romantic revolt against classicism, rationalism, and faith in the omnipotence of scientific method -- in short, the most formidable of the adversaries of the French philosophes and their German disciples."[5] Herder had a deep and sympathetic feeling, an *Einfühlung,* for the individual and the unique; it became the category by which he attempted to comprehend the appearances and forms of national developments, what contributed to their growth or to their decline; it made it possible for him to disregard monolithic theories, to immerse himself in a pluralism that made possible psychological and cultural tolerance and gave comfort and pride to those who sought to discover in their past those unique and distinct qualities, offering the needed and desired differences and origins of historical entities that could provide the justification for each individual survival and manifestation.

> Each form of human perfection then, is, in a sense, national and time bound and, considered most specifically, individual. Nothing develops, without being occasioned by time, climate, necessity, by world events or the accidents of fate. Tendencies or talents slumbering in the heart, therefore, may never become actual accomplishments.[6]

Illustrative of this sense for the peculiarity of *Volk* was Herder's description of the ancient Hebrews. Coupled with land, language, and clan was the amazing attachment of the Hebrews to the word *father*, which created reverential links between the generations and preserved not only a family tradition, but also a national bond. Not only language or climate, but the spiritual union evoked by the word *father* gave credence to the fact that external conditions, not permeated by spiritual threads, were insufficient to create the feeling for *Volk*.[7] In his attempt to discover the forces that spiritualize land and language and give to them decisive importance in the development of a people, Herder would also speak of "the happiest people in history." He could ask which people deserved such designation and could then answer: "I can only say that at a certain time and in certain circumstances, *each* people met with such a moment or else there never was one."[8] Human nature is like clay, assuming different form and character under different circumstances and demands. Climate, land, language, constitution are the categories by which we come to comprehend what is a people, knowing that with these categories we are left with an infinite variety of peoples, laws, and customs, denying us the right to ascribe to any particular one a unique and overriding force and judgment. Each becomes a microcosm having a life of its own showing its own laws of development and decay, leaving us with a Protean vision of ever-changing perspectives.

> Is good not dispersed over the earth? Since one form of mankind and one region could not encompass it, it has been distributed in a thousand forms . . . and even if it does not strive, as it keeps on changing, towards the greater virtue and happiness of the individual -- for man re-

mains forever man -- nonetheless a plan of a progressive endeavor becomes evident. This is my great theme.9

What we are forbidden to advance are those judgments of comparative value where one form of life is given greater credence than another. We stand before an infinite variety of forms and must feel a sympathetic *Einfühlen* with each. "Each age is different, but each has the center of its happiness within itself."10

Beyond this fatal skepticism Herder speaks of forces that transcend the individual and embrace it within a higher kingdom, a kingdom of God where everything has purpose and where cause and effect produce a higher meaning that at first is hard perceived in the immediacy of individual relationships. "Every reformation began with insignificant trifles which only later on became incorporated into a colossal, overall plan; indeed, whenever such a plan was deliberately drawn up in advance, it failed."11 History moves with passion and revolution; the guidance of reason, the divine hand, are figments of our imagination. We cannot, except in fancy, speak of a continuous progress of man toward a better world; at best we must depend upon the accident of a great man, or those quiet discoveries whose consequences only later generations have the insight to comprehend. "What Luther said had long been known; only now Luther spelled it out. When Roger Bacon, Galileo, Descartes and Leibniz made their discoveries they did so quietly."12 If all events belong to a higher purpose, the plan remains hidden. We are only aware that events and ideas bring forth consequences that at first are unknown and unexpected. We must observe from the perspective of later generations the meaning and importance of the work of earlier times. Herder betrayed that sense for distance that denied immediate judgments dominant validity. He had a fine sense for development and change, a sense for the accidental and contingent, for the unexpected and unknown. He was able to view the course of history with a prudence that allowed him to avoid molding events into preconceived laws of development and into unjustifiable ideological schematizations. This was the disease of "cold reason," which Herder knew could be prevented only where instincts and vital energies prevailed, were the driving forces of history, and which reason only later could comprehend. The sharpness of this separation made it difficult for Herder to comprehend that intimate relationship between reason and passion that made possible a dialectical development of human history that neither sacrificed reason to passion nor passion to reason. "The head and the heart are completely separated: man has unfortunately reached the point where he acts not according to what he knows but according to what he desires.''[13]

Herder balanced a sense of nationality with a cosmopolitanism that caused him to condemn both the abstractness that comes from the refusal to grasp the significance of the national entity and the barbarism that is perpetuated in the national entity that does not relate and absorb from others. ''The princes speak French and soon everybody will follow their example; and then behold perfect bliss: the golden age.''[14] ''But, on the other hand, that nation that turns in upon itself will, however, in time get set in its own ways. . . . Isolated by their self-imposed limitations, they [nations] continue for centuries in the most astounding ignorance like islanders who had never heard of fire, unaware of the simplest mechanical skills.''[15] This attempt to maintain a balance between uniqueness and dependence makes it possible for Herder to speak of the infinite possibilities that lie between the means and ends of national life, to become immersed in the innumerable contingent and accidental relationships that embrace the human possibility; to be caught in the quicksand of individuality as the unique category of reality. There is a vast panorama of contingent and unknown relationships making any attempt to grasp them in a meaningful whole the work of fancy and delusion. History has become the multiplication of individualities for the sake of individualities. Yet Herder is aware that in this abyss of change ''the same kernel of human substance and happiness can, and in all probability does remain virtually the same.''[16] Curiously, Herder, who had this eye for the individual, the unique, and the unexpected, interlaces these insights with equally sharp dogmatic judgments that startle and shock.

> There is no country whose civilization has been able to take a backward step and become for a second time what it was before. The path of destiny is as inflexible as iron: the scenes of that time, of that world, have passed by; the aims, whatever they were, are gone -- can today become yesterday.?[17]

It is at this moment that we comprehend that irreconcilable conflict between the understanding that attempts to grasp the infinite possibilities of contingent and accidental relationships, the dogmatic insistence that there can be no movement from the individual to the universal; that the universal is the proclamation of an iron law of history refusing the individual the source of universality and universality the embodiment in individuality, refusing each reality fulfillment in the other. The two moments remain in sharp and irreconcilable separation excluding the realization that in separation the ground of reunion and rediscovery is already present. The attempt to reduce individuality and universality to empirical concepts, i.e., to constitutive principles, imprisons these moments of reason, denies their heuristic nature, and confuses the concept with the idea, doing havoc to philosophy as the realization of a "natural dialectic of human reason." The philosopher is left with observations and reflections about history that delight us with their insight and imagination, but we are denied the endeavor to comprehend reason as the actual and the actual as reason; we are refused the task of philosophy that Hegel clearly enunciated as the comprehension that "what is *wirklich,* is reason." We have reverted to a constructivist metaphysics.

We find Herder asking how it is possible to comprehend this confusion that history seems to give us.

> We have ransacked and rummaged through almost all nations of our present age and through the history of all previous ages, almost without knowing what we are looking for. Historical facts and researches, descriptions of discoveries and travels, are available in plenty, but who will sort them out and sift them?[18]

Herder is correct that the accumulation of detail can be infinite and its availability without end, but the problem of meaning demands not an immediate grasp of facts; it is not an immediate seizure of purpose. Immediacy requires elevation to mediation. It requires reason, the realization that freedom is negation, that comprehension takes place in an already meaningful world and that the development of man is that encompassing of individuality in universality. Every state of human development is the embodiment of reason. In this comprehension man comes to an ever-deeper awareness that the movement of history makes it ever more possible for man to discover and reveal the reason that he is, as long as he is man, and that is the world even in its most depraved state. Herder was aware that historical observations and judgments had to be made, for where there is no reasonable discourse there is no history; where there is reasonable discourse there is historical development, there is that search for universality that is at the core of all thinking. Herder could say that "the smallest detail contains so much order along with so much confusion, so many perplexities along with the means for their solution, and both the order and confusion are a security and a guarantee for the rapturous splendour of the whole."[19] Herder continues with despair before the caprice and vast unknowability of history; he compares himself to Socrates, who recognized the limits of humanity, and could he, Herder, do less than proclaim his own minuteness in God's plan? Finally he asks, "Shall we be able to discern the end of the chain which links peoples and continents, observe how it forged its links hesitantly at first, then with increasing vehemence and clamor, until it began to weld the nations together, more firmly though less perceptibly?"[20] The question already implies its answer because Herder is aware that the constant and continuous search for the smallest detail, characteristic, and quality has made it impossible to grasp any concept, any regulative principle or idea that would make possible a comprehension of history. Individuality imprisons; it opens reality to chance and caprice; it denies individuality as the embodiment of universality; the extension of fate implies that any attempt to transcend individuality is fancy and illusion. We are condemned to a reason-forsaken world, ruled and dominated solely by sentiment and passion serving no purpose but the expression of vital energies, causing change and revolution without meaning beyond the circumference of the individual and its relationship with other individual entities. Truth appears beyond the human capacity already condemned to chance and contingency. We are all let loose to forge our own directions, for none are worth more than another; in the end the search for a meaning of history ends in scorn and discredit. Reason no longer commands; it has yielded to the arbitrariness of sentiment. The philosophical discourse becomes the pursuit of all, equally assured of their worth and validity, for if reality is the abandonment of truth, then all proofs, investigations, and projects are in vain; philosophy is no longer the comprehension of the rational; it has become random reflections and maxims, observations and insights into the geographic, climatic, political, linguistic conditions of society. But from this base it proceeds no further into the political and moral as the realization of man as a rational being. It explores no longer the progress of reason from its embodiment in family to society and to the state. It has lost its grasp of philosophy as "its time comprehended in thought." It has abandoned the idea that when a moment of maturity has been achieved it has already been surpassed. "When philosophy paints its grey in grey then has a shape of life grown old. By philosophy's grey in grey it cannot be rejuvenated but only understood." These most-cited words of Hegel reveal no iron laws or dictates of ideologies, but a subtle and sensitive comprehension of history that can be comprehended only when one age or form is passing on to the new. The philosopher is not the prophet or the artist, but the explorer and discoverer of reason in all its manifold and varied expression. In its realization through that universal law of negativity, in its denial of immediacy and the transformation of the reality of existence into a moment of reason, in this mediation it makes comprehensible and meaningful the course of human events. It realizes the moments of consciousness, it unfolds levels of freedom, it causes a deeper and more extensive grasp of that fundamental movement between universal and individual and prevents each moment from becoming that fixity that threatens thinking, that violence that finds its ground in the irreconcilable separation of the universal and the individual.

In 1784 Herder began his monumental work *Reflections on the Philosophy of the History of Mankind,* which is a panoramic sweep of universal history adding up to a series of insights and reflections on comparative civilizations, the factors affecting their growth and development and remarks on the ends of human nature. It is these remarks that concern us.

> God made man a deity upon Earth; he implanted in him the principle of self-activity, and set this principle in motion from the beginning, by means of the internal and external wants of his nature. Man could not live and support himself, without learning to make use of his reason: no sooner, indeed, did he begin to make use of this, than the door was opened to a thousand errors and mistaken attempts; but at the same time, and even through these very mistakes and errors, the way was cleared to a better use of his reason.[21]

The development of reason is born in necessity; it is awakened in the historical situation. In it man discovers the demands and challenges from which he develops moral and political life. Error becomes the source of progress; it is not to be disregarded as an aberration, but bears within itself the cause of positive consequences. This was an important recognition, but it fades away into discussions of the laws of climates and the identification between the temperate zones and forms of beauty, reason, and humanity. Nature's laws are the embodiment of reason, and the object of all meaningful exploration and research must be the presentation of these laws because they are the incarnation of that hidden harmony that allows us to avoid caprice and accident, forging a union between the external and the internal, giving us the source of explanation that makes human life clear and explicable. This reduction of man's life to natural laws leaves that realm of human activity we call freedom open to the unknown, unpredictable and arbitrary. ''Everywhere man is what he was capable of rendering himself, and what he had the will and power to become."22 The course of human development seems to embody a natural and predisposed law of growth and order that lies at the core of the species -- not an evolution from one species to another, but the achievement within the species of its potentiality. Whatever the course of development, the deviations, the "unruly passions" or "spirits of destruction," man has the power "not to entrust their flocks to these wolves and tigers, and even to tame them by the laws of humanity."23 The law of nature will have its way whatever the deviations in the species. It is this trust in nature's way that allows Herder to believe in progress toward a greater humanization of the species, toward a diffusion of knowledge and a lessening of the inhumanity and destruction that man brings upon his fellow man. Nature dictates this development; she made evils to challenge man to accomplish the good, poisons to bring forth medicine, storms to advance science, passions to drive man to confront the unknown. From the comprehension of nature man finds harmony and purposiveness; the more he trusts nature, the more he is capable of allowing contradictions to find their reconciliation.

Herder grants to reason the power to produce "unity out of multiplicity, order out of disorder, and out of variety of powers and designs one symmetrical and durably beautiful whole."24 Here we discover Herder's interpretation of reason as the essence of man, the expression of his humanity, i.e., of humanity; it is the "tissue of human history," it is man's guide. "He instructs, solaces and animates me, he is my brother, a sharer in the same soul of the World, the one human reason, the one human truth."25 We call it the one human truth, the source of life and permanency. This reason that Herder so profusely praises has its destiny determined by nature, fulfilling a purpose beyond itself, a tool of a higher power, denying to itself the freedom that could only come to it in its liberation from nature. Not within nature does it achieve itself, but in its attempt to overcome nature it begins to realize reason thinking itself as reason, the process of liberation that elevates man from immediacy to the realization of the eternal law of negation by which and through which whatever is positive finds the source of its beginning, and in which man moves from abstract person to subject, from family member to citizen, reconciling himself to himself, creating himself from what he does, realizing at each moment what it is to be man, the being with historical and social needs, the being who confronts and overcomes natural desire, the being who, faced with needs, creates himself in their overcoming. For Herder reason no longer links time with time. Is it not that totality in which every age must find both its differentiation and its belonging to the whole.

> Thus every return to ancient times, even the celebrated years of Plato, is a fiction, is, from the ideas of the World and of Time, an impossibility. We float onwards: but the stream that has once flowed, returns no more to the source. . . . History herself sings with a hundred voices, speaks with a hundred tongues.26

Although Herder speaks of the laws of nature and the inner harmony that they reveal, he was caught by the multiplicity and manifoldness of historical reality and resigned to its variety and uniqueness, knowing no bond that ties these unique expressions to each other or gives them a purpose beyond themselves. Immersed in them they seem lost forever in their individualities, subject only to that insatiable curiosity of man desiring to know more and more of their specific characteristics but not knowing if their existence has a purpose beyond their immediacy.

> The God, whom I seek in history, must be the same as in nature: for a man is but a small part of the whole, and his history, like that of the grub, is intimately woven with that of the web he inhabits. . . . Everything that can take place upon Earth, must take place upon it, provided it happens according to rules, that carry their perfection within themselves.27

Reason is the search for these rules. At its highest moment it is a mirroring of the natural laws to which all phenomena submit and find their unity. History compared to the grub is subject to the same understanding that organizes natural phenomena, the same timeless categories that make possible the experience of nature; the historical object is now fused with the natural object, the realm of values identified with the realm of nature. Thinking is no longer apprehended in thinking; "the free will which wills the free will" loses its validity in the reduction of reason to nature, this denial of the object of reason as the regulative principle of reality, this identity of reality with the objects of the understanding, with cognitive objects, the refusal to comprehend the dialectic that "engenders" and "dissolves every particularization of the universal" and prepares for a new form, a new moment of the realization of the universal. We lack in Herder the thinking of reason; we are resigned to a travelogue of descriptions and observations structured within a constructive metaphysics of natural laws. All the works of God have their stability in themselves, and in their beautiful consistency, for all their repose, within their determinate limits, on the equilibrium of contending powers, by their intrinsic energy which reduces them to order. "Guided by this clew, I wander through the labyrinth of history, and everywhere perceive divine harmonious order. . . ."[28] For Herder man is the observer and explorer of the creation. He walks through its history and observes the forms that arise and decay never to be repeated or recaptured, moments of uniqueness both of men and of nations making their specific and indelible mark on this panorama of human history, to be valued and preserved like monuments in a museum. We become collectors of these monuments, appreciating each for its intrinsic value, not allowing ourselves to compare or contrast, to value or devalue, attempting to create that amazing distance, *Urdistanz,* from each so as to give it its due and respect. Herder is revolutionary, for no thinker before him had so carefully held up before us the need to judge each historical reality in its own terms, to learn to appreciate every form that comes forth from nature as a necessary moment of the divine harmony. Not knowing how each piece fits, we nevertheless are bound not to rush into easy explanations and ideologies, but to wait in patience, with prudence, until we can comprehend the purpose that nature has assigned to each phenomenon, knowing and trusting her wisdom: that each part has a place, the importance of which is in its existence, part and parcel of a harmony known only to God.

In 1784 Kant wrote a review of the first part of Herder's *Reflections* or *Ideas* in which we observe the differences that separated their perspectives toward history. Deeper than these differences and perspectives is the manifestation of distant conceptions of philosophy. In Herder, Kant conceives a constructivist and dogmatic metaphysics, "even though," as Kant says, "our author renounces it, as fashion demands."[29] Herder constructs a philosophy of nature that finds its perfection in man, a construction that moves from the lowest level of being to the highest, in which every existent has its proper place and validity, every object has its being from the place which it occupies in this hierarchy. Place confers being and being is determined by place. Herder remains tied to a philosophy of being, denying the possibility that meaning and not being confers reality upon things. Kant claims that the purpose of the first part of the *Ideas* shows that the spiritual nature of the human soul, its permanence and progress toward perfection, is to be proved by analogy with the natural forms of matter, particularly in their structure, with no recourse to metaphysics. . . . But, what should we think of this hypothesis of invisible forces acting on the organism; and then how should we regard the design which aims to explain that which one does not comprehend by that which one comprehends even less?[30]

The reduction of man's spiritual nature to analogies with natural forces and forms eliminates that profound division between objects of the understanding and the object of reason, between the regulative and constitutive principle of objects, and denies all validity to the meaning of the aesthetic and rational idea; it proclaims the God of nature and leaves abandoned and godless the realm of the mind, its freedom and source of movement and development: the eternal law of negation. This idea of an organic force, Kant claims, belongs to speculative philosophy, is a regulative principle that when transfigured into a constitutive one plays havoc with natural and spiritual reality, reducing both realms to mechanical and predetermined laws to be mirrored and recorded, eliminating that vital tension between the natural and the human order, between being and meaning, necessity and freedom, between that desire and need to explain and to prove, and that need to understand and to think. Central to the whole discussion of Kant's reviews[31] was Herder's denial that the moral and rational development of man did not belong to the peculiar nature of the human species, but lay "completely outside it in an understanding of and instruction by other natures. As a result, all progress in culture would only be a projected communication and fortuitous proliferation of an original tradition."[32] In this vast realm of the unknown and indeterminable instruction by other natures, man is no longer allowed, or morally obligated, to bring forth a meaningful moral existence, to orientate himself in the world, to realize his potentialities, and to forge that political constitution that makes possible the concepts of human rights, the exercise of critique, the release from self-imposed tutelage, and the right to be happy.

Implied in the Kantian critique of Herder's *Ideas* is the fact that man is not simply a knower, but a doer. Higher than knowledge is action.[33] Man acts from ideas and acts as a being who bears within himself the force and capacity to change things, and it is with this capacity that man can comprehend the passion that is at the root of historical change. Kant in the "Canon of Pure Reason" advances the "interest of reason" to the point where it becomes clear beyond doubt that the object of reason, different from the objects of the understanding, is the source and impetus to man's action in the world. The "idea" can arouse the person to a degree that is beyond the capacity of knowledge. Action, like the idea, refuses the world that *is* and puts before it the *should be;* it is this confrontation between being and meaning that makes the meaning of history a possibility. Three problems face us when we attempt to comprehend the category of action: "what we ought to do if the will is free, if there is a God and a future world."[34] We face what happens with *what ought to happen.* We are not captives of nature, bound by our senses and limited to our experiences. Freedom is a fact that is proved, not by an investigation of origins -- if such is ever possible -- but through its consequences. Freedom is, because it has effects. In every particular situation where the moral problem arises -- for it can only arise in a particular situation -- historical morality confronts pure morality, and it is in this confrontation that decision and action take place, endeavoring not to fuse the historical with the pure, but to relate them to each other as moments of freedom, revealing the dialectic of the universal and particular. In the needs and dependencies of man, the confrontation is constant and free; it is a confrontation that can be comprehended as a continuous interpretation denying the fixity of being for the openness of meaning. Kant was certain that if philosophy yielded a deeper concern for ideas than it did for knowledge, it was because philosophy was inseparable from the need to find the meaning of human life, that thinking was orientation in the world, and that decision to view reality *as if* there were a highest intelligence, a creative reason and simple mental substance, was possible only because there is a "natural dialect of human reason." The ideas of pure reason "arise from the very nature of our reason; and it is impossible that this highest tribunal of all the rights and claims of speculation should itself be a source of deception and illusions."[35] From this natural dialectic we do not construct relations; we think relations. For philosophy we think the analogy of qualitative, not of quantitative relations; we discover the relationship between things, not what things are. We are involved in that continuous interpretation of reality, the search for heuristic principles and paradigms, the need to elaborate what Kant meant by separating quantitative from qualitative relations. The ideas that arise from this natural dialectic of reason are heuristic, regulative principles, the *as if* affirmation that does not pretend to construct reality, but only to understand it; not to find explanations, but only to elaborate it. Reason finds its expression in the "relative supposition" that we must not assume to be absolute. "This distinction has to be reckoned with in the case of a merely regulative principle. We recognize the necessity of the principle, but have no knowledge of the source of its necessity. . . ."36 To think the possibility of the existence of being that corresponds to a transcendental idea does not necessarily allow me to confirm th existence of that being. In this duality between thinking and existence there lies the need for decision and action.

The gap between thinking and existence creates an estrangement that posits the ground of its reconciliation, *Faden der Ruckkehr*. Kantian duality implies a natural, not an imposed dialectic, the objective dialectic of the subject, that dialectic discovered in the reason of the subject manifested in reality, in the realization of negation, the ground of the subject actualized as reason. Kant affirmed:

> I shall not be entitled, but shall be constrained to realize this idea, that is, to posit it for a real object. But I may posit it only as something which I do not at all know in itself, and to which, as a ground of that systematic unity, I ascribe in relation to this unity such properties as are analogous to the concepts employed by the understanding in the empirical sphere.37

Thinking requires qualitative analogies, metaphors, symbols; it is the search for the meaning of reasonable life, for its history, i.e., its development, its decline, its hopes, ends and moral demands. The problem is not to know the object of my idea

> according to what may be in itself; it is to give meaning to the object I know. The idea is the ground of the relationship which I establish between myself and my situation, the basis of my actions and conception of the world, the realization of my moral and political responsibility; it is a regulative and heuristic principle. The vocation of the idea, different from the unity of the objects in a cognitive concept, is the unity in reason: the unity of a system and this systematic unity does not serve objectively as a principle which extends the application of reason to objects, but subjectively as a maxim that extends its application to all possible empirical knowledge of objects.38

This idea of systematic unity is beyond all experience and is at the same time the source of the possibility of experience, yielding, however, no exemplification of systematic unity. The impossibility of finding for the idea an adequate manifestation, making it problematic and not "real absolutely and in itself," makes it possible to grasp the idea as the source of experience but not identifiable with it. The relationship between the idea and experience must be thought analogously, as a qualitative relationship, assuming the possibility that the world has its source in a creative reason. Their relationship belongs to the natural dialectic of reason, to the objectivity of subjectivity, to that dialectic of the subject that is objective. The objective dialectic of the subject reveals that in the separation of the idea from reality there is already given the source of their relationship, the endeavor to overcome what has become determined and fixed, what lies in the quantitative relationship as given and measured, and what remains embodied in being not transformed and transfigured in meaning, making it impossible to give purposive unity, "to regard all order in the world as if it had originated in a purpose." This is the interest of reason. "The idea of such unity is, therefore, inseparably bound up with the very nature of our reason. The same idea is on that account legislative for us. . . ."39 Not only are the ideas necessary if the object of thinking is the meaning of reasonable human life, but the idea is legislative; it causes us to think ourselves as lawgivers, as capable of structuring reality and giving it meaning, but here we come face to face with Kant's warning that "to take the regulative principle of the systematic unity of nature as being a constitutive principle and to hypostatize, and presuppose as a cause, that which serves, merely in idea, as the ground of the consistent employment of reason, is simply to confound reason."40 Kant has given us a structure in which we can think the problem of historical meaning and interpretation. The difference he draws between the regulative and constitutive principle is fundamental; it is the difference between the idea and concept, between the objects of the understanding and the object of reason, between thinking and explaining, between the search for meaning, order, and purposiveness and the desire to fix reality in quantitative relationships. The idea remains a guide for meaning and unity; it functions to deny and refuse the absoluteness and totality of any moment of reality. The idea is the realization of the eternal law of negation; its history is that of pure reason, it has preserved the possibility of what Kant calls the critical path: "to secure for human reason complete satisfaction in regard to that which it has all along so eagerly occupied itself, though hitherto in vain."41

"From the very nature of our reason" there arises the need and interest which we must and should take in the meaning of human life, in its history and purposiveness; it is from this nature that we derive ideas for the guidance and elaboration of experience, ideas which we can call "heuristic principles"; principles of the understanding, i.e., "undetermined without the schemata of sensibility," yielding rules or principles for unity, enunciating the need for meaning to be more vital than the acquisition of knowledge; bringing together knowledge and value, showing the meaninglessness of their separability, making us more and more aware that fact and meaning are one. The "interest of reason" gives forth in "maxims of reason," but whatever be the particular maxim used by the thinker, the "interest of reason" is singular: to seek the meaning of human life, to make possible that action and decision that enhance the moral and political value of life, knowing that the "interest of reason" is the expression of freedom that determines no-thing and is the possibility of everything. When we think of history as the struggle, not of the individual, but of the organized groups against violence, we think of society and the individual who, knowing that he cannot struggle alone against violence, seeks the group, in which and through which, morally and politically, the individual becomes man, not as subject to the arbitrariness of the state, not in opposition to the state, but through the state to that freedom and infinite validity that is in man as moral and political subject. History is the exploration and elaboration of this movement of man through the varied forms of organized life, to its highest moment, the state, and to the realization of that freedom which is actualized at every moment of organized life. Kant maintains in the *Critique of Judgment* that man could not be considered only as the physical end of nature, "but as the being upon this earth who is the *ultimate end* of nature, and the one in relation to whom all other natural beings constitute a system of ends."[42] Man, we suppose, has the will and intelligence to give purpose to his existence, to make himself more than a "link in the chain of physical ends"; he has the capacity to choose, to realize the development of this capacity; to choose in freedom. Kant calls this culture. Man meditates upon his history. He conceives and analyzes the forces that have brought it about, the violence and passion that are its motive powers; but no matter how deeply he knows himself to be rooted in these forces, he believes that he has the force to change its direction. We study our diplomatic and political history, we perceive periods of intellectual "break-throughs" and "breakdowns," we shudder before the calamities of war, but we are resolved that the knowledge we acquire, the insight we achieve, and the moral agitation that stirs up must become spurs for developing to their highest the talents and virtues that can suppress, overcome, and go beyond these forces, elevate our sense of freedom, increase our capacity to communicate ideas and to make comprehensible that concept of humanity that is embodied in the "universal feeling of sympathy" and in that faculty "to communicate universally one's inmost self" showing that "social spirit" that raises man above the animal. Yet, it is not only the ability to communicate a social spirit or the inmost self, but it is that historical spirit that links age to age, that through separation of time and space forces the threads of return that thinking creates between one epoch and another, realizing that rational path that developed in confrontation with dogmatism and skepticism, and that is embodied in the political and moral dimensions of reality. The realization that history is the present comprehending and interpreting the past, that this comprehension of the past is at the same time the present overcoming itself, preparing not for the coming of a future, but for the "break-through" of the universal in the present. This poses many questions about the meaning of history for the philosopher and philosophy. Is not history the dimension in which freedom, the humanity of man, finds its actualization? Is freedom born from itself or in situation, responding to the needs of man searching for meaningful life and who knows that meaning is decision and action, who knows that knowledge is value and that freedom is negation, i.e., the source of the manifestation of reason in political and moral life?[43] The meaning of history belongs to that constant retaking, *reprise,* of the past from and by the present, i.e., from a perspective of values diametrically in conflict with those of the past, but which elicit from the past meaning for the present, meaning that is transformed in and transforms the present. This thinking takes place in the moral and political existence of man, not as the lonely individual, but as the being whose individuality is the source of universality. Kant justly stated this development when he said that "human knowledge begins with intuitions, proceeds from thence to concepts and ends with ideas." We can parallel this development and speak of the movement from family, civil society, and state, raising from the immediacy of the natural being to the freedom of the reasonable being who in the reasonable state finds those laws which recognize the value and meaning of these reasonable needs and desires of the citizen.

Returning to the question of the meaning of history, we are faced with Kant's radical statements that express the pure objective moral law, that forces a moral demand upon a world given to absurdity, lawlessness, and violence; in other words, Kant causes us to think universality and transcendence; he requires us to think the universal in the particular, the pure in the impure, the timeless in time.

Now, moral-practical reason within us voices its irresistible veto: *There shall be no war*, either between thee and me in a state of nature or among states, which are still in a lawless condition in their external relations with one another even though internally they are not. . . . We must, however, act *as though* perpetual peace were a reality, which perhaps it is not, by working for its establishment and for the kind of constitution that seems best adapted for bringing it about.[44]

What Kant indicates in these and many similar statements is that philosophy is thinking transcendence, ideas that move toward universality and universability because thinking stands already in universality and is its actualization; we are always moving toward, we are always incomplete and inadequate for the transcendence that confronts *what is* with what *ought to be*. But it is in this tension and demand that we grasp in our individuality, in our historical situation, the eternal, the universal. From this point of view we can say that philosophy is thinking the universal. Every period of history is what Weil has called a "breaking through" toward universality.[45] On the historical level it is this "breaking through" that characterizes the most significant moments of our history, our autobiography. This "breaking through" is accompanied by the "breaking down"; the idea is not realized, there is no final "breakthrough" nor "breakdown"; there is continuous movement toward universality and universability. The final end is the hope that has stirred philosophers from Plato to Hegel, and it is from this hope that we assume the duty to the moral law in us; imagining that it can deceive us, that we can pervert it, we surrender to animality and to the mechanism of nature. Our struggle is not for the realization of a new future world, but for meaning in the present. Philosophy is not the surrender of the present for the future, but the realization of the present as the embodiment of the universal, of the universability of the moral law and of our duty toward it. We write the history of mankind from within history, i.e., from that struggle for and "breakthrough" toward universality at every stage of our autobiography.

If we look back at the thoughts of Herder we can agree with the judgment of Isaiah Berlin:

Finally I come to what is perhaps the most revolutionary of the implications of Herder's position, his famous rejection of absolute values, his pluralism. Men, according to Herder, truly flourish only in congenial circumstances, that is, where the group to which they belong has achieved a fruitful relationship with the environment by which it is shaped and which in turn it shapes.[46]

These are reflections and observations adding up to maxims of wisdom yielding little in the form of a philosophy of history, a comprehension of the relationship between the universal and particular, that "breakthrough" of ideas into historical reality, that tension and confrontation between historical and pure morality, between the demands of the *ought to be* and the resistance of what *is,* between the absurdity, lawlessness, and violence of historical life and the constant struggle. The "breaking through" of universality and universability is the breaking through of the moral into the immoral and amoral. With Kant the meaning of history becomes a philosophical problem;[47] it is no longer a random preoccupation, an outline of historical laws, observation on political techniques, geography, language, and climate; and above all, it is not "poetic imagination," the source of dogmatic metaphysics denying that there is a fundamental difference between the object of reason and the objects of the understanding, between ideas, the qualitative relationships that are the architectonic of reason, and the quantitative relationships that are the measure and definition of empirical reality. It is the history of the "breakthrough toward universality" that delineates the autobiography of man's struggle for reason.

5

Hermann Cohen and Kant: A Philosophy of History from Jewish Sources

One of the most interesting developments of Kant's philosophy was its transformation and expression in the philosophical work of the head of the Marburg School of Kant interpretation, the philosopher Hermann Cohen (1842-1918). We can speak of a transformation because the last two works of Cohen, *The Concept of Religion in the System of Philosophy* (1915) and *Religion of Reason out of the Sources of Judaism* (1919; 1929, 2nd ed.), attempt to enunciate a philosophy of history rooted in the philosopher's endeavor to discover in Jewish sources an ethic and a messianic vision that could be comprehended as the consequence and fulfillment of Kant's moral philosophy. The link that Cohen attempted to establish between Kant and Judaism implied a conviction and belief that a historical religious faith -- its history, and its peculiar endurance -- witnessed a sense of history deeply rooted in values that posited a belief in the *ought to be*, in the refusal to accept as fate the *what is*. This faith was capable of structuring a vision of the future that neither rejected nor devalued the present, but placed before it a teleology that brought to clarity the struggle and confrontation that the ethic of the pure will realizes within the limitation of the historical moral situation. Cohen was a believer, having that faith in reason that has been the philosopher's from Plato to Hegel, but this faith found embodiment not only in the love of ideas, but in the love of a people's metahistorical history and in the moral significance which that reality bore for the history of mankind. The ideal of humanity belonged not only to its theoretical expression. Cohen assumed that the respect and admiration that Kant showed to Job was identical to the reality of the suffering and loving Israel, the suffering servanthood of God, which if understood from an ethical perspective would yield insights into that cosmic conflict between ignorance and reason. At the end of his essay on "What Is Orientation in Thinking," an essay that Cohen deeply admired, Kant said,

Assume what appears most believable to you after careful and honest testing, whether it be facts or principles of reason; but do not wrest from reason that which makes it the highest good on earth, i.e., the prerogative of being the ultimate touchstone of truth. . . . To make use of one's own reason means nothing more than to ask one's self, with regard to everything that is to be assumed, whether he finds it practicable to make the ground of the assumption or the rule that follows from the assumption a universal principle of the use of his reason.[1]

While it is true that Cohen turned to the sources of Judaism to explore and comprehend the question of the meaning of history, it is equally true that his attempt to grasp the meaning of history from within Judaism appeared as a deviation from reason. In fact, it is Judaism which is embraced in reason and is expressed and transformed in it. The unique position of Cohen is centered on his affirmation that reason is the "touchstone of truth" and that a great religious and historical tradition, given a cosmic historical interpretation, is a realization of the conflict between the profane and the holy, the delineation of a messianic age embodying the idea of reason and peace. This can be revealed from within the ideas of reason and made meaningful to those who trust and believe that reason embraces the deepest and most extensive needs and dependencies of man and mankind. It was also Cohen's belief that the meaning of history lay beyond the narration of facts and the proof of theories; that history was inseparable from morality, from the theomorphic reality of man, from the universalism that is embodied in a God whose presence is the incarnation of an ethical imperative that commands every man to see in the other an end and not a means. History deepens and extends our feeling for the human and makes possible that deepest of all relationships: the correlation between man and man and that between God and man.

In the "Conjectural Beginning of Human History" (1786) Kant reflects upon those moments of moral awareness that indicate a movement away from sensuality toward a sense of decency, *Sittsamkeit*.

Refusal was the feat which brought about the passage from merely sensual to spiritual attractions, from mere animal desire to love, and along with this from the feeling of the merely agreeable to a taste for beauty. . . . In addition there came a first hint at the development of man as a moral creature. This came from a sense of decency . . . by concealing all that which might arouse low esteem. Here, incidentally, lies the real basis of all true sociability.[2]

Cohen was deeply attracted to the idea of refusal because he knew that it embodied neither a simple rejection nor an abstract negation, but was the source of positive reality. It was unending judgment, *das unendliche Urteil*, the unending moral activity; it was the refusal to reduce the uniqueness and peculiarity of the moral law to a credal-dogmatic statement, the refusal of all fixity. The Oneness of God, the idea of humanity were no longer secular ideas for Cohen; these were transformed and transfigured in the history of Monotheism. The Oneness of God is yet to be realized; it belongs to a messianic history that embraces and fulfills the idea of humanity. The history of mankind is inseparable from the history of God. His Oneness is yet incomplete, it has not brought forth the oneness of mankind, the two remain estranged, the struggle for the one is the struggle for the other, the Oneness of God is the responsibility and ideal of mankind. Cohen refused to consider these ideas as theoretical speculations, as the foundation of ethics. They had to respond to the need for meaning, to the needs and dependencies of moral life in situation, to the need of man to comprehend the moral demand of God as unending judgment and privation, as that peculiar and distinct Oneness to which no numerical figure is adequate, but in relation to which all numerical figures are insufficient. Cohen wanted to comprehend the reality of Israel, which for him did not symbolize, but actualize the struggle for God's Oneness. It is in the unique reality of Israel that Cohen takes his philosophy beyond Kant. Is it a leap into a historical tradition and dogma? Is it a fantasy to attempt to reconcile a religious faith and history with the ideas of reason? Should or must our commitment to one exclude the other, or is there not a ground of similarity that makes it possible for each to enlighten the other? Each has grown from man's need to comprehend the meaning of historical life and create that reasonable discourse that is imperative for the believer in reason. Cohen incarnates this discourse into the correlation between man and man and man and God. He embodies it in his belief in the dialogue that has taken place between Israel and God, in that profound moral confrontation that he envisioned between messianic humanity and the profane speculations of skeptical, eudaemonistic, and dogmatic attitudes that deny that longing for universality characteristic of the discourse of monotheism and its vision of messianic humanity, but at the same time prepare for it through denial. Just as Job's friends failed to turn him from his trust in God and strengthened his resolve to confirm Him in his

sufferings, similarly Cohen believed that the sufferings of Israel were the source
of her strength, her realization that her partnership with God brought forth not
only its own redemption but also God's. This partnership with God, *Bun-
desgenosse Gottes*, was Cohen's most courageous transformation of ethics into a
cosmic divine human drama in which both God and man in deepest dependence
found redemption in each other. The intimate dependence of God on man and
man on God gives to human history a dimension of redemption hardly spoken of
by philosophers of former ages. Cohen fused divine and human history not in
the individual, but in the historical destiny of Peoplehood. No longer was this a
history of secular events, but an openness to the transfiguration of every secular
dimension into a divine significance. The Holy and the Profane were joined in
the present, but their exclusivity was to be overcome when the Oneness of God
would be realized in creation. The unfinished divine odyssey is paralleled by the
incomplete and yet unrealized moral inadequacy of man. Just as man has made
but few steps toward the moral, toward that "breakthrough to the universal," so
God is only slowly emerging in His divinity, grasped so imperfectly by man,
whose moral life is at its beginning. The dynamic that Cohen sets forth to embody the historical meaning of that correlation and partnership between God and
Israel removes all limitations to an heroic responsibility that man and the people
must and should take for God's needs. It appears that Cohen, deeply conscious
of man's central position in this moral struggle for God's redemption, brought to
a level of moral vision and responsibility man's role and responsibility as human
and divine rarely contemplated or revealed. Cohen attempted a transformation
of Kant's doctrine of virtue that was elaborated in the *Metaphysics of Morals*.
He transferred the doctrine of virtue to the correlation between Israel and God.
He transfigured the doctrine into a world drama, a philosophy, and theology of
history. He raised it to a level where man's strength to fulfill his duty is surpassed by a people's strength to fulfill a trust given to it to reveal a moral law
that is none other than the Oneness of God embodying the oneness of humanity.
The strength to fulfill such a responsibility was from the beginning the destiny
of Israel, the purpose of its creation, and the need that God had for articulation
and actualization. The meaning of history becomes a theodicy, and it is this
theodicy that Cohen elaborates. Kant has revealed the absolute nature of the unconditioned Ought and at the same time showed how easily "mean, natural beings endowed with reason who are unholy enough that pleasure can induce them
to transgress the moral law, even though they recognize its authority. And when
they do obey the law, they do it reluctantly, and so under constraint."3 For

Cohen the collective strength of Israel would fulfill its destiny when that trust which was placed in her showed a capacity to be true to that archetype of all commands, the "Sanctification of the Holy Name."

With the virtue faithfulness, *Treue*,[4] we go beyond the individual to the faithfulness of a people. The virtue of faithfulness links the generations. From the Covenant with Abraham to what Cohen believed to be his covenant in faithfulness, there has been forged this partnership with God, with the truth that is embodied in a relationship that does justice not only to reason, to the work of culture, but to the meaning of monotheism, the equality of all before God, before that God who in covenant with Abraham covenanted with all mankind. Cohen, bound to this covenant, drew God in to experience and converted secular history into a history of covenant. Kant had made it clear that religion was a duty of man to himself. "Again we have a duty with regard to what lies entirely beyond the limits of our experience but is yet encountered, according to its possibility, in our Ideas, e.g., the Idea of God. It is called the duty of religion: the duty of recognizing all our duties *as if* they were divine commands."[5] Kant refuses to go beyond the idea; he negates the fact that we have before us a being "to whom we are under obligation for in that case the reality of this being would first have to be shown (revealed) by experience."[6] With Kant's denial and Cohen's affirmation we arrive at the parting of ways of the two philosophers. We must not simply rest satisfied with this separation; we are concerned with the consequences for morality. Whatever belief Cohen was willing to accept, whatever tradition he was capable of belonging to, he was careful to remain loyal to a conviction that went deeper: his faith in reason and the moral law. If he confessed himself a son of Abraham, Isaac, and Jacob, he was also a son of Plato and Kant. If he refused to accept Kant's reasoning to place respect before love,[7] it did not mean that love now replaced respect but that in the context of the biblical faith the love of our fellow man bore witness to the love of humanity, and it is in the love of our fellow man that we come to love God, the love which God has actualized in us, the spirit of His holiness, the love revealed in our heart. Cohen was willing to accept this biblical faith because it implied a social and political consequence that was intimately tied to messianic peace, the goal of moral thought and action. If the philosopher had any purpose it was to reveal the messianic age, and if Judaism had a purpose it was to delineate this messianic peace. In this Messianism Cohen believed Judaism achieved its historical meaning. The central problem to which Cohen's speculations are addressed is the meaning of history. The more we attempt to understand why

Cohen turned to the history of Israel to expand his grasp of Kantian ethics, the more it seems that the problem of history became more and more fundamental to his thinking. Without a messianic age that we could experience in the religious calendar, there would be no concretization of those ideas of reason, no struggle or confrontation with the profane, and no need for that courage and faithfulness that determine that correlation between man and God in a world that remains indifferent and contradictory.

The actualization of the messianic age is peace. It is the purpose of Israel to reveal the messianic age, to achieve the significance of the original covenant, to redeem suffering, to fulfill a cosmic mission, to realize reason, and to give hope to a humanity that longs for meaning and purpose.

Peace requires an acceptance of the universal divine kingship, of a kingdom of faith and of an eternal faithful people. It is a kingdom in which eudaemonism and sophism have been negated. Its values lie beyond the worldly material attractions; its truths have only begun to be revealed. The accompanied sufferings are not unknown elements, and at moments of great moral heights they are transfigured into "sufferings of love." Though the messianic age might be delayed for thousands of years, there is an assurance that in the truth of the divine providence the day will surely come. It was this reconciliation with the coming of the messianic age that made the path to peace a holy one. It was also a path that could avoid the despair that clustered around this messianic peace and drove men to reject the world. Belief is not adequate, for without knowledge true peace is unattainable. The way that God shows cannot be known by belief alone, and the command to do justice, righteousness, and loving kindness is not fulfilled without study and learning. The knowledge of God is the love of God; from His Being and attributes flow those commandments for justice and righteousness upon which the moral universe depends. The freedom from injustice prepares for the messianic age, an age in which the knowledge of God will be the concern of man. Although Cohen clearly separated philosophy from religion in all his previous works, it appears that in this final work the division vanishes, for in the messianic age the goals of philosophy and religion are united. The universal domination of knowledge is necessarily linked and bound to the messianic destiny of mankind. If Israel is the mediator in this destiny, there is joy in this knowledge and a spiritual peace that reflects its truth.

Cohen struggled all his life against philosophies of feeling, pessimism, and skepticism; he knew of their political effects for his fellow Jews. The Messianism of the Torah gave to Israel the uniqueness of her lot, a universalism that struggled against hate and atavism. In hate lies the roots of perversity; this Cohen had already noted in the *Ethics of the Pure Will* and had observed that the rawness of hate was usually and attractively disguised by sophisticated national and religious motives. *Humanitaet* was the weapon that could hopefully negate these cultural perversities. But *Humanitaet* assumes a world that arises from reason in a practical-moral sense, a noumenal world centered in man as subject of morality. Cohen adds to the ethical speculations biblical texts whose validity, although not contrary to ethics, is nevertheless grounded in religious faith. As an example he cites "Thou shalt not hate thy brother in thy heart" (Lev. 19:17); this is a text man must know and believe, for in accordance with it he must act. The world is created through correlation; its moral reality should become concomitant with the Being of the Creator. Man's moral activity redeems a creation that is yet unaware of its truth and the source of its reality. The meaning of creation and revelation is unfolded in the contrast and mutuality that fill correlation. Correlation on a cosmic scale embraces symbolically a messianic kingdom that ties, through love and justice, the uniqueness of God to the oneness of mankind. The highest endeavor of reason has become the clarification of the divine purpose of creation.

Hate is derisive.[8] It tears man from man and nation from nation; it is vanity. *Aller Hass ist umsonst.* Hate is moral violence. It diminishes and finally destroys the subject of morality, moral man; it is the death of the person. To suppose that I hate another is the realization of violence, and with it crumbles the human dialogue, the world; terror is its consequence. The depth of Cohen's insight into the problem of hate is his firm dismissal of attempts to ascribe even false reason to hate, when the essence of hate has in fact, no ground. In this lies its terror. As long as the possibility of hate exists, be it my own or that of another, there can be no peace. Cohen had already made the link between hate, cruelty, and sexual perversity. Their embodiment in a political ideology followed naturally. The dehumanization expressed in disgust, *Ekel*, was already assumed in a hate that was *grundlos und eitel.* Kant had already shown how deep this dehumanization went when he pointed to the utter inability of beautiful art to represent that which excited disgust:

> The Furies, diseases, the devastations of war may even regarded as calamitous be described as very beautiful, as they are represented in a picture. There is only one kind of ugliness *Haesslichkeit* which cannot

be represented in accordance with nature without destroying all aesthetical satisfaction . . . that which excites disgust *Ekel*.9

Hate terrorizes the human, morally and aesthetically. It shows neither contrast nor contradictions that might be gathered into new harmonies, and it destroys the human substance and reduces man to bestiality. Hate penetrates only where the spirit weakens, hope fades, and the practical-moral values and beliefs decline.

Closely related to the problem of hate is that of pessimism. Cohen radically opposes all attempts to ascribe to evil a positive power. In such mystical schemes where the power of the evil and the power of the good are in eternal conflict, the moral substance of monotheism is destroyed. More deeply moral than any other belief of monotheism is that which declares that before God, man is made innocent. The *Shegaga,* unintentional sin, is the limit of man's fault. Man's guilt is but momentary. To ascribe to man an evil character is an excuse to lessen or diminish the moral and religious task placed upon him. The purification of man takes place before God. It is the trust in Him, in His truth, that is the ground of the new truth, the new beginning, and the new hope. Every man can assume the task of holiness; it was given to him as an eternal obligation by a God that is Holy. Eternal Israel is that pure demand of holiness that characterizes her universal significance for all mankind. It is in her midst that God is hallowed.

In contrast to eternal Israel, man must be ever seeking purification, a new heart. This is the purification before God that renews the strength for moral redemption; only before God does man find purification. Religion became a sublime defiance of all attempts to reduce man to the woes of his positive condition, to sufferings and to his despair; it is in the very midst of these realities that the truth of God is proclaimed in faithfulness. The symbol of suffering Israel gives lie to pessimism, for it is the eternal embodiment of the symbol of redemption. Philosophies of pessimism have no place in Judaism, ethics, and Messianism. In the *Ethics of the Pure Will* Cohen pointed to the danger of these philosophies, both for the history of rational thought and for the historic mission of monotheism. He never wavered in his belief that his own philosophy had stood in the tradition of Plato, Maimonides, Leibniz, and Kant, and that moral optimism is coterminous with a belief in the rationalism of man. Cohen believed that the eternal movement and development of thought unfolded ever-new dimensions of reason; in Israel's Messianism lay the monotheistic redemption of mankind;

the two are ultimately one. Universality in philosophy is the self-consciousness of purity; monotheism is the truth of God in His Oneness and uniqueness, the truth of unique purity. Philosophy and religion join in the oneness of reason and the uniqueness of God; they effect a similar universal task in knowledge and ethics.

Peace is a feeling that comes over us when we become aware that someone has done a good action; it assumes a susceptibility and a feeling for the moral and the sublime. There is a joy in this feeling and a desire and a thirst for its continuance, but joy is even more an expression of our receptivity -- not only for the moral, but for each act of repentance that helps unlock the "Holy of Holies." Although joy seems to have yielded to suffering in Cohen's theodicy, joy in faith is one of the deepest expressions of the truth of his belief, and of all belief both religious and philosophical. Joy emanates from within the believer; it embraces peace as the supreme virtue, the culminating point of justice and courage, and proclaims its messianic reality. The feeling of joy is the limit of suffering, the obstacle that opposes its fall into sadism and pessimism. Joy is the sign, *Wahrzeichen*, of peace, but even more it is a cry of its strength and power. In the *Ethics* the representation of the virtue of *Humanitaet* gave rise to a sense of moral power through which man feels himself superior to nature and becomes aware of the sublimity of his moral destiny. Cohen in the last pages of his *Ethics* could declare that this feeling is all, *Gefuehl ist alles*. Joy, on the other hand, is our awareness not so much of our moral destiny as it is a foreshadowing of the divine peace that is reflected in the reconciliation between both God and man, and man and man. This peace takes place at every moment of human history; ;in Israel, redemption and suffering are the motive forces that inhere in the fabric of its historical life. Peace is the redemptive moment that belongs to each suffering event. The longing for reconciliation, for the good in an indifferent world, is man's search for peace. Joy is the expression of this messianic peace. It regains for man the equality lost in class distinction, in poverty, and it is in this peace that man can reconcile himself with himself as a moral person.

The joy of the religious celebrations reveals and expresses those moments of eternity that fill our longing for the knowledge of God and join all men as seekers of the same end. With pointed concern and purpose, Cohen slips in the remark that these celebrations, and the joy attached to them, can in no way be related to the dionysian or bacchanalian with their orgiastic fascination with intoxication and ecstasy. Cohen was always aware of the threat to his religious and moral position that was real in these romantic excesses, and in the philosophers who glorified them and built ethical systems upon them. He viewed the joy that was imbedded in the festivals, e.g., the Passover, as the joy in the freedom from slavery, the formation of God's people, and their symbolic representation as a kingdom of priests. The joy in the giving of the Torah, a joy in the law, *Gesetzesfreude,* this is the true moral and religious feeling that accompanies these monumental events of human history; they embody the struggle for the being or nonbeing of moral man and universe. Cohen celebrated them and felt their overpowering sublimity. It would be difficult to imagine the vast impact that the religious made upon him if he had not been so deeply devoted to Kant and the moral law. Religion came as a fulfillment of the religiosity of his philosophy, of his philosophical belief. The depth of his moral commitment and his passion for the ideal of humanity hover closely to the religious. The Jewish attachment to Messianism in all its ethical implications seems to have determined Cohen to bring together the best of both worlds.

If Judaism had given to mankind only the *Shabbath,* it would have brought the most significant symbol of peace and joy. Abysmal is the separation between the joy of the bacchanalia and the joy of the *Shabbath;* the separation is profound, for its consequences brought two worlds into existence, unbridgeable in their political, social, and economic realities. The joy and peace of the *Shabbath* arise from the contemplation of the fulfillment of creation, of the end of injustice, and of the monotheistic mission that will someday spread to all men and reconcile the truth of God with his creation. The *Shabbath* is a moment of eternity that breaks forth into the profane. It hovers over existence and proclaims its inadequacy and limitedness, its subjectivity and arbitrariness. This Cohen profoundly experienced in the *Shabbath.* The messianic dimension of the *Shabbath* is analogous to Kant's realm of ends, *ein Reich der Zwecke,* but the latter is only an ideal and requires a *new being* who is without need and whose power is adequate to his will.[10] That no such being is or can be without God's grace is clear, the ideal remained mere ideal. The *Shabbath* did not demand a new being for its realization; it belonged to and was experienced by the Jew not only in joy and peace, but it brought concrete moral obligations, anticipated a future whose messianic reality was not in doubt. In correlation there is assumed the moral and religious adequacy of man; the world of correlation is rooted in that cosmic dialogue between God and Israel from which the moral emerges as task and obligation. For, as Israel is moved by her God, she reveals to man the eternal mission of monotheism: to transform through knowledge and justice the incompleteness of creation into messianic humanity.

The deep separation -- the fallen world of man and the pure world of grace and redeemed man -- has always dominated Christian thought and is clear in Kant. Cohen, on the other hand, expressed that strong belief in man's capacity to sanctify both body and soul, to refuse all dualism that can threaten the moral task, for Cohen believed that this moral task borne collectively by Israel would bring a new future and a new hope. In Israel the division between the holy and the profane, between the material and the spiritual, was healed, and it is for this reason that with the history of Judaism the history of religion was just beginning. Her monotheism has not yet transformed the world; its revolutionary nature is still to be experienced. Peace, that ultimate reconciliation of creation, is the meaning of the Messiah; it is Israel's message and her martyrdom. In her religious celebrations moments of this peace are enjoyed; there is a freedom from the anxiety of self-preservation, and the individual can live that reconciliation that is the essence of religion. To be yoked to the Law is to be yoked to the Kingdom of God; this is the symbol of peace for all people. The Law and its symbolic form as God's kingdom are the driving force of Cohen's Judaism. Israel announces the Kingdom of God; this is the truth that she embodies; it is her "imperial message": the Kingdom is peace, the ultimate and supreme consequence of correlation. In Cohen there lived that vision and imagery, those symbols that made it possible to see in the people of God this actualization of the messianic hope for redemption. In every instant of the present a moment of reconciliation between creation and Creator is occurring through the mediation of Israel. Peace is the summary of all values; it is the realization of the path of the virtues. In peace they have their end. The human enterprise is meaningful when the end, *Endzweck,* is peace.

Kant's pietism would have him say: "I will that there be a God, that my existence in this world be also an existence in a pure world of the understanding outside the system of natural connection, and finally that my duration be endless."[11] Kant was also certain that the conflict with Satan never ceased to fill man's soul. Luther had reduced the geography of the combat for man's soul to each individual. In Cohen the vast Platonic world returns, but now it is reformed and redefined in Judaic terms. If it could be said that at a certain period in Cohen's thought Kant had found an interpreter or that Cohen's philosophy meant a "return to Kant"; it finally could be said that in Cohen not only the Kantian ethic, but the metaphysics of Plato and Leibniz were ultimately vindicated. In fact, the vast drama of suffering and Messianism etched in the *Religion of Reason* is a theodicy whose moral-religious dimension and significance incorporate the insights and values that Cohen had identified, on the one hand, with the history of reason that had begun with Plato and ended with Kant, and on the other, with the monotheistic truth of creation that lies at the beginning of all reality and is at the same time its redemption and transfiguration.[12] To philosophize was a religious act, and it is apparent that Cohen believed he had found reconciliation both on the level of thought and in the meaning of Israel. Philosophy and religion could be joined in the love and knowledge of God. It was the reconciliation between the temporal and the eternal that Cohen called peace. Israel was for mankind a symbol of that messianic peace that redeems both evil and death. There is no death in Israel; all reality, historical and metahistorical, transfigured into the eternal life of Israel. The prayers, the festivals, the Law are forms of redemption and "Sanctification of the Holy Name" in which the creation is regained for the messianic humanity and the peace that is its truth. The moral universe is a consequence of divine incomparableness. In Israel's divine odyssey the way is found to the days of the Messiah, that messianic peace that is the goal of all the virtues that Cohen had declared to be signs and paths to this peace. The great struggle to reveal this truth of monotheism is thus the supreme religious and philosophical task, for upon this eternal verity of verities depends not only the moral universe, but the ultimate realization of that spirit which God implanted in man and which in correlation is known as the Holy Spirit, the spirit by which man takes his task to become holy from the Holiness that is his God.

Cohen's religiosity surpassed and fulfilled his attachment to Kant. The writing of a philosophy of religion from Jewish sources, and from the conviction that Israel was the embodiment of an eternal truth, the truth of monotheism, made it necessary for Cohen to think in terms of a religious metaphysics. In Israel, past, present, and future are transfigured in eternity. Messianic hope and peace are the supreme virtue and meaning of Israel's eternity. Her historical presence is the witness to a truth that the future is yet to reveal, but that Cohen believed the Jew embraced in the *Shabbath,* the Day of Atonement, the Passover, and in the cycle of the religious year. It is under the Yoke of the Law, willingly accepted, that the Jew lives in the Kingdom of God, for it is in this kingdom that the holy is separated from the profane. The purity and pureness that permeated all of Cohen's works is symbolized in the Israel that bears within it the verity of verities. Israel was for Cohen that symbol of truth that fills all rational life from logic to ethics to aesthetics. The virtues are not ideals, but preparations to servanthood, the goal of the universe God had determined as creator.

Man alone is no longer the center of value, but in correlation became a coworker, a suffering servant on behalf of God. The days of the Messiah will bring forth peace, men will end injustice, there will no longer be hate among men and nations. The ethical realm, reflecting the mutual obligations among men, is validated no longer from within but from divine command; God's oneness will encompass all realms. Israel suffers the martyrdom of this monotheistic encompassing. What is deepest in Cohen is the rejection of the Christian doctrine of sin and grace, that separation between salvation and damnation. Israel is the spiritual and physical redemption of man and the world; evil and death point only to our inadequate and insufficient knowledge, the yet-incomplete relationship between monotheism and the world. Israel was for Cohen the collective name for the pious of the world.

If we return to Kant's writings and think again what he tells us in his *Religion within the Limits of Reason Alone* we are struck with an idea that remains consistent and messianic: the love of the law. "But the highest goal of moral perfection of finite creatures -- a goal to which man can never completely attain -- is love of the law. The equivalent in religion of this idea would be an article of faith, 'God is love.'"[13] God is the "archetype of humanity," but He is also the need that each person has to honor the source of his creation, to honor that moral law in him that is the ground of his humanity. In honoring God man reveals the fact that God needs man to be His *causa cognoscendi* and man needs God to be his *causa essendi;* each in mutual dependence embodies that circular truth showing that the idea and its manifestation are mutually dependent, for the one has no reality without the other. Even Kant was willing to admit that "though it does sound dangerous, it is in no way reprehensible to say that every man *creates a God,* nay, must make himself such a God according to moral concepts in order to honor in Him *the One who* created him";[14] to respect that dignity of humanity in oneself and the human destiny for which we are all responsible. With all this Cohen was in agreement, but he was a member of a minority whose historical situation was permeated with nationalism, myth making, hero cults, and aphoristic philosophical styles that threatened the survival of the individual. This brought forth from him a clear and firm enunciation that the individual is inexhaustible, *das Besondere aber ist unerschoepflich,* that the meaning of history is the struggle for and the concern with the particular, the minority. Cohen never failed to stress the need to show compassion for the suffering of our fellow being, *Mitmensch,* to repeat again and again that God loves the poor. When we attempt to comprehend this stress we find that it stands in close relationship to the sufferings of Israel, to those sufferings that are intimately tied to divine responsibility and to the reality of the law, that messianic expression of the Kingdom of God. This feeling for the suffering of our fellow being witnessed that passion of the suffering God whom Israel bore into exile, the exile of monotheism in a polytheistic world, the exile of purity in the impure.

The concept of the particular, *der Begriff des Besonderen,* is inexhaustible; there is no reconciliation of universal and particular, there is only approximation. The particular is the refusal of redemption and absorption in political or economic ideologies; it is the foundation of the legal state. The whole educative process of state must seek to destroy those myths and cults created by religion and the nation to justify its historical hatreds and its self-glorification. The virtue of practical wisdom, *sophrosyne,* the "eye" for particularity and peculiarity, embodies the strength to expose and to root out these aberrations. The ideal of the rational state embodies the ideal of virtue as *Humanitaet.* Cohen spoke of this *Humanitaet* as the law of moral harmony, the harmonizing power for all the melodies of the moral spirit, *die harmonierende Macht fuer alle Melodien des sittlichen Geistes.* This was Cohen's answer to the Treitschke dictum: "The Jews are our misfortune." The misfortune could only be in the denial of the concept of particularity and in the affirmation of an all-embracing naturalistic nationalism. Cohen struggled to forge a philosophy of values grounded in the universal-categorical dictates of reason that could counter an historicism capable of justifying the ideologic and mythologic historical thinking of contemporary politics. The virtue of *Humanitaet* regards man not merely as a natural being, but as an animal endowed with reason, with *Menschengefuehl,* the feeling for the human. We are limited by our conceptual power; life surpasses comprehension but is confirmed in our trust of the human, *Menschengefuehl.* It is this feeling which links aesthetics to ethics and is the source of great art because it affirms in man the humanity of his person as the ideal of beauty. Great art, as Kant reminds us, "requires a union of pure ideas of reason with great imaginative power even in him who wishes to judge of it, still more in him who wishes to present it."[15] In Cohen's language, the art of the ideal is the art of humanity. In this feeling for the human in its particularity and finiteness lies the source for a concept of humanity. The progress of civilization is rooted in diversity and pluralism, in the virtue of *Sophrosyne.* Cohen's thought reflects a conflict of values that nineteenth-century Europe had seen sharpened by the development of nationalism and its chauvinistic social and religious consequences. In Cohen, as in Kant, we realize the shortness of our lives and the weight of the moral task.

It demands moral faith and a belief in the future, the strength of virtue and a bit of irony. Kant expressed the historical dimension of the development of man's capacity to use reason in a way that makes us aware that the heritage of reason belonged, belongs, and hopefully will belong to mankind as its truth and responsibility. Its development requires time: "Since Nature has set only a short period for his life, she needs a perhaps unreckonable series of generations, each of which passes its own enlightenment to its successor in order finally to bring the seeds of the enlightenment to that degree of development in our race which is completely suitable to Nature's purpose."[16]

The virtues are the guides and the ideals; upon them Cohen placed his faith in the future. This was a moral faith, a moral feeling, a moral hope; it was the expression of a philosophy of history rooted in his faith that Israel's mission was moral and universal. It was the struggle for the Oneness of God, the oneness of humanity; it was that passion that drove through hate and suffering, that "breakthrough to the universal" is the justification of philosophy. What Cohen loved in Israel, Kant loved as the truth of reason; what Kant could state as pure objective law without historical development, Cohen could reveal only through theologic history. In the thought of Kant's most loving follower, history found its fullest expression and need; in the meta-historical reality of Israel, the moral law, the love of the "yoke of the law" became an historical force. If we posed the question of the meaning of history to Hermann Cohen he would refer us to that tension that exists between the inexhaustible quality of the particular and the Oneness of monotheism, between the sufferings of love of Israel and the moral indifference of mankind, between messianic age and the incompleteness of the here and now, between the love of the law as the embodiment of the Kingdom of God and profane existence. He knew that these conflicts did not separate unbridgeable realities. In the tension between the historical moral situation and the pure will there communicates the real discourse of morality in which each moment finds its meaning in the existence of the other, discovering in conflict its meaning, and showing in this meaning the movement of history and the hope of reconciliation. In correlation and partnership Cohen discovered a philosophy of history in which human and divine realities realized themselves through each other. He brought to the fore the moral dimension of the divine human exile; in this he achieved a philosophy of history whose meaning we are only now beginning to comprehend.

6

Eric Weil:
History as the Reality of Reason

Eric Weil was born in Parchim in Mecklenburg in 1904 and died in Nice in 1977. He completed his doctorate with the philosopher, Ernst Cassirer, in 1928 in Hamburg. In 1933, he left Germany and settled in Paris. Weil joined the French army in 1939 and was interned in 1940 as a P.O.W. He completed his French doctorate with a major thesis, *La Logique de la philosophie* (1950), and a minor thesis, *Hegel et l'état*. Both books have become landmarks of contemporary philosophical thought. Weil, being a systematic thinker, completed the *Logic* with a *Philosophie politique* (1956), and a *Philosophie morale* (1961). His other books include a volume on Kant, *Problèmes Kantiens* (1970), and three volumes of collected essays, *Essais et conférences* (1970, 1971, 1982). If we ask what tradition Weil's philosophy reflects, we might answer that it reflects the thinker who ponders the discourse of philosophy from Aristotle to Hegel. He is concerned with an elaboration of those categories and attitudes which make possible the comprehension of ourselves as reasonable beings attempting to grasp the meaning of a world which we have not created but which is, nevertheless, receptive to reason. These categories are elaborated in the *Logic of Philosophy;* they embody the categories of Aristotle, Kant, and Hegel. They reveal the dialogue of philosophy, the continuous universal discourse of reason which defines philosophy as the determination of the concept, a determination that is expounded not only in the forward movement of thought, but also in the rethinking which is the source of philosophic movement. The encompassing achievement of Weil's *Logic of Philosophy* is yet to be realized. It is one of the great monuments to systematic philosophy. In the chapter on twentieth-century philosophy in France, Yves Belaval could state, "It is still too early to appreciate the profound influence of his teaching" (*Histoire de la philosophie,* Pléiade, 3:1061).

Eric Weil was no stranger to American journals. He wrote several articles for *Confluence: An International Forum,* among which are "Propaganda, Truth and the Mass Media" (1953), "Tradition and Traditionalism" (1953),

"Religion and Politics" (1955), and "Education as a Problem of Our Time" (1957). He wrote six articles for *Daedalus:* "Philosophical and Political Thought in Europe Today" (1964), "Science in Modern Culture, or the Meaning of Meaninglessness" (1965), "The Languages of the Humanistic Studies" (1969), "Humanistic Studies: Their Object, Methods and Meaning" (1970), "Supporting the Humanities" (1973), and "What Is a Breakthrough in History?" (1975). His concern for political and moral philosophy is inseparable from the movement of thought revealed in the *Logic of Philosophy.*

To begin a reasonable discussion of the political requires certain assumptions which connect the problem with history and morality. Not only is it necessary to relate the political to morality and history, but to comprehend its relationship to philosophy. The political and historical belong to the philosophical; we can say that they would be impossible if the philosophical had not developed the categories in and through which they could be thought. The philosophical must first, for example, realize the category of action to make it possible for the political and historical to be thought as reasonable action. We can say that the political comprehends reasonable action, attempts to discover its meaning and the structure in which it is possible, and, if possible, what its consequences are. We can also say that the political is one of the dimensions of universal discourse, dimensions which can also be defined as categories. Eric Weil has stated that the political is a "philosophical science which reveals what is in its philosophical category through concepts which are proper to it and which we call 'political categories.' We understand these as fundamental concepts in this domain, analogous to, for example, those which structure physics without rendering the existence of a physics philosophically comprehensible."[1] What we are concerned with when we speak of the political is a comprehension of those categories which make the political comprehensible and meaningful to the thinker who needs to grasp these categories, making it possible to think the nature and implications of reasonable action. Reasonable action presupposes a theory of state and society; in fact, it demands that we think the possibility of thinking, i.e., we think the structure in which thinking becomes thinking about the nature of man as a historical, moral and political being, a structure which posits the state as an eternal form. "It would be legitimate to affirm that the truth (the nature) of the state is eternal. It is not always and everywhere known, but as soon as it is known, it is one and the same. Nevertheless, each moment of history must grasp for itself this truth. The end of thought can, indeed, be independent of the road which leads to it, but this is an indemonstrable, irrefutable and gratuitous affirmation. Without this road which begins in history the eternal would only be a form without meaning."[2] Profound and challenging is Weil's attempt to comprehend the significance of the state as eternal, but the question which is posed by its eternity is whether it is possible to think the political as a philosophical category without the affirmation of the state as the eternal form, in and from which the discourse of politics begins and category develops from category. Reason can now be revealed as history. History is the comprehension of reason as discourse, man's autobiographical consciousness as action and thought.

If we assume that the discourse of the political and the historical begins with the eternal form of the state, then we affirm that every level of human organization from the family to society is comprehended from and through the state, i.e., comprehended in reason as history. We are saying that the whole must ontologically precede the parts, that the parts realize the whole; that the nature of every part is to find its logical relation to the whole; and that the whole is only knowable in its parts. Accepting the fact that man is a political and historical being, we accept the equally clear observation that man without community is either a brute or a god. Weil would say that the "reign of the arbitrary is the eternal dream of the slave."[3] If the reign of the arbitrary is the slave's dream, then the purpose of the state, from the individual's point of view, is the existence of the free and reasonable individual, the realization of reasonable discourse, the rational organization of work. In the state men develop their capacities. Nonviolence is the positive consequence of our comprehension of violence as the source of reason and the motor force of history. If arbitrariness is the morality of the slave, then we affirm that reasonableness is possible only within the universal. The individual who claims to be reasonable, who attempts to grasp the political as a philosophical category or dimension of universal discourse, realizes the universal within his individuality, he discovers the true measure of his humanity. Universality which embodies reasonable freedom is assumed to be possible for every man.

Freedom can be understood in terms of what reason refuses. This negative comprehension of freedom is an openness to every positive possibility which in the course of man's development becomes part of his thinking reality. Neither freedom nor reasonableness is yet fully within man's thinking and action. Would not this imply that the struggle for the meaning of State has only just begun? The state is not to be identified with society nor with government; it is the form of reason, it is reason as reasonableness and rationality, it is the structure in which we think family and society, in which we think every form of community from individual states and their morality to the relationships between them, their international organization and interrelationships. Within the structure of state we move from what is arbitrary and yet unrealized to what is reasonable and self-conscious. "Everything indicates that the struggle for the state is not ended and that it is only beginning as a *conscious* struggle. Having become conscious struggle, it has also become struggle on the level of consciousness, and will again become violent struggle only to the degree that the first universal, i.e., society and calculating rationality, do not impose themselves successfully."[4] What we can begin to understand is that every historical and logical movement of political development from society to state takes place within the eternal form of State, because it is this form which is the very embodiment of reasonableness and rationality.

Every particular historical moment in the development of society and government, or what we call constitution, takes place from the perspective of the State as reasonable and rational law, as the highest form of human community. In the State, the individual is not submerged and eliminated; he finds the realization of self, freedom, and reasonableness. This highest form of community is inseparable from the universal discourse of reason, of which it is the embodiment. The State is not society, nor is it government. It is realized imperfectly and unconsciously in the contemporary state. It has the possibility of realization, it is the negation of what *is*, the source of its overcoming. The State is the potentiality of higher and more conscious self-realization. "The state is raised above every historical reality other than itself, because it alone gives birth to and brings to life among men this awareness of its own imperfection, not as a desperate awareness, but as conscious will, the will of consciousness, rationality and reason."[5] Here we touch upon the central theme of Eric Weil's political and historical philosophy, which is deeply imbedded in the political thought of Aristotle, Kant, and Hegel. This awareness of state as the eternal form for political thinking corresponds to the eternal form of reason whose structure makes possible that universal discourse, in and through which reason reveals the categories of thinking, i.e., man's awareness of self as freedom and reasonableness, as a political and moral being.

Before we can comprehend the importance of reasonable discourse we must confront the meaning of violence in Weil's political philosophy. Violence is not only the motor force of history, it is the source of reason, i.e., its dialectical *other*, the eternal ground of reality. Violence in and for itself is meaningless, but as the *other* of nonviolence it is the possibility of its meaning and the ground of its existence. Violence and nonviolence belong to each other. They are revealed in dialectical relationship. Nonviolence which is conscious of itself without violence is meaningless and blind. It is dead identity. Its significance and value can lie only in the realization of its *other,* the source of itself. "It is, on the contrary, probable that it (nonviolence) could never be attained if the possibility of violence were forgotten. . . . Violence, in itself, is the negation of all meaning, the absurd in a pure sense, but we would come into the most violent and inevitable internal and external conflicts if we were convinced that it is sufficient to speak of nonviolence and the good life in society; we would founder in the most stark violence if we deprived human existence of all meaning by limiting it to what society can limitlessly offer it."[6] Society offers means to satisfy our needs, it perpetuates our individuality in its struggle for acquisition. It feeds the competition which sharpens our power of calculation. Society is the source of conflict, antagonism, social experimentation. It expands our rationality, but it does not seek its own overcoming; it refuses the dialectical *other* as a higher form of community. It seeks nonviolence in and for itself. Society is the embodiment of rationality; its goal is self-evidency. Its refusal to be more than calculating reason arises from the dialectical realization of its limitation through negation, the source of all thinking about reality, the force of social progress, the hope that moves toward change, toward that rational and reasonable satisfaction of man.

Society and the State are the two universal moments of reason whose interdependence and interrelationship are evident in the course of reason's development from self-consciousness to reason. But there is a moral dimension to this relationship between society and State. The State is an ethical demand in its universality and universability. It is the demand of reason, refusing that demonic possibility in the particular to be in and for itself, to be totality. The State as reasonable and rational law is freedom, the eternal negation which is its reality. The State is the source of reality, the dialectical *other,* the *other* to what appears. The struggle and history of the State is only just beginning. We are not dealing with a Kantian idea, a regulative idea, which allows us to think and rethink the history of reason. The State is a constitutive idea thinking itself, returning upon itself, understanding what has been understood, but understanding through negation rising to new levels of self-consciousness. What is our task in all this? Is it not "to form a world in which nonviolence is real without suppressing the *nonsense* of violence nor the positive meaning of man's life?" We want to realize nonviolence, but this *non-sense* must have meaning and this has always proceeded from the force of violence, from what it has sought to create in history and what it continues to search for today by violent means. The struggle with violence is not simply an attempt to curb arbitrary and individual actions, but the conflicts among the individual states. It is the antagonisms and class divisions, economic inequality, social hierarchy which make it possible for us to grasp the moral dimension of violence, to realize that in and through it we comprehend the moral and political actualities of our age. We confront the universality of reason in its particular and individual form. We face moral-political problems at the level of their finitude. Decision and prudence supercede clarity and self-evidence.

Just as State and society are never discovered fully but develop; reason, active reason is in time, in history and is never fully revealed nor discovered. Every epoch is reason manifested. Every state is responsible for the education of its citizenry, every statesman is an educator, "he is an educator and cannot but be one." Every statesman is responsible to the morality which the state embodies, which is born from within the state. The State does not inherit an external morality; it does not find one given to it; it discovers it in itself. Morality comes to be through the experiences of the state. No statesman can avoid the morality of the state; he finds it there, is responsible for what he discovers and knows; he cannot violate or ignore it. He employs and enhances it.

The struggle for the state as reason is yet to be won. Reason has had but a short history. The danger is to want to ignore the moral, to think of the political as a calculation, as rational, and not historical, to confuse the calculating rationality of society with the historical morality of the State. There is no actualization of state without society, and no society without the idea of State. The sense of morality and critique, i.e., reasonable discussion belongs to society because it is derived from State. If society is "calculating violence," if it develops institutions to restrain and dominate this violence, then we are forced to perceive society as dominated violence. The reason which grows within it forms the common interest that comprehends violence as evil and forces us to grasp the reasonable, public discussion, as the source of meaningful communal life. "Violence has been and is still the motor cause of history. Nevertheless, political conscience seeks progress toward the elimination of violence. This is its *final cause*. Conscience does not arise from conscience but from its contrary. The will for peace is born from war and struggle."7 We deal on this level with dominated violence and not with morality. On the level of society the individual becomes the potential slave. Within the structure of rational calculation every human activity from passion to ruse, from lie to deception, becomes manipulative possibility in the struggle for prestige and power. The aspirations of reason, of reasonable discourse, remain potential and at moments become actual. They are powerful even in their overcoming. If we ask at this juncture what philosophy demands, we reply that it cannot prescribe what is to be done, that is for the political activist. It shows the problem, reveals what are its limits and what are the consequences to human affairs when reason is renounced, when violence is manipulated calculation, or when nonviolence has no more meaning than theoretical or abstract pacifism. The problem remains the realization of the State as reasonable and rational law.

We have affirmed that the philosophical-political problem is inseparable from that of moral consciousness. The political problem was not revealed by a supreme wisdom nor will it be resolved by one. The self-evidency which ties philosophy to mathematics and analogously analyzes political forms, denies that reason is in life, acts upon it, and, in turn, is acted upon by man's decision to affirm or deny what seems good or bad for him. If reason is man's capacity to refuse the meaningless, to attempt to discover meaning, then the development of this reason is the realization in history of the structure of reason which every historical manifestation reveals partially. Man's comprehension of himself as a reasonable being is not a definition which creates a reality. Man's reasonableness depends upon community, in and through which he emerges as an individual. As a political animal community is a necessity, but community is a development to higher and more complicated forms. The development is not the consequence of the discarding of one form for another, but the realization of the lower form in the higher. The lower forms are overcome, they are sublimated, realized, and preserved. This formula-like analysis only attempts to provide a philosophical, non-scientific structure to think the relationship of society and state. We need to think this relationship, because man in search of meaning, of reasonable and moral existence, finds no self-evidency. Man must satisfy his needs, and we would distort the nature of society if we denied that they were materialistic.

Society is materialistic; this formula is a description and not a value judgment. The value judgment arises as a negative judgment at the moment we define either society, or, the historical state as the only dimension wherein men's lives are formed and pursued. Most contemporary political thought forces us to choose between society and the state, calculation and morality. It is a comprehensible error, since it is from the historical state that the problem of concrete morality is posed, and it is modern society which is opposed to the historical state. Nevertheless, it is a dangerous error, because in it we discover the origin of most metaphysical theories of history."[8]

What are the implications of this separation of society from the state? The struggle against nature does not belong to the individual; he would be destined to defeat. The struggle is an organized one, and it is this organized struggle against nature, against violence, which we call society. "Every human society is essentially in conflict with external nature. This does not mean that man, at every age, considers himself in conflict with nature; on the contrary, this manner of interpreting the relations between man and external nature is the result of a long and complex evolution and characterizes man as such. But even where this awareness is lacking and where other interpretations prevail, the fact is that men are not content with what nature puts at their disposal. They transform the given, which becomes matter, *materies*, materials of construction."[9] The conflict with nature, the emergence of forces needed to change and transform it, the overcoming of the dissatisfaction which is the source of human achievement and development brings in its wake only a deeper dissatisfaction. It reflects man's distinction as that being who refuses to belong and accommodate himself to what is, but who through the word and the deed has the power to overcome. Not only what society does for him, but what he can achieve in and through society is what makes him the essential factor in the struggle against violence. Society is organized struggle against violence. This achievement makes it possible for man to fashion a society of work, form the institutions in and through which society develops. If we return for a moment to the dangers which lie in this separation of society and state, and if we consider the consequent metaphysical theories of history, we can comprehend the nature of the danger. Metaphysical theories imply the discovery of unique forces, in and through which we are capable of explaining the meaning of history, and the subsequent programs of political actions. "It is of little importance that these explanations and extrapolations, whose numbers would suffice to awaken suspicions, discover this unique motive in the society of work, abstracting from all that is for society *only* historical, or, on the contrary, they envision salvation in the return to the *true* history of great deeds, grand principles, eternal or national morality, neglecting, as is convenient in this case, the work of humanity and the desires of men in society.''[10] We are comforted by grand principles whose eternity provide convenient interpretative principles and justifications for political actions. But, are we certain that these principles are eternal and that what they project and structure is unchanging and a-historical?

Reason is born in history and attempts to comprehend it. It does not create it. Whatever we say about wars and revolution, about class struggle and violence, whatever be the projected theory about the origins of our modern society, its growth or its demise, theory refuses to allow the fact that there is already given in society the source of its own remedy, and control of the forces that cause conflicts and disorders. In other words, what brings forth revolution and war, brings with it the possibility of this overcoming. The universality of revolution becomes the principle of a world society and makes it possible for rationality to engulf all of mankind. The revolution behind the revolution is what must be taken seriously. Metaphysical theories of history are true, but only within limits. The limits reveal what is explained, but not comprehended, and are only comprehended when explanation supposes not only itself, but what is its other. This is no longer explanation, but comprehension. Without limits these theories of history become pure categories which order reality and make it possible to resolve the problems that are in it.

From society to society these metaphysical theories claim self-evidency, but beyond society is the State, the organ in and through which we think those universal moments of community which belong to the Idea of the State. Not without expectation Weil declares that ''with the risk of shocking we must say that the ancient theory (the Aristotelian in particular) of the State as a moral and educative institution is true. It is not totally true for us because . . . the world in which it developed did not know the *progressive* struggle with external nature; the idea of a world society of work could not be conceived. Man's liberation -- to be exact, the liberation of some men from need -- depended upon the work of other men considered and treated as natural forces, and this liberation could only be realized by the abandonment of the idea of the real liberation of all men.''[11] What the ancient theory accomplished and which we consider to be its supreme value and truth is that the State is not a tool established by society for its protection. The State is the structure in which we think the nature of man as a political animal, in which we think contract, property, corporation, family. Through the State the ties and traditions, the mores of a living community, are comprehended. The State is the structure of reason. From it we can comprehend the

nature of the political, and man as a political animal. The realization of this nature depends upon the actualization of the idea of universality and universability.

If put negatively we would say that man cannot be condemned legally to
slavery because modern society is convinced that one man should not be the
property of another and confirms this legally. This does not prevent man from
becoming a slave by his refusal to accept moral and political responsibilities, to
be reasonable and rational. "Man who only lives on the level of society is a
slave accepting this meaning of the word, whatever be his social importance, influence and power. He has no master in the modern world, but being free
legally, he is no less a slave as long as he does not come to the thought of the
concrete universal."[12] The essential concern of political philosophy is the reasonable freedom of the individual from which we draw two consequences. We
can say that the reasonalbe individual is above the State. We can, at the same
time, affirm that the individual is nothing without the State. These are the contraries which Weil arrives at, but they are contraries which complement and are
necessary for each other. They are dependent upon each other. Man is above the
State because it is the State which made it possible for him to think the universal, to think himself free and reasonable. "It is not in wishing to abolish the
State -- a nonsensical design -- but in leading it to its perfection that man will
realize himself as a reasonable being in a community with a morality, which
thinking itself, wishes reasonable."[13] To be above the State as a reasonable and
moral being means that in the State man knows himself to be free. It is from the
State that man rises above the state; being above the State depends upon being
in the state. The two statements make it possible for us to comprehend man as a
being who should realize that his nature is political and moral. Without the State
there is no structure in which man can know himself. The violence which he can
undergo in his choice for slavery implies that man does not have to choose to
think; he does not have to be reasonable nor moral. Man can choose animality.
Man can choose slavery. The question of social justice arises only if we are
willing to pose a concrete universal problem, one that implies the development
of man as a free and reasonable being, the being for whom language begins in
negation, where the need and capacity to say no is the first level of self-consciousness, the beginning of the moral.

If the nature of man as a political animal is realized in negation, i.e., in concrete universality, then we are attempting to comprehend what it means to speak
of particularity and universality, finitude and the infinite, subject and object. To

put the problem more concretely and within the political dimension we would pose it as a question. Are the historical states capable of "surpassing themselves and becoming in the consciousness of their citizens and their governments . . . what at present they are only in themselves, i.e., moral particularities within world society . . . could they become morally free communities, recognizing the necessities of work and organization in regard to the realization of reason; could they give to all men the possibility of being satisfied with the dignity of their reasonable and concrete freedom, in *virtuous life?*"14 With this question we face the challenge of the idea of the true State, that embodiment of reasonableness and rationality which although not yet achieved remains as the *ought to be* of political philosophy, a universal moral imperative which makes it possible for us not only to grasp the universal in its concreteness, but to comprehend the particular in universality. Here it is that philosophy sets the problems for political thinking. This is why we said at the beginning that the political is a category of the universal discourse of reason, inseparable from philosophy, the demand of the universal. Hegel recognizes this to be Plato's fundamental insight. "Plato gets hold of the thought that a genuine constitution and a sound political life have their deeper foundation in the Idea -- on the essentially and actually universal and genuine principles of eternal righteousness. Now to see and ascertain what these are is certainly the function and business of *philosophy*. It is from this point of view that Plato breaks out into the celebrated or notorious passage where he makes Socrates emphatically state that philosophy and political power must coincide, that the Idea must be regent, if the distress of nations is to see its end."15 If it is true that a meaningful political life is dialectically related to the Idea, then we are saying that every positive political development is a "breakthrough" to the universal and that it is the moral obligation of every particular state, recognizing man's natural violence, to educate its citizenry to think in terms of the concrete universal, to think a purpose and meaning to political existence, to act with moral responsibility, to think reasonable discourse. The universal is the moral critique of particularity in all aspects of political life. It is the source of science, morality, religion, and art. It stirs the awareness and creates dissatisfaction in those who find satisfaction only in particularity and feel secure in it. It is the negation which refuses permanence to every finite institution; it comes forth as the denial and refusal of every metaphysical theory of history to explain, define, and offer fixed and immutable laws of social conflict, political action, and historical development. The universal remains the *yet-to-be* in face of what is, the freedom which negates the inclusiveness of finiteness. The universal is the source of history as the discourse of reason.

Man's problem refers not only to the universal and the particular, but to the danger of a universal that is not concrete that becomes a romantic fantasy, a myth, veiling sublimated violence. It refers also to a particular that refuses mediation and claims totality, a particular which becomes demonic. The fact is that man lives in both the State and society. He can arbitrarily set one in opposition to the other.

> We find the opposition of the modern historical state and society a very real difficulty for the individual, not placed between the two, but in the two at the same time. For him, the conflict is between "moral" virtue which historically and traditionally gives meaning and dignity to the individual's existence, and "social virtue," that of the worker, the organizer, the efficacious man, without which the former would have no possibility of subsisting and power of self-realization. Historical loyalty toward the historical morality of the state does not suffice for everyone; rational virtue does not produce positive meaning.16

There does not exist a contemporary state which satisfies these two human needs. We think back to the ancient *polis*, it comforts us greatly, but not meaningfully in our attempt to join moral and social virtue. Loyalty to society distorts our devotion to the State. We are forced again and again to choose one over the other. For the thinking man the dependence of one upon the other is the dialectical and practical necessity for living an ethical life. Thought, however, does not resolve the practical and historical conflicts which are inherent in the differences which both universal moments of reason demand of us. We easily attach ourselves to one moment or the other. We become loyal to one and disloyal to the other. If we think about the political in which the State is the highest form of political life, the embodiment of reason, we are compelled to transcend both the historical state and society, to historical, moral and social virtue. We become disloyal to both in thinking, for thinking forces us to transcend and overcome, to grasp the State as the form of the future because it is the eternal form of reason, to realize that it *is* and is *yet-to-be;* that it is only partially and inadequately manifested as Idea in society and the historical state. "The State is the highest form, because it is the conscious form of the common life of men, i.e., the State to come; but the concept of this State also justifies the present State which it already contains unconsciously and imperfectly. What is true can give reality to the 'true' state which through education, law, responsible discussion, leads men to a dignified and meaningful life."[17] We return again to the thesis that the struggle for the State has only just begun, our confrontation with language and education both reflect the struggle of violence and reason, the birth of reason in negation. "The true, concrete negativity of the language sign is *intelligence* since by this the sign is changed from something outward to something inward and, thus transformed, is preserved . . . the word gives to thoughts their highest and truest existence. . . . Just as the true thought is the very thing in itself, so too is the word when it is employed by genuine thinking."[18] In reference to education, Hegel spoke of the struggle for liberation from subjectivity and the arbitrariness of feeling as the source of knowledge. "The disfavor showered on education is due in part to its being this hard struggle; but it is through this educational struggle that the subjective will itself attain objectivity within, an objectivity in which alone it is for its part capable and worthy of being the actuality of the idea."[19] I cite these few comments of Hegel to indicate that the struggle for the State is inseparable from man's experience with language and education. Both are realities of reason and historical development. They are the consequences of violence, the attempt of reason to rise above the arbitrariness of subjectivity, to comprehend dialectic as the "culmination of self-conscious reason," the mind in its freedom. What it means to consider a thing rationally is the realization that this does not imply the imposition of reason, "but to find that the object is rational on its own account."[20] The universal is not imposed upon reality but is in reality. This is always clear to us. Only where the infinite-finite discourse is the reasonable discourse does man discover himself as a reasonable and rational being, he comprehends the object in the subject and the subject in the object. Thinking is both a moral and intellectual commitment, it is the search for the dialectic of reality, that discourse of opposites in which we hear the Logos. We can say with Eric Weil that the dialectic "is born subjective, to reveal itself in the course of its development objectively, i.e., universally and necessarily, objective from the beginning where it sought, but did not yet find itself."[21] What we are here discussing is the nature of universal reasonable discourse.

The violence which threatens the universality of discourse is born in what we call the unmediated particular. This particular claims to be the unmediated universal: no thinking, no self-consciousness, no freedom. We have a refusal and rejection of discourse. This violence is the end of discourse. Discourse is doubt and possibility, subjectivity and objectivity. The language of particularity is the embodiment of *intelligence* surpassing all mediation and conflict. It is the search for absolute surety and certainty. From this perspective we comprehend modern totalitarianism. The consequences are political and intellectual myths, the illusions of fixed positions, the tyranny of facts, anti-intellectualism and cultural pessimism disguised as highly developed and sophisticated intellectualism. These infuse our societal life with fixed realities, stifling reasonable existence and discourse. Nationalism, regionalism, religious and ideological fanaticism have their roots in the particularism that assumes universality. The unmediated particular is the refusal of discourse. Discourse is reduced to fact and silence. Here we have that radical denial of what Paul Valéry called the belief "in the human word, spoken or written" which he knew to be "as indispensable to human beings as to trust the firmness of the ground."22

We can say that man identified with the particular has no language, if we mean by having a language what Hegel calls the realization of concrete negativity, otherwise language is a tool that the man of the unmediated particular uses to manipulate purpose, and justify his activity. He does not believe himself created through language, but assumes to be its creator, seeks its domination, and through it society and the state which now become expressions of himself. Reality is created in his personal language. He does not become reason through it. He does not comprehend the realization that history is a man's struggle with violence. Particularity creates a world in its own image, but this world has a fixed purpose and is organized and directed by a positive idea; it remains embodied in what Hegel called the "arbitrariness of feeling as the source of knowledge." What is opposed to it must be destroyed because it hinders its realization and future projection. The language of its expression is enthusiasm, sentiment and passion. The sincerity of this sentiment is created from itself. It is challenged neither by reason nor discussion because it puts these aside as its enemies, nonsense, not to be considered, but to be eliminated. Language no longer deals with men, it is concerned with masses, their feelings and pleasures. No longer is meaning significant, but sentiment and passion, obedience and command. We have arrived at the opposite pole of Hegel's comprehension of education as the "liberation from subjectivity," of Weil's conception of the political as the "thought of reasonable action." Weil made this clear from the beginning of his discussion when he said that we must comprehend reasonable action within a philosophical system "where it is seen as one of the categories of human thought or, if one prefers, as one of the dimensions of discourse, autonomous as is every dimension, not reducible to others, nor comprehensible without them.

What we call the political is a philosophical science. . . ."[23] The category of the unmediated particular ends the comprehension of the political, it is the refusal of reasonable discourse; it is violence for the sake of violence.

We have returned to the point from which we began. Man wants to be reasonable, to reflect upon the moral. Man knows that he does not create reason but is created in it. Man is the being who can choose not to think. The reasonable individual is the critique of the empirical state. He "becomes a fully living individual through his action in the state, in the morality of his community, and on all the moralities of all communities."[24] The category of action is fundamental to the comprehension of the historical and political.[25] Action seeks its end not in an already-given reality, endeavoring to acquire it and finding satisfaction, but in an end *for* reality, an end to be given reality so as to orient and transform it. The category of action is the source of the meaning of history. It is here that action assumes its true meaning. Man in revolt is protestation against condition in condition, of meaning in meaning. This reflect's man's desire to dominate not only nature, but the human condition, to dominate not for the sake of domination, but to confer meaning. Man is the creator of history. Man cannot simply be an instrument of progress, it must have meaning for him. It should be at his service. We are not dealing with action for action's sake, but with action that creates meaning and, therefore, history. Action is not arbitrary. Man bears in himself the history of action. The philosophical justification and purposes for which men have acted are a source of the category of action. Man becomes himself in action, its necessity, its historical necessity, becomes objective necessity. History is the meaning of this objective necessity. The struggle for reasonable action is the highest realization of the political. This is the same struggle which man undertakes to actualized himself as a reasonable and moral being. Man as an acting and thinking being is the commitment which he makes to his political and moral existence. The assumption of social responsibility is the highest achievement of his being-in-the-world, the actualization of his freedom in negation. Is it not in political and social existence that he comes to the awareness of the concrete universal, to the realization of himself as a reasonable being, the subject of the categorical imperative? This reason he finds in the world as command. This makes it possible to comprehend the reason which he calls his own. The unity of philosophy and the political is attained only where that union of action and thought is no longer disdained or discarded by the philosopher. Holding one apart from the other gives justification to each in its distorted separability, refusing relationship to the universality of discourse, in and through which alone they become moments of the coherent discourse, the discourse of reason. In their separability they fall into self-identity, into unmediated particularity. In thought they belong to each other in systematic dependence, coming to terms with their limitations, discovering their validity in confrontation with the other. In practice, philosophy is the logical in the political; the political in the moral. Philosophy is the comprehension of all in the State.

From what we have said we can now affirm that the "reasonable State is the necessary condition; it is even the sufficient condition in so far as the individual cannot reasonably require of the state more than this State now offers him; but it is not the sufficient condition in the sense that it elevates every individual to the perfection of which this individual is capable. The sufficient condition, thus understood, would be the negation of freedom."26 The question which concerns philosophy, and is perhaps at the limits of the political, is the nature and content of the life of the reasonable individual, whose rights and dignity are recognized wherever and whenever philosophy comprehends man not only as a being of needs whose satisfactions are given over to rational calculations, but whose happiness is in reasonableness and freedom, in that "breakthrough" to the universal which founds the discourse of community in which violence is overcome. This overcoming of violence speaks to the quality of a civilization, the values which it embodies. If these are the issues of our moral, philosophical, and political life, then the commitment which we make to them establishes the level on which they can be discussed and acted upon. Morality has meaning only for the man for whom it is a problem, and who has the freedom to assume it, who is dissatisfied with the world about him, who desires to change it. He believes that this change is still possible, that the world is receptive to it and that neither violence, immorality, nor shallow skepticism, denying and rejecting the worth of moral and political life, can suppress the fact that reason is capable of actualizing the human potential in ways which we cannot as yet foresee, nor dare to limit.

Assuming that the individual is reasonable only within the universal, he nevertheless remains the individual whose reason and freedom are limited by what his reason refuses. This refusal implies a search for meaning, for happiness and that rejection of despair which is the source of cultural violence and myth. "Because man's world, the world of history and action, is *meaningful* we can *seek the meaning* of his existence in it, seek and find it not as an object nor as an event, and an already made doctrine, but seek and find it in the vision of the universal, with reasonable freedom, which refusing what refuses it, finds its content by comprehending itself as a view of the whole which grasps the whole, but which is always a partial view, and that must be formed completely before it can comprehend that it seized this whole completely differently than it had already been grasped from another point of departure and under a completely different image."[27] Weil brings us back again to the concept of philosophy in which the political is thought in the circularity of discourse in order to realize the reasonableness within the discourse possible only within the State. The philosophical discourse, simply because it is philosophical, is systematic and circular. Its beginning is truth. This beginning is at every moment of the discourse, justified in its negation. In this justification lies the meaning of philosophy, which is the comprehension of the linear-circular movement of thinking. The realization of reasonable discourse is in and through the struggle with violence, the primal condition of morality and politics. The search for meaning and reasonable action, is the essence of philosophy.

The philosophical discourse is man's autobiography, it is the discourse which every age forms in its attempt to "break through" to the universal, to the meaning of the finite-infinite dialectic which is born in that eternal form that is called the State. Here we discover the essence of history: the struggle for the universal. Philosophy reveals the oneness of the universal and the varied categories man needs to grasp it: "it reveals a truth present in the morality of every reasonable community, in the life of every man capable of perceiving living nature, not using it as brute matter. The truth is present in art, religion, and in every universal human feeling."[28] Philosophy, like poetry, is eternally the same activity. Both are derived from doing. Man, the doer, transforms and transfigures *reality*. The creativity of transcendence and negation inhabits what we call thinking, for what else can thinking be if not the search for meaning and the nature of transcendence? In the poetry of negation lies man's precious intercourse with the ground of reality. This is the sacred discourse of philosophy, the discourse in and through which we attempt to comprehend the political and the moral. Weil concludes his discussion of the political with remarks he made at the beginning of his reflections:

> rational and reasonable discussion remains the sole guarantee of the presence of the universal among men, the sole protection against the atrophy of law, institutions, and traditions. This discussion is not possible everywhere and at every moment of history. . . . The existence of the reasonable individual justifies the State. He knows that he can only en-

dure in the reasonable state, that only the state educates in reason and allows the presence of reason even in its least theoretical forms.29

In the State man comprehends what it means to be moral or immoral. It is in it that man reflects upon what he does, he reflects upon the meaning of negation. The truth of man's individuality does not lie in its empirical reality, but in that confrontation and relationship with the universal, with reason, with the categorical imperative. Only in and through this confrontation does man comprehend human action in history, history as human action. In universality human action and history gather meaning.

Reflection upon the political is reflection upon the philosophical and historical. We live in a world in which man must pose the question which is posed to him from the world, the question of truth. It is not man who poses this question, but the world which he confronts. The world is the center of concern, not man. Thus, it is from the world that man comprehends himself as freedom and limitation, as finite and temporal. We become what we are because this world is receptive to our reason and can be transformed and ordered by us. We are not only created but create. We are reason because the world allows us to realize the reason that we are. The fact that the world is, is the measure through which we comprehend our existence. Never is this existence merely receptive and not hostile, pliable without challenge and demand, acceptance without rejection, enticing and, at the same time, menacing. But these are the constraints through which man comes to terms with himself through the realization of his dependence and freedom, challenges which evoke the imagination and bring forth the poet, the doer for whom the demand, the menace, and the adventure are the very materials of life. Man is *homo faber*, he can change and surpass the reality about him. He is the political animal whose potentialities find their condition in family, society, and state. "Only the citizen of a reasonable state can be a man in the strictest sense of the terms, a completely developed and *virtuous* man, but even such a state does not guarantee that all its citizens will realize their possibilities."30 Knowing that violence is the motor cause of human action, that the State is the highest form of man's reasonable existence, that societal existence is the suppression and constraint of violence, that government is the rule of passionate men, we comprehend Weil's insistence upon reasonable and rational discussion. He stresses the philosophical faith in the universal discourse of reason, in the possibility of a meaningful politic. He follows that "wager" in faith which philosophers from Plato to Hegel have known to be the source of their affirmation, of reasonable and moral action, their rejection of violence as the *bellum omnium contra aomnes,* as the immorality which confronts and contradicts universality and universability. The moral and political problem is inseparable from the universal with which we can never be identified, which for him is always task and obligation. The universal is always to be rediscovered and realized, we draw close but never embody it; "infinitely distant and infinitely approachable," the universal is the conditioned and conditioning condition of political and moral life. Since we cannot embody the universal, for it would then no longer be the universal, but the demonic, we move toward it in hope, not of the heart nor of feeling, but the hope of reason, a hope confirmed by the freedom of reasonable choice, a choice given in reason and freedom, a choice rooted in universality, but nevertheless the choice of a finite acting being. The universal is our deepest concern. It is our freedom from the particular, the negation of the given, the *yet-to-be* that challenges every *is.* Thus, for Eric Weil, meaningful discourse concerning the political and the moral belongs to the universal. Nothing remains more destructive to thinking than the attempt to grasp finite and reasonable being only as finite, as object and as instrument. The moral and political consequences of such an attempt have already given us the demonic result: violence for the sake of violence.

History is inseparable from the moral and political, from the struggle for the universal and universality. History is the elaboration of the reasonable discourse that man discovers and forms through time. History is the search for meaning in the finite universal dialogue. The dialogue is the constant rediscovery of reason, the categories of discussion that bring it within our experience. In this experience we find our condition and conditioning limitation; we also discover the meaning of negation as freedom. History is not an attempt to organize the events of politics, the creations of the imagination or the purpose of some destiny or law of development, it is the revelation of that divinity that lives in man as reason. History is the autobiography of the *Logos* that man learns to hear and attempts to comprehend. Man is always in history through condition, but he is always beyond it through the freedom of his reason. The universal that confronts him is the eternal Thou that commands as the Categorical Imperative. History is man's response to the Thou. Nothing is more dangerous than man's affinity for the particular, his rejection of reason as nonsense, the refusal of the universal as a figment of the imagination. History is elaborated in that dialogue of opposites where the finite moves toward the infinite in love and the infinite approaches the finite with command. History is the linear-circular movement of thought discovering and rediscovering the inexhaustible reality of reason. We cannot think of history without the eternal Thou, we cannot comprehend the Thou without history.

PART II

Theological Discourses

7

The Philosopher and the Theologian: The Friendship of Raymond Aron and Gaston Fessard

The friendship of Raymond Aron and Gaston Fessard is the concern of this chapter. I have little desire to be a psychologist or en explorer of the "soul" and I do not look into dreams or hidden corners of personal life. My interest is the intellectual content of a friendship that lasted for almost half a century. Aron died in 1983 and Fessard in 1978. Aron was the political theorist who dwelled more deeply with Max Weber, Alexis de Tocqueville and Carl von Clausewitz than any other thinker of his time, while his friend, Father Fessard, ventured into the world of Hegel and Marx but never failed to perpetuate his enduring and widening insights into the *Exercises* of Ignatius Loyola whose revolutionary method he compared with that of Immanuel Kant. They were men of innovation and from their works the generations that followed developed spiritual and intellectual responsibility and tasks. Aron was a philosopher devoted to the dignity and efficacy of human reason; Fessard, a theologian, for whom the message of Christ and his Church were the source of man's freedom and truth. These men were companions in the struggles against Nazism, Fascism and Communism with all their varieties and expressions. The fight for truth and freedom made their friendship possible. Aron had little concern for theology. He had hardly any interest in the Judaism of an assimilated family tradition but there was a later, strong allegiance to Israel and its survival. Aron was the model of the assimilated French Jew. France, and French culture demanded his loyalties. Fessard wrote a book on Aron, *La Philosophie Historique de Raymond Aron* that was posthumously published. Aron spoke of Fessard in his *Mémoires* and in a talk which he prepared for a conference in Rome at the Centre Saint-Louis des Français held on May 18, 1983, "Gaston Fessard devant 'l'actualité historique."[1] Important ideas developed from this friendship between the Jesuit theologian, devoted to his Church and to freedom and the philosopher of practical reason, a journalist, and above all a man committed to the intimate and necessary relationship between thought and action.

Aron's initial remarks at Rome gave a precise delineation of Fessard's attitudes and perspectives. He said: "Father Fessard, to the end of his life, was engaged with the moral, political and theological debates that stirred the Church of France for half a century. As a philosopher, Fessard never referred to Thomism which he criticized for the absence of the sense of historicity. Fessard, from the 1930's on, dedicated his works to historical actuality in the light of his Christian faith. Although a theologian, Fessard was, at the same time, a philosopher; he expressed both his theology and philosophy in essays or books which for the most part were related, in one way or another, to *historical actuality*."2 Theologian, philosopher, polemicist, political commentator and activist, Fessard was a thinker for his time, he reacted sharply and quickly to the immediate political and moral problems. He was in the public arena advocating a point of view, awakening public response, angering and befriending people and the Church. In these activities there was a single demand: truth and freedom must and should never be compromised. From his book, *Pax Nostra-Examen de conscience international* (1938), to his critique of liberation theology and in particular the maxims of Jules Girardi, in Cheétiens marxistes et théologie de la Libération (1978), there was this unceasing political, theological, and philosophical activity. Each new book and article was a confrontation with an immediate issue. When we are away from the events and their demands we write a *Republic*, an organized and aesthetic tyranny. We leave historical actuality to those who have the peculiar talent to comprehend its qualitative differentiation, its need for decision, political subtlety and the special sensitivity that is synonymous with *phronesis*, that peculiar practical wisdom that knows no definition or explanation, but is seen in political decision. The philosopher who luxuriates in his mystical expressions or who spins a Penelope web of theoretical calculations only to have the pleasure to unravel the patterns is like a magician whose only concern is the momentary disbelief and incredulity of his audience. This philosopher would understand little of the courage and prudence that accompanies Fessard's work. Historical actuality is not peculiarly realized in the passions or in sentiment. Political engagement requires moderation and perspective. Again the Greeks gave us the word: *sophrosyne*, that unique and distinct *harmonia* that brought passion and sentiment under the reason. Fessard's friendship with Aron developed in and through their shared practical wisdom. They had qualities that are rarely dispersed among men.

If we would venture a judgment as to Fessard's most extensive and structured work we would, without hesitation, proclaim his studies of the *Spiritual Exercises of Ignatius Loyola, La Dialectique des Exercises spirituels de Saint Ignas de Loyola* which appeared in two volumes in 1956 and 1966. These are not only theological studies but philosophical, political and logical ones as well. Fessard clearly delineated in the first pages of the first volume the problems that had been at the center of his thought. "Those who have followed with some care our books and articles will have no difficulty, after they have read this present essay, to perceive from what source we have been inspired each time we have encountered the problem of freedom and truth in history, particularly, as it has been posed in our time by Hegel, Marx and Kierkegaard. For those who have read more superficially, it is only necessary to indicate the relationship between history, freedom and truth. The dialectic of Pagan and Jew, Master and Slave, Male and Female, which are fundamental themes referred to constantly in our analyses of historical situations, are from my point of view of the same kind as the dialectic of the Before and After of Election in and through which we explain the structure of the *Exercises* but also closely related by content."[3] When Fessard referred to the point or source of action he referred to the free decision by which man brings forth and influences both individual and public reality. Again and again he returns to historical actuality as the ultimate realization of that undefinable freedom that is in man. This freedom to decide and to act upon decision is man's unique path from non-being to being. The awareness of the absence of freedom, of those forces that make freedom difficult and impossible is, at the same time, the awakening of freedom's possibility. We could agree with Fessard when he said that "good and Being *acquire existence* only in relationship to an Evil and to a Non-Being *tempore prius*. This complex composition has only one end, i.e., to permit the self to *pose itself* as the freedom *to be what it must be*."[4] This theoretical formula is concrete in political and social terms through decision and action. Man can realize his political and moral nature, the good which is his end, only in a free society that makes possible man's political and social decision.

Fessard's further remarks about freedom are profound. They permit us to comprehend his fundamental opposition to Fascism, Nazism and Communism and to every attempt to reduce political and social thought to Marxist formulations and jargonistic cliches. "Like all intrusions of freedom in the physical, social or religious world" Fessard believed, "their appearance in the Self is directly nongraspable. Nothing is more hidden than *the Before* and *the After*. The point of passage is without apprehension precisely because we are not dealing with a *thing* but with an *act*, not with a *fact* but with a *Fiat*, not with a *given*, but with a *Giving* (Donnant)."[5] These observations are remarkable for the preciseness of the opposition. When we speak of freedom we do not refer to a thing, to a fact or to a given. In relation to them there is no need of freedom. To put aside the question of freedom means to speak of things, facts and givens. Freedom belongs to the act as an immeasurable source of change and possibility. The act in historical actuality has the power to negate; it is the source of negation. We are speaking here of a freedom which in its subjectivity is objectivity, i.e., whose objectivity is its subjectivity and where subjectivity is its objectivity. Fessard reminded us that "the freedom becomes true freedom, objective freedom, freedom that determines itself, at the same time, that it is determined by God."[6] The realization of the objectivity of the subject is the fundamental insight into the divine indwelling and the sacred dignity of the human soul. Believing in the sacred dignity and divine determination Fessard's philosophy of freedom is an expression of man's unique purpose and beauty in the created hierarchy of Being. The salvation of man's soul is the untouchable foundation of all his activities and his struggle for truth. Every attempt to reduce man to an historical and mechanical development does violence both to his freedom and his destiny. It destroys the beautiful in his creation.

We could easily say that these are pious words and are as jargonistic as Marxist terminology. The problem lies in the consequence for human dignity. The struggle that Fessard waged against tyranny must be remembered if we are to appreciate his theological-philosophical position. From 1933, Hitler's rise to power, to the end of World War II, Fessard fought against Nazism and Communism which he later identified with Nazism. The events that moved him deeply were the Spanish Civil War, Mussolini's aggression in Ethiopia, the *Front Populaire* in France, the *Anschluss,* the Munich agreements, the Czechoslovakian invasion and the outbreak of war which Hitler now desired because of his military strength. Without entering into the articles and books which these events brought about we know that a fundamental attitude penetrated his life: opposition to every ideology that destroyed man's search for truth and freedom. In his short but very informative "Bio-Bibliographie du P. Gaston Fessard" Michel Sales reports that "on December 15, 1940, at a conference held in the Church of Saint-Louis de Vichy, Fessard spoke of the impossibility of collaborating with Nazism and at the same time showed the parallel between communism and Nazism."[7] This was a radical parallel and found few supporters both within and outside the Church. Fessard was, however, no novice to opposition and incomprehension. He always knew that the greatest love he owed to his opponents was truth. He knew that his openness deeply affected his reputation and his life.

The qualities that Fessard exhibited could not fail to endear him to Aron who, for the greatest part of his life, followed the same path. These friends were the "active philosophers" who responded to the needs and demands of their time, men who refused the traps of totalitarianism. Philosophy was at the service of the event; it challenged morally and politically the forces of irrationality, totalitarianism and terror. The struggle for a sense of humanity did not belong exclusively to meditation, the lecture hall, or the academic conference. It was needed in the immediacy of the moment and in this it required the prudence of decision, the courage of thought and the strategy of procedure. Aron mentioned that Fessard was intransigent in his opposition to the two totalitarian regimes he believed were inimical to the force of truth and freedom. He said that "after the war Fessard criticized numbers of Catholics, Jean LaCroix, for example, for admitting that Communism went with a sense of history." He was intransigent in his faith and in "the inviolability of his Church and he affronted, often, the Church hierarchy and Catholic intellectuals who were less clear in perspective than himself."[8] His faith was uncompromisable and many saw in it the inquisitorial spirit. This was true only if we believe that there is compromise with evil. If we believe with Fessard that every régime that is committed to the destruction of freedom is evil, then we are fellow believers whatever be our strategy and procedures. If we cannot follow him in his belief in eternal salvation through the Church, we do believe in the power of the giving spirit and in dependence upon a transcendent God. Commitment demands faith. Action demands commitment. Do not action and faith form that sacred union from which is possible that persistent opposition to the forces of totalitarianism? We may not agree that the struggle is exclusively between Moscow and Washington; we might believe that the legions of terrorists and the centers of terror have made both Washington and Moscow conservative capitals with much in common, but if the danger is now international terror, then the commitment against it must be firm and unflinching. Fessard's intransigence is the source of freedom from which no one can flee who feels deeply and knows intimately the dangers of both communism and terrorism.

Within the Western world there were two movements that had to be constantly fought because the world contained within it dangers that threatened the survival: materialism and pacifism. Could a society survive that had lost the will to fight for its values? Could a society endure that turned to itself and had lost its responsibility to its neighbors and to the community of nations? Aron noted that the 1938 Czechoslovakian crisis had revealed the consequences of these dangers. Fessard had earlier reminded the public of this attitude in 1936 in his *Pax Nostra*. Aron analyzed Fessard's opinions with these comments: "Pacifism is the degradation of the spiritual élan towards peace and it risks self-contradiction and self-denial. Because it refuses unconditionally war it ends up by allying itself with the enemies of the country. It becomes the accomplice of all those who in the name of an anti-Christian ideal prepare for the universal revolution (Fessard is thinking of the complicity of the pacifists and communists) of all those who do not hesitate to rearm while at the same time demand disarmament (Fessard is thinking of the Nazis)."[9] What the pacifists lack in realism, the nationalists lack in idealism. The failure to see beyond one's own country, proclaiming the love of country to be the virtue, shows that the lover can be the enemy. Where the particular is glorified exclusively the universal is lost. The question is how to find the universal in the particular and the particular in the universal.

During the war and the occupation Fessard fought against collaboration. In November 1941, he published a brochure, "France, prends garde de perdre ton âme. Cahier clandestin de Témoignage chrétien." This and other clandestine brochures were disseminated to show the dangers of Nazism and the collaborationists. In the brochure Fessard wrote: "At first sight, it seems impossible that the Nazi mystique could penetrate us and overcome authentic Catholicism. As a result of a long tradition even our unbelievers are filled with the Christian spirit and the great mass of the people are attached to freedom and remain deeply oblivious to the mystique of race and blood. . . . Once the principle of collaboration is accepted a common action will cover a French-German agreement on every level. With the pretext of constructing a pacifist Europe, the propagandist of the III Reich will associate the French in a perverse enterprise."[10] This perverse endeavor was the struggle against the Jews. The issue of anti-Semitism was fundamental for Fessard. In 1928 the Vatican had stated: "by Christ and in Him we are the spiritual descendents of Abraham. . . . Anti-Semitism is inadmissible. *We are all Semites.*"[11] The task that Fessard saw in 1941 was the radical opposition against every attempt of the Nazis to enlist France in its racism and to pervert its Catholic heritage. Fessard knew that Christianity could not adapt itself either to Nazism or to Communism; it had adapted itself to liberalism and democracy because there were possibilities for freedom in the commitment to individual rights and governmental procedures. He said that the language spoken by Nazism and Communism was not that of Christianity. These ideologies had brought new languages into existence and these were based on the lie. The language of the lie had become a most serious enemy.

Both Aron and Fessard took strong positions toward the widely publicized Christian-Communist dialogue. In 1948 Fessard wrote, *France, prends garde de perdre la liberté*. In 1941 he had warned the nation of the Nazis and their collaborationists. Now he cried out against the communist danger. This voice of Cassandra reacted with pain and anxiety to what he knew was communist perversity, the lie. He said: "Five years ago our denunciation of the Nazi peril confronted incredulity from every part of French opinion. To unveil the hypocrisy hidden in the Vichy government was to undermine the authority of a 'legitimate' head of State, to disunite the French, to prepare for civil war and to prepare the ground for communism. Now there is a completely different part of French opinion who blames us for breaking the unity of the Resistance, dividing the country and making us allies of business and fascism."[12] What Fessard had witnessed and understood was the character of communist deception and its use of the lie. To say one thing and to do another, is to proclaim democratic intentions and, at the same time, use these intentions to destroy democracy; to formulate principles of social development in order to bring about a crushing bureaucracy and a dogmatically controlling Party which determines what is truth and falsity. Fessard understood well the dangers of bureaucracy and hierarchical domination; he comprehended the perversity of power when employed for destructive purposes; he knew there was a difference between good and evil.

Fessard had not only seen the similarities between Nazism and Communism, he had also known that rationalism was inadequate to give man eternal salvation and that these same rational forces could be used for destruction. Fessard spoke of the inhumanity of these two totalitarian mystiques and this he attributed not only to the absolute character of their ends but also to the cynicism of their means, their disregard of morality. These two characteristics, their absolutism and their cynicism, brought with them a third which Fessard did not mention, nor did he foresee its international character: terrorism. If rationalism was supposed to form the essence of Marxism, the consequences of its absolutism could be anarchy and contemporary world terror. It is this terrorism that threatens both democracy and communism, because it does not share the traditions of rationalism or the deviations that are in it: historical actuality. Terror is the absence of a sense of society. It is destruction for its own sake.

Aron delineated with real clarity Fessard's theology of history. This was Fessard's major contribution to the understanding of historical actuality and from it we see why his political and moral thought lay in a firm and committed faith in revelation and history. Fessard thought with oppositions. He believed that they were the structure that allowed us to comprehend history. He believed that we should pay particular attention to the opposition Pagan-Jew. From the *Pax Nostra* Aron cited these characteristic lines: "The opposition of the Jew, the chosen people, and the Pagan, who is indifferent to the (divine) promise, dominates and explains all history *before Christ;* the opposition of converted pagan and of the rejected Jew explains all of history *after Christ.*"[13] The Christian, being the consequence of this opposition, causes within himself the idolatry of the Pagan and the sceptical non-belief of the Jew. From these two realities he is never free because redemption is not in history, but beyond it. The kingdom of God rejects all immanence and is therefore never identifiable with political or social revolutions or with any particular form of government. It is eternal opposition, the historical negation to what *is.* From this negation arises the eternal critique of human life and its pagan attempts to seek totality. It, likewise, stands against the scepticism that refuses every transcendence, that perpetuates Idealism drawing God from the *Cogito.* Fessard knew the inherent dangers that lay in rationalism that refused to deny its invincibility. He comprehended the irrationalism from works embodied in it, but lived from the rationalism it objected to and condemned. He did not analyze the relationship between irrationalism and terrorism that became the formidable political antagonism of contemporary political life. Idolatry and incredulity remain at the source of human conflict but the depths of their meaning belongs to the thought of every decade, to the quality of our comprehension of historical actuality. Within the conflict Jew-Pagan the conflictual nature of our society is more forcefully revealed to us.

The antagonism of Jew and Pagan is the model for all the antagonisms that inhabit human society. In society we struggle to limit the degree of conflict but we know that these conflicts remain the forces from which society develops. In fact, it is in and through antagonism that society refuses every attempt to find the unique interpretation or the final solution. Speaking of history Fernand Braudel wrote in his book, *La Dynamique du Capitalisme:* "There is no book written for all times and we all know it. . . . For historians as well as for all men of objective science there will always be an America to be discovered."[14] In human affairs antagonism is the realization of metaphysical truths which are imposed upon thought in its attempt to comprehend freedom and subjection.

Fessard never believed that the antagonism that he elucidated could be resolved within the here and now. His faith in the Church as the *Corpus Mysticum* made it possible for him to "know" that only in the Church do conflicts find their reconciliation. The belief in the immanence of this Mystical Body is the source of man's destruction. "The temporal replica," he said, "of the Corpus Mysticum will suppress the transcendent mystification only to become itself, here below, the most extreme mystification."[15] We are aware, however, that this secular mysticism belongs not only to the totalitarian state and its myths, but to those forces that seek societal destruction *per se* because they recognize neither reason nor society. The threat to the antagonism that is valid for societal growth proceeds from the mystifying power of the "final solution," its jargon and banalities.

Fessard's structures of conflicts form his theology of history. From this theological history there emanates a philosophy of history. In relation to the Pagan-Jew conflict we could say that "the survival and dispersal of the Jewish people, the movement of the Jew toward rationalism, and faith in the sufficiency of reason for the organization of life and the assurance of peace is explained by the dialectic of the election of the Jew, his consequent rejection, and the idolotrous converted pagan."[16] The fear of idolatry created the Jew. The movement toward rationalism was his persistent attempt to ward off the dangers of anthropomorphism, divine immanency, exaggerated sentimentality, pessimism and fatalism. Rationalism was identical with the critical study of the law, with experimental medicine and fluidity of business relationships. The Jew spoke less of love and more of deeds and responsibility; he spoke little of God and more of the varieties of justice and intricacies of legal commentaries. Rationalism drove him to scepticism and he became the great opponent of the human idols. The Pagan who had no comprehension of the transcendent remained the believer in the immanent Absolute whether it was metaphysical, historical or political. He felt attracted to fatalism and unresolvable conflicts which reduce man to the child of the Furies; he spoke of tragedy, its irreducible contradictions, and its denial of free will. Where does the Christian emerge from the Jewish faithfulness to his non-corporeal God and the Pagan devotion to his deification of human nature and history? If the Christian converted and redeemed the Pagan it would be assumed that he overcame his idolatry. But the idolatry of the Pagan is never overcome and the Christian lives with this inheritance. He lives with the Jewish bond to the Divine Covenant, he lives with Abraham, Isaac and Jacob. Does the Pagan forgive the Christian for condemning and depriving him of his idolatry?

Can the Jew comprehend the Christian for his Incarnation of divinity, for giving the aesthetic dimension of divinity priority over the ethical? The antagonisms that Fessard raised are overwhelming in their implications. We witness paganism in Nazism and Communism. If Judaism bore within itself rationalism it also had a fierce attachment to its Covenant. Its radical opposition to idolatry cannot be applied to rationalism and scepticism because where rationalism is accompanied by reasonableness it discovers modesty, i.e., the ancient but never surpassed *Sophrosyne*. Christianity inherits from the Jew faithfulness and reason, from Paganism, idolatry.

If we turn to another antagonism we can understand more about the Jewish-Pagan conflict. Fessard believed that in Nazism and Communism we grasp the two moments of the master-slave relationship because "the dialectic of the master and the slave allows us to comprehend the kinship and hostility of Nazism and Communism. The former envisages the universal realm of the masters, the latter emphasizes work and the creation of the new man. Marx understood the dialectic of the slave and master from the point of view of the slave. Hitler understood it from that of the master. . . . Both attacked Christianity; Hitler because he saw in history only a natural struggle, Marx because he believed in the universal mission of the class struggle . . . after which the classless and stateless communist society would begin. . . . Marx could thus conclude that Communism has resolved the mystery of history. He knew that he has resolved it."[17] Why do both attack Christianity? If we read Fessard closely we realize that Christianity is the realization of the overcoming of idolatry as it is expressed in all forms of paganism from the ancient to the modern world whether it be Stoicism or Epicurianism, Rationalism or Scepticism. These forms of thought are idolotrous from the moment they accept themselves as truth. Pagan idolatry passes into the myth of the State in the form of racism, atavism and the exclusiveness of nationalism as romantic mythology and historical illusion. Both Nazism and Communism are idolic forms of romanticism because they are the creations of utopian mythologies: racial and historical mythologies exhibited as natural law. Christianity stands forth as the primordial negation of myth and of economic and political utopianism. Christianity rooted in intransigent monotheism and radical opposition to idolatries stands opposed to these idolic romanticisms of earthly salvation. The living Church is the stumbling bloc to every social, economic and political utopia.

In relation to the Jew the problem is complicated. The Jew remains bound to the Abrahamic covenant and stands forth as God's chosen people. The rejection of this chosenness made the Jew the exponent of rationalism. The system of Spinoza is the consequence of the rejection of chosenness and the Covenant. Rationalism is, however, the purification of the sensible; it is the clearest and purest realization of thought that is possible. Rationalism is, at the same time, the most decisive and sharpest rejection of transcendence. If Kant was the last theistic metaphysician in his refusal to mediate the *should be* with *what is,* then it was Hegel who most profoundly exploited the concept of mediation which made it possible to discover a divinity that was embodied in the power of conceptualization. In thought what is real *(wirklich)* can be thought of as reasonable. This was the loudest clarion call of modern rationalism. Was it peculiarly the heritage of the Jew? This would be difficult to affirm. In the form of scientific research the rationalism that remained inseparable from experimentation and empirical observation became the form of thought that most seriously questioned the reality of transcendence. If Christianity cannot overcome the Pagan and his idolatry, it, equally, finds itself powerless before the inundating onrush of rationalism. Christianity bears within itself both the mythologies of the one and the scientifism of the other. Where does it stand with these two forces in its body politic? The fundamental question for Fessard always referred to this conflict. Truth neither coincides with the mythology of paganism or with the exclusivity of rationalism. Fessard was certain that truth belonged to their overcoming in the Church. Truth belonged to God and his Church and from the perspective of God's radical Negation every human activity remains incomplete and partial. If we state it theoretically as Fessard did in his work on the *Exercises* then we say that from the view of the Absolute "non-being has as its consequence to bring forth Being in existence where it is realized. At the same time this Being takes from Non-being its false existence, it assures its truth."[18] The realization of Being from Non-Being is the way by which man discovers through negation the true nature of Self as the constant movement from Non-Being to Being. In human life the movement is unending. Historical actuality is always the fluidity of truth and falsity; it refuses every absolute as a denial of its reality.

Before Fessard died he had completed two books. One was called, *Église de France prends garde de perdre la Foi!* What was crucial for Fessard was to show the impossibility of a dialogue between Christianity and Communism. He was deeply opposed to every Christian movement into which Marxist jargon had seeped and had undermined the vitality of Christian theology. The warning that was expressed in the title of his book and which were the same words with which he ended it stemmed from his belief that the words of Lenin's representative, Litvinov, at the Court of Arbitration at The Hague in 1920 had remained true of all later Soviet policy. Litvinov had stated that the Soviet Union was the systematic enemy of arbitration except in technical cases and in litigation concerning private law. "We asked him (Litvinov) to clarify the reasons for his attitude, 'that it is impossible to find an impartial judge in the world.' He replied: 'It is important to state that there is not *one* world but two *worlds*, the Soviet and the non-Soviet world, or if one prefers the Russian and the non-Russian world.' He emphasized the incompatibility of the 'material and intellectual interest' already encountered. The latter eliminates the possibility of establishing a jurisdiction between the members of the two worlds."[19] This message which the Soviets gave early to the world expressed their categorical obligation: "the *historical mission* of the proletariat is destined to liberate humanity from all alienations by liberating itself." This historical mission will overcome the two worlds, the difference in language, of intellectual and economic conditions. Fessard's attitude was stated in his reply to the question of the French communist leader, Maurice Thorez: "Is dialogue possible?" Fessard's words bore the weight of his experience with communism: the communist is a man who does not have a "knife between his teeth but has the lie in his mouth." The issue between the incarnated Word and the universality of its significance and the lie of Marxism was for Fessard irreducible. The struggle between the lie and truth had become the singular moral and intellectual issue of his thought.

With our intellectual sophistication we feel uneasy about such reductions of problems to good and evil, truth and falsity. To see the simplicity that is in the problems that we face does not imply a simple-mindedness, but rather a clarity that allows us to act. The virtue of simplicity is refused only by the fuzzy mind that can only grasp detail and the frenzy of conflict. Fessard stood firmly with his message of Christianity and he opposed persistently the lie which he believed to be Marxism-Leninism-Stalinism. Whatever the variation and changes in Soviet policy he believed that the Litvinov statement was valid. The fundamental dogmas of class struggle and historical materialism had become scientific explanations formulated and reformulated by the Party and made inviolable. Wherever these dogmas had influence they weakened the power of transcendence. Fessard fought against the Marxism of the worker priests and later against the theology of liberation. Against the latter he dedicated the second of his last publications, *Chrétiens marxistes et théologie de la Libération*. It is a book that demands careful analysis because it shows the danger that occurs when Marxism infiltrates religion.

Never far from Fessard's thought was always the problem of the Jew. His friendship for Aron was expressed in an unfinished manuscript that was published after his death, *La philosophie historique de Raymond Aron* (1980). In conversations with Jean-Louis Missika and Dominique Woltan, Aron referred to the book of Fessard. "Gaston Fessard," Aron said, "interprets me in a way that makes me essentially a semite. It is his privilege. In spite of my great friendship for him I was not convinced of his interpretation."[20] Aron did not have a Jewish education. He claimed to be more familiar with Christianity than with Judaism. He considered himself a Frenchman of Lorraine and this remained his attitude until his death. Aron felt close to Israel's struggle for independence and her constant struggle for survival. There was a solidarity with the historical struggle of his people. Aron opposed DeGaulle's attitude toward the Arabs and he, more and more, constructed bridges to link himself to Israel's intellectual life. He could not escape the image of being France's leading Jewish intellectual. The question is what determined Fessard's attitude toward Aron's Jewishness? Fessard believed that no Jew could escape the Abrahamic Covenant. The Jewish people lived the historical consequences of the Covenant and with them historical actuality had more significance than with any other people. The incarnated Word lived in that historical actuality more fully than in any other. In 1973, an interview with Fessard was published in "France catholique-Ecclesia" on the subject of the "Mystery of Israel."[21] How did he understand his friend Aron? If we reflect on his comprehension of this mystery of Israel we can clarify the problem. In answer to the question: "Would you say that Judaism has an irreducible vocation and a place in the religious destiny of our world today?" Fessard replied that whether or not the Jew believed in his religion the world would always see him as a Jew. "Opposition is to his honor because the pagan shows that the Jew has the responsibility to make present the true God. The pagan, who is always alive in the Christian who must ceaselessly seek to convert himself, feels in the atheistic Jew the possibility of a negation of his idols. In fact, the presence of the negative transcendence of all idolatry is peculiarly specific to the Jew. This is his election, his proper vocation, and it always exists, even when he denies it."[22] This is truly an amazing statement of metaphysical importance. The Christian must ceaselessly be converted from paganism; the Jew to the eternal negation of idolatry. In essence the survival of Judaism is necessary as long as there is idolatry. Idolatry is, however, the eternal human condition. The Jew is eternal as long as the human condition endures because idolatry takes on ever new forms of intellectual and moral sophistication. Rationalism is another form which the Jew uses to express his opposition to idolatry. If Fessard wanted to comprehend Aron as the Jew it was not difficult to see in Aron's work that deep devotion to reason, critique and limitation as the peculiar marks of his agnostic Jewishness. He and Aron struggled against the idol makers of their time, both were threatened by their existence and both knew there could be no compromise with these or any form of idolatry. The question of eternal salvation belongs to the Church and not to Israel. The work of Israel is divine and historical and in service to the universal church of Christ. In this respect the Church and Israel live together in brotherly love, each given by God its unique and peculiar role in salvation. The role of Israel remains historical, that of the Church universal and eschatological because she is not only of the world, but its purpose and end. She is the universal expression of Israel's particularity.

In his *Mémoires* Aron spoke in more detail of his position in relation to Fessard. He referred to his theory of history. "I distinguished," he said, concerning his *Introduction à la philosophie d'histoire,* "natural and human history; I did not categorically eliminate sacred or supernatural history. I reserved for myself the possibility, or if one wishes, the blank space. Father Fessard fills in this blank with faith in Christ."[23] Aron remained the man of practical activity. He was immediately engaged in the events and ideologies that occurred in Europe from 1933 to 1983. His life was devoted to those human values we call freedom, pluralism, liberalism and reasonableness. Human events had to have human explanations. He remarked in relation to Israel's independence that "nothing in the formation of the State of Israel and in the persistence of the Diaspora defies ordinary historical explanation."[24] In relation to Fessard's desire to make him into a son of Israel with theological implications he said: "I don't believe he is mistaken; I only maintain: the sentiment of kinship does not surpass human, profane history. Thousands of years of history have left in the depths of the Jewish soul indelible traces among which the intuition that all Jews, despite their dispersion, share the same fate. All Jewish communities feel concerned, menaced when one is persecuted. If this community is called Israel, how can this "kinship" not come forth irresistibly removing with it the film, mysterious if you wish, from our eyes?"[25] Aron hoped that relationship with Israel could be explained historically and sociologically. Whether this truly revealed his feelings we will never know. We know only what he said. Fessasrd had something else to say. He wanted and needed Aron to be more Jewish. He believed that Aron's rationalism never made it possible for him to comprehend his solidarity with the history and destiny of his people. It hid his feelings; it suppressed the depths of Solidarity.

Fessard's discussion of Aron's relationship to the Jewish people is based upon an analysis of Aron's book, *DeGaulle, Israel et les Juifs* (1962). This book was published at the time of DeGaulle's famous news conference at which the general said of the Jews: "An elitist people sure of itself and dominating." "Peuple d'élite, sûr le lui et dominateur." The book is a collection of articles. Fessard said of them: "Of the sixteen articles which form the core and the major part of this work, I will say nothing, but that in rereading, from a distance, they bear witness to Aron's extraordinary lucidity and his competence in the field of international diplomacy and strategy."[26] The issue was not Aron's competency as a scholar of international diplomacy but rather Fessard's theology of history which is structured in and through the antagonism of Jew and Pagan. Fessard, like Aron, was convinced that religious solidarity preserved the people of Israel in their dispersion, but this religious solidarity had deep cultural significance and forced from itself the values that are intimately connected to rationalism and to those arts and sciences that depend upon the moral and intellectual dignity of man. Fessard delineated the fidelity of the Jew with the intransigence of monotheism. This intransigence belongs to the unique and jealous God who man must never image nor see face to face.[27] Accompanying this intransigence is the absolute prohibition of image-making. This refusal of idolatry is the categorical imperative of the Jew's moral and intellectual life. He remains critical in thinking; he struggles against the myths and ideologies of societal life; they are the source of his destruction. If his faith refuses him the world of "sight," toward which he must be sceptical, it demands of him a sensitive and commanding world of "obedient listening" (ob-audire). This commentary of Fessard is deeply significant. He comprehends the Jew attached to the world of thought. Fessard remarked that this "negation of sight predisposed the Jew's intelligence to be more dependent upon hearing, a sense of time whose flight is only retained by the caring and pensive memory remembering the words heard and recorded by Scripture."[28] These words are remembered not through mere repetition but through the tradition of interpretation, historical analyses, linguistic analyses and literary commentary. The art of hermeneutics belonged naturally to the art of listening. The subtlety of discussion formed an intricate part of Jewish intellectual life. Fessard believed that he had given sufficient reason to explain the "practical reflectiveness of the Jew and his extraordinary capacity for assimilation and adaptability."[29] Fessard was willing to accept the fact that the Jewish passion for intelligence and universality explains his great contribution to the philosophical and religious life of the West. The long and detailed commentary of Fessard on the role of the Jew paralleled his undeniable belief that hid friend, Aron, embodied these characteristics and was more deeply Jewish than he liked to admit. Aron was Jewish through destiny even if his Spinozeatic rationalism made it possible for him to be critically distant in his analyses of his feelings. The paradoxical faithfulness of the Jew to the Abrahamic Covenant and to rationalism which is the expression of his non-believing belief enters Christianity with its antagonism intact. There they face paganism and the struggle for its conversion. On this depends the Church.

Do not all of Aron's historical studies show the basic dimension of Jewish existence: historical actuality? We have spoken of the primacy of the word, of hearing, and the sense of time that belongs to memory, but we have not mentioned the meaning of history. Here we encounter the history of a people and a God whose will is unknown and whose freedom deprives man of the securities of the fates, fatalism, and an inexorable destiny. God's freedom is Israel's history. Fessard stated that it "is expressed less through the creation and direction of a Cosmos entirely subordinated to His pleasure than by an address, a vocation given to individuals: Abraham, Moses and the Prophets and to Israel itself. From this there arises the idea of "election" implicit in the Promise to Abraham, made precise in the giving of the law to Moses, the Sinaitic Covenant, which is renewed at crucial moments of Israel's life and becomes the center of the cult created to preserve the people's fidelity."[30] Fessard made the role of the Jew pivotal in the history of Western religion. This role was of such significance that without it the return to idolatry would have occurred long ago. The totalitarianisms of this century could be fought by Christianity only because Christianity embodied within itself the Abrahamic Covenant. The converted pagan is a possibility only because of Jewish history. From Fessard's theology the victory of the universal Church is intimately tied to the historical actuality of Israel and its fierce opposition to idolatry.

The separation that exists between the thought of Aron and that of Fessard was deep, but there was ground enough for them to share similarity of interests and oppositions. We could call it "dialogue between a philosopher of tolerance suitable to the non-believing rationalist and a philosopher of intransigence proper to the believer in a religion of salvation. Both were opposed to the intolerance of secular religions."[31] If we seek the reason that Fessard believed that the role of Israel was a preparation for the truth of the Church, then we must

find the answer in his ultimate rejection of Israel's peoplehood and his acceptance of the Church's universality. The essence of Israel's role in the scheme of
salvation belongs to her particular Covenant in which particularity has within itself the universal. Israel, however, remained the particular. The Incarnation was
the universal that lived in the particular, i.e., in the historical actuality of Israel.
Fessard's theology of history is a clear acceptance of Israel's uniqueness and the
Christian dependence upon it. Christianity could only emerge from it and remain
historically and ontologically tied to Israel. Even in her universality the Church
remained dependent. If she believed that the universality was the true meaning
of Israel's particularity and was already embodied in it, she could be universal
because Israel was and is particular. Whatever divided Aron from Fessard is
dwarfed by the community that exists in their religious heritage. They both remained unalterably opposed to idols of Communism; this opposition was born
from their solidarity with the intransigence of monotheism. Their dialogue was
possible because of their historical community and their loyalty to freedom and
truth which they knew they had to defend.

Fessard was an intransigent fighter in the struggle for truth and freedom. He
fought against every form of spiritual collaboration with Nazism and Communism. In this intransigence lay gentleness and compassion. The words of Aron
tell it all. ''It is impossible to present the man. I would simply say that he is the
most gentle, open, the least capable of evil that I have known. He was the most
attentive of men.'' He, more than any other, knew that ''the language of the
Communists, whether in or out of power, is that of the lie.''[32] Aron admired his
courage, his faith in truth and freedom. From the political perspective they were
staunch liberals. History was choice, decision and the search for truth, but never
the truth. We, today, see new and dangerous forms of terrorism that threaten all
societal forms. Whenever the dangers arise men must develop the diplomatic
and military strategy to oppose them. We must never lose our faith in universality and transcendence. As long as we remain devoted to freedom and moderation we are inseparable from the struggle against idolatry. Fessard and Aron
were friends in the deepest of all communions: the common struggle for truth
and freedom. The Christian and the Jew belonged together in the theology of
history. Fessard more deeply than any other theologian or philosopher developed a comprehension of history in which the meaning of Israel and the Church
found their divine role. What emerges from their relationship is beauty of form
that bears witness to God's plan and purpose. Fessard was unique but this
uniqueness must yet be discovered. His books await those who are sensitive to

his concerns. His friend, Aron, could not follow him in his deepest theological speculations and in the strength of his religious faith, but he pointed us in his direction and for this we owe Aron a deep debt.

The historical, actual dialectic of Jew and Pagan does not belong to a nontemporal speculative value and truth. It is the living, historical experience of religion in the West. Fessard's great contribution to speculative and political philosophy lay in his capacity to determine the Jew-Pagan opposition, dialectically and historically. In this he gave us the categories in which we understand the political and moral conflicts of the age. Theology became historical actuality.

8

The Dialectical Forms of Human History

The dialectical forms of human history are correlative, but there is an intrinsic *sense* to their relation: Good, and Evil.

There are no beginnings and ends when we are thinking the thoughts of a fellow philosopher and theologian. We comprehend the thinking of Gaston Fessard if we assume that his thinking is an attempt to explore and venture into the reality of freedom. Freedom embraces not only human thought, but what lies at the source: God's reality. If there are no beginnings there are preliminary remarks which enable us to grasp the *fact* that a beginning is already the embodiment of what will be revealed in the course of our thinking about the beginning. The beginning is not temporal; it is logical. We begin with abstract remarks and it is from these that we develop the theses that the dialectical structures of Fessard's thinking are rooted in two Ideas: truth and freedom. From these Fessard developed dialectical categories to explain those relationships which introduce and embody the meaning of human and divine history. In the development of these categories we find that we are confronted by others that have been drawn from Totalitarianism. In Nazism and Communism Fessard found an incontrovertible perversity that distorts and threatens the Ideas of freedom and truth. From the actuality of the perversity freedom assumes a profound importance. At the beginning of his study of the *Spiritual Exercises* of Ignatius Loyola, Fessard described, in abstract terms, the problem of human freedom. He noted that "the opposition of Evil and Good placed the self before the ambiguity of its being in order that it might freely posit itself and be what it must *be*. Being and Non-being, Evil and Good *are only possible* in relation to a Being *natura prius*. The priority of nature is reversed in the representation. Good and Being *acquire existence* only in relation to an Evil and a non-being *tempore prius*. These complex oppositions have the one purpose of allowing the Self to *posit itself* as the freedom of being what it must be."[1] Freedom exists only where there is political, moral and social conflict. Conflict refers only to valid alternative positions and values, not to positions that are fundamentally destructive to the continuing interplay of these alternatives. Wherever and whenever positions are maintained that persistently aim to destroy the conflicting reality of life, there totalitarianism arises as the deification of a human alternative and the consequent perversion of every competing one. The struggle for freedom begins only when and where evil and non-being is one.

If we now turn to Fessard for a more concrete statement of his position in relation to Nazism and Communism we get both an abstract and concrete reality. In other words, the clearer the abstraction, the more precise its concreteness. In reference to Nazism and Communism Fessard elaborated the triadic relationship of Paternity, Maternity, Fraternity. He declared that the ''classless and stateless presupposes a maternity of the *materia-mater* without the paternal principle; it presupposes a pathenogenic or virginal one. The master race, on the other hand, which prohibits their members all sexual intercourse with slave states in the name of *Rassenschande* . . . promise these states, however, a superior civilization . . . presuppose that they exercise in relation to these slave states a quasi-adoptive paternity. In these two myths humanity is conceived either as Women . . . without . . . men or as Men . . . without . . . women. We easily see the difference from the Christian representation where the fundamental relationship between God and Humanity is given by the loving model of the man-woman relationship. Only this model establishes universal human fraternity that has its foundation in divine paternity and the human-divine maternity of the Church.''[2]

There are three dialectical forms that Fessard structured into the architecture of his thinking: Woman-Man, Master-Slave, Pagan-Jew. These oppositional forms are not exclusive of one another; they imply each other and are dependent upon one another. The Master-Slave opposition is the natural dialectic form of human relationships from which society and the consciousness of freedom take their first conscious steps. The Woman-Man conflict embodies the Master-Slave but builds the structure of human relationships in and through familial life, the core of civil society. The Pagan-Jew conflict is the fundamental struggle by a realization of the Idea of Humanity. The unending opposition to Paganism takes on the form of a continuous struggle against fatalism, racism, mythical and utopian concepts of history, all forms of totalitarianism that seek to end the conflictual nature of civil society. Each dialectical form bears witness to the fundamental problem of freedom, to that difficult movement from Non-Being to Being. Each form, whether it be natural, human or historical, bears within itself the distortion and perversion of the Non-Being that it cannot drive from itself.

The dependence of these forms upon each was clearly noticed by Fessard. He remarked "that the contrast between the Man-Woman and Master-Slave dialectic is the origin of the relationship of Paternity, Maternity and Fraternity in the supernatural as well as the natural order and that it would not be an exaggeration to say that the dialectic of Pagan and Jew is the motor principle of History and the guide of Christian thought in search of the meaning of its faith. In this light the three mysteries of Trinity, Incarnation and Redemption are revealed. . . . It was for the apostles and Paul to show in Christ the achievement of the Promise, the truth and reality of the figures of the Old Testament. . . . How would this theology progress without recourse, either implicitly or explicitly to Paulian dialectics which set in Christ the One in whom Jew and Gentile are one; 'He has made the two one and in her body of flesh and blood has broken down the enmity which stood like a dividing wall between them' " (Eph. II, 13-15).3

If the dialectic of Pagan and Jew is the motor force of history, then it is the foundation from which the architecture of a philosophy of history is formed and developed. It is this architecture that makes it possible for us to comprehend the meaning of the struggle against idolatry. Where idolatry implies the deification of any form of temporal reality there the threat to freedom becomes serious. The deification solidifies forms of reality and prevents oppositional forms to enter into conflict with them. These solidifications are the idols of ideologies, ideologues, and myth-makers who project either maternal or paternal forms of ideal societies. But whether the form be a deification of the paternal or the maternal, the consequence is the perversion of freedom and the truth of divine transcendence. The idolatries of our world were, for Fessard, Nazism and Communism. From these spin off various forms of fanaticism, racism and mysticism that bear within themselves the inner perversions that accompany every form or non-form of human action and organization in which freedom is not simply threatened, but systematically crushed. This destruction of freedom is the object of Fessard's analysis and its dialectic procedure. What is of profound significance is the realization that the threat to freedom is at the same time the threat to the philosophical and religious tradition. Where this threat exists and is effectively active philosophy and theology die. The dialectic in every form that is described by Fessard implies the question of freedom. Man, in his comprehension of the dialectical forms of thought, realizes in himself the freedom of his being. In and through the dialectic he moves from the "before" of his being to the "after" of Being.

Fessard accepted the undeniable perversity of all forms of totalitarianism simply because of their immediate inhumaneness, because this perversity was the Non-being of Paganism, the absence of Goodness from which there was no movement toward Goodness, the manifestation of Evil whose force could only be destroyed through physical power. The Paganism that assumed the forms of Nazism and Communism were different in their perversity. Fessard explained the differences that lay in their common substance. He stated that "Communism and Nazism were diametrically opposed in their conception of history's point of departure and its end. The former spoke of *work* and the creation of *classless and stateless society;* the latter of the *death* struggle and the domination of the *master* people. They agreed only on the means of leading history to its end. For both it was *political struggle* but for the one it was understood as the *revolt of the slaves* and revolution; for the other the *national wars* of the masters and the victorious peace."4 The latter was driven by the will to power, the former by the desire for possession. Deep within each form of totalitarianism is the struggle of master and slave. This natural struggle, already in the glance of the eye, is the fundamental condition of natural life and the basis of human life. In the master race, or in the proletariat, the struggle is the core of the ideology and the myth. In communism the slaves search through history for their promised mastership while the master race seeks in that same history to find its natural place as the guardian of the inferior peoples and the destruction of those whose survival would only be a constant threat and source of perversion. The Master-Slave relationship is the foundation for the utopia of either the masters or that of the slaves but in every utopia lies the hidden hell which destroys the forces that are barriers to the utopia. These forces are always a disguised expression of freedom because their existence would maintain the right to the legitimate meaning of conflict. The struggle to death is a natural condition, because the slaves, conscious of themselves as slaves seek through work and struggle to enjoy the possessions that are in the hands of the master. It is not through work that the slaves seek to become the masters, but in the realization of a fundamental condition of life: the struggle to survive between the weaker and the stronger, or to emerge from the constant battle of friend and foe to an equilibrium, which for the moment we call peace. The Master-Slave reality is the foundation of human life. Within it man's efforts to reach a degree of civilization, to universalize his efforts and to create conditions of sophisticated human life become possible through the multiforms of work. Work that is physical and spiritual, individual and collective, technical and artistic expresses the societal power of man to imagine and invent, transform and transfigure reality. Every effort is a movement from slavery to mastery, but mastery creates slavery in the circular process of natural development. Where master and slave are ontological categories their abstractness denies them their existential and historical variety, possibility and contingency. Where they are universal historical categories history is glorified and structured in their image and destroyed as human history. Freedom, which must be identified with possibility and the unexpected, is reduced to the expected and to necessity.

What is always significant for Fessard in every dialectical comprehension is his deep faith in man's freedom to surpass every barrier of slavery, and his faith in the fact that the degenerative forces that permeate the master finally reduce him to slavery. The movement from non-being to Being occurs because prior to every human and societal conflict there is Being in and through which the dialectic has its freedom as dependence. In this dependence the dialectic has its architecture and validity. The truth of the natural and human dialectic is founded in this fact. Its historical truth is in the Jew-Pagan conflict. Fessard found that their dialectical forms were the condition in which human activity as such could be thought, but if such activity was raised to an exclusive form and hypostatized it reduced the universality of the condition to an historical circumstance and to an activity. As a circumstance the condition is no longer a category of thinking. Fessard would draw these consequences from Marx's attempt to put work before the Master-Slave relationship. Marx believed ''that in putting work as the first historical fact he could preserve all the benefits of its Hegelian analysis. In fact, by this inversion he cut away the universalizing and humanizing root of work.''[5]

Work has significance when it is exercised by the person who has learned fear and courage in the situation of suffering and challenge. In the Master-Slave relationship man learns the possibility of being born into humanity. This takes place in mutuality of recognition, the *co-naissance*, which is at the same time the mutuality of birth. In this mutuality man gives birth to a sense of humanity and universality. But this recognition emerges from the ever existent reality of stupidity, ignorance and indifference which are fundamental human conditions of both slavery and mastery. The philosopher Hegel spoke of this dialectic because he knew that in recognition man discovered himself. This recognition depended upon conflict in which there was a constant realization of conflicting moments, of their development and degeneration. The slave does not necessarily become a master, but more thoroughly a slave, and a master does not naturally degenerate into a slave, but can develop into the statesman. The dialectic means nothing where there is a necessary consequence. Without the unexpected and unrealized possibility of new forms the dialectic is a natural and mechanical process.

The primordial significance of the Master-Slave relationship was clearly and precisely recognized by Fessard. He wrote that "it represents not only the *original social tie* and the origin of political society, but even an *essential moment of the genesis* of human reality, i.e., a movement *which is repeated at each instant and at every level of social relationships* from the least contact between two individuals to world conflicts."[6] If the Master-Slave relationship is the structure in which we comprehend the nature of recognition then it forms the categories and attitudes in and through which man and societal existence become meaningful. This universal dialectic supercedes the ideologies and myths which attempt to negate the dialectic to particular or individual forms of thought and existence. As universal as the Pagan-Jew, Man-Woman, dialectic, this Master-Slave form is the *sine qua non* of natural existence. All the forms that develop from it bear within them this dialectic. This dialectical form can be suppressed but not eliminated, controlled but never forgotten. From whatever perspective we consider human life the Master-Slave relationship remains as the fundamental instance. From a systemic point of view the fundamental categories of reason constitute the architecture of existence. This is an architecture that is constantly developing and realizing the nature of the categories that constitute its forms. Where the human discourse loses its meaning is at that moment where man attempts to comprehend it exclusively from one categorical perspective to the detriment of the other. The world conceived from the perspective of the slave or from that of the master distorts the understanding of the forms of mutuality which are necessarily assumed in their relation to each other. The attempt to absolutize a category and to develop from it an exclusive attitude reduces reality to totalitarianism. Man is projected into a utopia or paradise from which he delineates the character of hell. Fessard was the philosopher for whom freedom was essential, and from this faith in freedom's efficacy he drew the strength to oppose every totalitarian form. In the depths of his faith lay the courage to act in opposition to Nazism, to Vichy and to Communism. Fessard understood deeply the wisdom that preserved the unity of abstraction and practice. From his clarity in theoretical matters came his decisions for practical action. From the Master-Slave relationship Fessard comprehended the nature of political life; from the perspective of valid alternative conflicts to the demonic suppression of conflictual life and the false messianism that form heavenly Jerusalems in human garb. This corresponds to the millennial thinking of those who create paradisial visions in order to construct political and social totalitarianism.

The Master-Slave relationship embodies more than the theoretical conflictual expression of human life. It goes into the fabric of contemporary political life. The struggle of the ruler to suppress the ruled is more than physical domination. It aims at the destruction of human life in which the lives of the oppressors are as deeply distorted as are those of the oppressed. Within the ruling class the same distortion is at work. The ruler is suppressed by the forces with which he rules. The magnificence of Hegel's schemes is reflected in the innumerable relationships that grew from those first vague and abstract forms. The qualities of the rulers are as varied as the degrees of suppression which are forced upon the ruled. Those in power will yield one day to subordinates who will become more orthodox in attitude and commitment. The suppressed will bring forth from their ranks those for whom the memories of freedom are deep and for whom they are meaningful. The ruled learn with greater and lesser ease what it means to lose culture and language. Their adaptability to new conditions depends upon the intelligence and firmness of the rulers. The rulers become more demonic when they realize that physical subjection yields to more effective distortions than arise from the deprivation of history, books and memories. Destroy these memories and the people will in turn embrace the new culture, language and history. The heads of statues fall easily and new ones arise quickly to point to the new directions that society and nations follow. Milan Kundera, the Czech novelist, remarked that Prague in Kafka's novels "is a city without memory. It has even forgotten its name. Nobody there remembers anything, nobody recalls anything. Even Joseph K does not seem to know anything about his previous life. . . . Time in Kafka's novel is the time of humanity that has lost all continuity, with humanity that no longer knows anything nor remembers anything, that lives in nameless cities with nameless streets or streets with names different from the ones they had before, because a name means continuity with the past and people without a past are people without a name."[7]

The Master-Slave dialectic draws us into the perplexities of all forms of life in which the struggle for freedom comes up against those varied totalitarian methodologies that seek new histories, languages and cultures for which they are eager to destroy the old and remove it from memory. These new forms of Master-Slave relationships have now taken the place of the friend-foe, hunter-hunted, or stronger-weaker opposition that belongs to the simpler and more basic forms of human relations. The novel and complicated forms of suppression demand not only our philosophical interest, but more seriously our political and moral comprehension and action. The evil which they have developed does not go away in debates, conferences, dialogues and pseudo agreements; they require of us the power and will to physically destroy evil societies. Whether this can be effected through economic, moral or other more subtle means depends upon the prudence of statesmanship. There are conflicts in political and moral life that become contradictions with which we cannot morally and politically survive. If there is movement from slavery to freedom it is not forced by rational determination. What can be said theoretically about the Master-Slave relationship merely delineates the terms in and through which serious thinking begins to encompass history and politics. These political actualities are not the creation of philosophical thought. They can be comprehended, but remain undetermined and uncontrolled. In the face of them we begin to grasp how deeply and intimately what is undetermined and unexpected deprives us of fantasies that reveal a desire to impose reason on a world that mocks our efforts.

Silence is another consequence of the Master-Slave relationship. It is closely tied to the extinction of memory. This is the imposed silence of the rulers, the quiet and painful way that is used to end the memories of history, forbidding the historians to continue their work. The rulers bring forth the ideologically pure historians with new terminology and perspectives. The quiet violence of such a profound transformation of cultural life is the tranquil weapon of the rulers to tranquilize the life of the ruled. The rulers have already become the subjects and objects of their own ideological silence. The wonder of human perversion is as ungraspable as are the depths of divinity. The violence of imposed silence spreads through language and disrupts the nature of human communication. We are slowly awakened to the fact that in the tenor of silence humanity is losing its discourse with the past. Numerous worlds of discourse emerge in which intercourse is silenced and the languages that are spoken convey meaning that is difficult to comprehend and even more difficult to define. Fessard, repeatedly, advanced the notion of a violence that spreads through language tearing the present from the past. This reduces the discourses among men of different ideological positions to words without meaning or words of corrupted meaning.

The past is silenced by the questions that are put or not put to it. The questions and answers that are controlled by the masters determine the shape of the past that comes forth for the discourse of society. When the questions lose dominance to the answers the world that is *yet to be known* fades away into the world that is known. The struggle to know is a fundamental human need, but knowing without thinking becomes a human terror. In this world the master and the slave become each other. The master knows but doesn't think; the slave neither knows nor thinks; he simply does, but his doing is a knowing, a knowing what to do, without knowing if the doing should or should not be done. The totalitarianism of the masters is embodied in the gods of humorless seriousness. These gods tolerate few jokes and humor breeds suspicion and fear. Through humor man regains master over himself and his world, and it is this humor that the masters are forced to check and eventually to deny. The Master-Slave relationship furrows deeply into the soul where it harbors the innumerable suppressions and the deepest forms of rejection. These existential attitudes have profound ties to philosophical abstractions because only where philosophical categories and existential attitudes are joined is there serious philosophy. In the finite world that has been purged of its variety, possibility and ungraspable shades of meaning, philosophy has no significance. Philosophy refuses to remain abstract, it wants to walk through the world of human action, decision, hope, despair and imagination. In this world it wants to keep alive man's physical life, his family relations and his societal responsibilities. In these it knows that man finds freedom and expression. What Fessard has forced us to do is to remain in the realm of the political. The Master-Slave relationship has made us aware that without its vitality there is no movement toward those human relationships that liberate the master from his master, and the slave from his slavery. In a society of meaningful alternatives, conflicts, and discussions, there are neither slaves nor masters; there are human beings who decide, who think and who act.

Fessard refused to allow us to think outside of societal problems; never can we jump forth into the sterility of philosophical argumentation divorced from historical actuality. We can be neither religious nor political without being moral and courageous in action. Religion and philosophy remain inseparable from political and moral responsibility. From every dialectical speculation there should emerge a deeper understanding of our being as responsible action. In this understanding lies our awareness of the perversity of totalitarianism as the suppression of individual action. In this action lies the more profound human experience of freedom: the capacity to say no, to grasp the meaning of negation. The Hegel whom Fessard admired was the Hegel who understood the meaning of negation as the source of thought and historical and societal development. This was the Hegel who was closest to Ignatius. The freedom that lay embodied in negation was at the core of Hegel's philosophy of society and man. The freedom that earlier filled the *Exercises* was the revolutionary force of the sixteenth century. The significance of this freedom never failed to guide, as a beloved daemon, the thought and action of Fessard.

In the Master-Slave relationship we discover innumerable relationships through which these terms take on differences in meaning and possibilities. Every dialectical relationship implies others. A dialectical relationship is not an isolated phenomenon constructed in the mind of the philosopher. The philosopher discovers this given relationship, gives it form and attempts to show its universal applicability. Fessard moved from one dialectical structure to another knowing that the validity of each was rooted in the other. He had understood the dialectic of the *Exercises* as man's spiritual truth and from this truth all other aspects of man's life could be comprehended. From the Master-Slave relationship Fessard moved to the Man-Woman dialectic and he asked if "this relationship of Man-Woman is not itself the source of a dialectic as universal and rigorous as that of Master-Slave and which realizes precisely the interaction of all the elements which Hegel and then Marx analyzed on the basis of becoming. For Hegel the becoming was phenomenological, for Marx it was historical. We do not need extensive reflection to see that the relationship of Man and Woman yields to a dialectic of exactly the same type as that of Master-Slave but whose elements are intrinsically reversed."[8]

In Marx's *Economic and Philosophic Manuscripts of 1844*, Fessard discovered a text which he stated to be fundamental. The mystery of the relationship between man and man "has its *unambiguous decisive, plain* and undisguised expression in the relationship of man to woman and in the manner in which the *direct* and *natural* species relationship is concerned. The direct natural and necessary relation of person to person is the *relation of man to woman*. In this *natural* species relationship man's relation to nature is immediately his relation to man, just as his relation to man is immediately his relation to nature -- his own natural destination."[9]

This dialectic bears within itself the natural struggle of the love struggle in which each seeks to find in the other the recognition of the self. In his search for recognition lies the unending conflict between man and woman. The conflict never ceases to find ways to reduce woman to man or man to woman, but is at the same time a conflict that draws from both the potentiality that lies within, the self. The very being of the relationship, of the need for recognition, forces each partner to reveal to the other what constitutes the self. The conflict for recognition spreads into all forms of relationships and reveals the essential conflictive nature of human relationships. The first moment of the man-woman relation is in struggle, but this struggle finds its purpose in the fulfillment which each has in the other and in the fruition of this fulfillment: the child. Of this fruition Fessard remarked:

> A solemn moment for both man and woman because both perceive in the child not only humanized nature, a source of pleasure for the master and knowledge for the slave, but a nature that has become man *hominisée* . . . truly having 'become man' as Marx wanted it . . . where they show the bond of their perfect unity the double relation of man to man and of man to nature.[10]

If the relationship between Master and Slave realizes the multiple ways that the rulers suppress the ruled and, in this suppression, end their own mastery, then we can view the relation of man-woman as the counter-force in which both find fruition in the love of other, through the child. When the master and slave become *man* before they become husband and wife, mother and father, they have nevertheless not yet become rational beings. They have not yet become conscious of the universal nature of right and wrong.

In the man-woman relation a form of oppression is reconciled. In this relationship we find the natural and necessary relation of person to person. In this relation man and woman discover that in mutuality each comes to recognize what is natural to the other. The dialectic becomes the paradigm of the free and responsible society. Man needs to find in society the opportunity to bring forth the capacities that lie in him. He needs recognition from his peers and responsibility for his fellowman. He learns mutuality in family and society. He overcomes the selfishness and egocentricity that prevail where everything is determined by the friend-foe relationship. In the man-woman relation man's sense of humanity begins. In the respect and obligation to oath man finds the notion that every societal relationship is dependent upon oath, upon the respect that he owes to his fellow human and which he demands is owed to him. From these contractual relations man forms societies and nations. Fessard stated that "if social life, in which the human being discovers man and woman, is so precious to him, is it not because it unveils the foundation of his own being as a 'life of relations' in which, in the most hidden intimacy of conscience, he engenders and con-

ceives himself, and bears himself as in a long gestation, and finally gives birth
with a word which is a work, a verb which is an act, and shows to everyone his
power and fertility.''11

If this relation is man's "natural destination" then man has discovered his
architecture of the relationship in which he realizes his natural and human capacities. In familial life man discovers the moral and in this discovery prepares
himself for the legal. How deep is this natural relationship can be understood
from that important letter of Franz Kafka to his father "Letter to His Father"
because in and through this letter we discover that familial relations not only
bear witness to the pains of love from which some reap wonderful benefits and
others destructive consequences, but we perceive the depravation and unfulfilled
desires and hopes that find in parental relations the natural and human needs that
are crippled and made perverse.

The Kafka letter is more than a personal tale of woe and unfulfilled dreams
of companionship and communication; it reveals the tensions, pains and dissatisfaction that tears apart familial life. The dialectic of man-woman extends to all
aspects of human relations which seek to find equilibrium and satisfaction. The
need of man for communication and relationship is rooted in that primordial
need for recognition that man seeks on every level of life. Where this recognition is threatened and denied man suffers physically and spiritually. Recognition
is the source of man's societal life and when it suffers, at its most crucial relation, that of man-woman, of family in all its forms, then the human being is torn
away from his natural ties and into this gap corruption and distortion assume
their more violent societal consequences. We read this letter of Kafka with a peculiar and serious empathy because we know how deeply violent is the chaos
that proceeds from the destruction of the human familial dialectic. Kafka remarked how deeply pained he was by his father's indifference to his writings.
He explained how "you (the father) struck nearer home with your aversion to
my writing and to everything that, unknown to you, was connected with it. Here
I had, in fact, got some distance away from you by my own efforts, even if it
was slightly reminiscent of the worm that, when a foot treads on its tail end,
breaks loose with its front part and drags itself aside. To a certain extent I was in
safety; there was a chance to breathe freely. The aversion you naturally and immediately took to my writing was, for once, welcome to me. My vanity, my ambition did suffer under your soon proverbial way of hailing the arrival of my
books "Put it on my bedside table! (usually you were playing cards when a
book came), but I was really glad of it, not only out of rebellious malice, not

only out of delight at a new confirmation of my view of our relationship, but quite spontaneously, because to me that formula sounded something like: 'Now you are free!' Of course it was a delusion; I was not. . . .''12

Kafka could never imagine himself free if this meant putting aside his father. All the elements of conflict were present in his relationship to him, propounded by the realization that there was no escape. Nevertheless, we may free ourselves from one burden only to bear it within ourselves in another form. Kafka's father would always dwell within him as the man dwells within the woman and the woman within the man. The father lives within him as the unachieved recognition, the love that failed to bring forth comprehension, to realize what is natural in human relations. When this love is absent the fraternity that belongs to relations turns into animosity and resentment. The power of resentment turns men and peoples into antagonistic forces that refuse reconciliation, but seek to level fraternity into contradiction.

Fessard, who knew that the Master-Slave relationship needed to be complemented by the one of Man-Woman, asked why this is not more clearly recognized. "If such is the importance and value of the Man-Woman dialectic should we be surprised if the conceptions of the world that are oblivious to it and are limited to using only the dialectic of Master-Slave cannot explain the genesis of human reality and do not succeed in wanting to direct it, but only in exacerbating the divisions of our world?''13

Fessard remarked often that his books and articles from 1936 were written in response to historical actuality and were replies to the fundamental problem of that historical actuality and freedom that is necessary to comprehend man as the being who can and should make free decisions. But from where does this capacity to decide freely arise? Is it born in the Master-Slave dialectic when the forces of suppression continually seek to envelop both master and slave or when work, spiritual and physical, is the source of man's liberation from the domination of nature, and man and society? This liberation from slavery is an illusion as long as it belongs only to the relationship of Master-Slave. The recognition of man as man belongs to that activity that comes through the relation between man and woman, through that love that creates a fraternity between maternity and paternity. The natural relationship should be more properly termed the human relationship when man is humanized and recognizes himself as man. This recognition begins in the family. It comes forth as the love toward the child, the communal activity of man and woman who are now mother and father. The humanization of the individual belongs to familial confrontations. In this dialectic man begins to comprehend the meaning of the oath, collective and individual responsibility. The family is the primordial step toward the awareness of the idea of humanity. The work of the family is the spiritual and physical work of mother and father, brother and sister, each term bearing in itself moral and physical meaning. In the depth of the family tie lies also the depths of its negation that stems from man's shortsightedness and his egocentric reality. In the family the egocentricity is suppressed and overcome but in this suppression it lives as the deep power of potential destruction and perversity. Fessard would remind us that ''as soon as we understood that the dialectic of Man and Woman is as basic and essential as the dialectic of Master and Slave we see that the concrete genesis of humanity is not realized without creating between these two dialectics a continual conjunction of contact of the two movements which are proper to them.''14

The relationship between these two dialectical movements is comprehended within our continual discovery of the dependence of each dialectical movement upon the other. The dialectic belongs to the discoveries which man makes through reason and it is in this reason that he finds the source through which is revealed the ever deepening dependence of dialectical movement upon each other. The Master-Slave dialectic is the primordial form for our comprehension of natural man. The Man-Woman dialectic is the comprehension of the human dialectic ''man'' through which we grasp the societal nature of man as it moves from one level of societal life to another and bears in the higher the forms of the lower to be suppressed and preserved. From the Master-Slave dialectic the dialectic of love struggles to realize fraternity. In fraternity the love of each suppresses the need for domination and attempts to realize the quality of individuality through mutual conflict, to heighten the force of love as the source of procreation and the passion to create. In this love of procreation and the procreation of love man discovers his humanity in the humanity of the beloved, in the child of their work, in the mutuality of their search for beauty. We know that the genesis of humanity can only develop from that core of relationships where the concept of paternity, maternity and fraternity have their source and that occurs only in the dialectic of man-woman. In a similar way the reality of the dialectic of humanity as both secular and sacred has its origin in the Pagan-Jew relationship. The Master-Slave dialectic is the natural condition to which man always returns when the human dialectic fails or when violence of states and men returns to a condition of chaos to which we must respond with force in order to reestablish equilibrium. The Master-Slave dialectic is the condition that permeates every other dialectic and to which they yield when their structures collapse. This return is physical as well as spiritual. It is a return that lives in every man, society and state. It is the fundamental dialectic of life that threatens every attempt to bring forth that freedom and truth that constitutes man's humanity. The Master-Slave structure is the primordial architecture of life in which every form of spiritual existence attempts to rupture and deny. The sublimity of man's spiritual adventure is his attempt to subordinate the Master-Slave condition to that fraternity of man-woman relation, the fundamental basis of civilized society. The consequence of its destruction is the dehumanization of the world in which every level and distinction is reduced to the natural condition of subordination and domination.

Fessard believed that the bonds that held together the individual human family extended into all other human relationships. Those of the state and the nation assumed different characteristics although the sense of loyalty and community remained essentially the same. Fessard observed that "fraternity is not satisfied by the multiplicity of the abstract duality of man and woman. . . It turns back upon paternity and maternity and finds the means to establish the universality of these relations although they are individual. In the *cult of the dead* the recognition of the children immortalizes the existence of those to whom they owe recognition. Familial fraternity is the source of the paternity and maternity of the nation. The unity of men among themselves appears also to be the unity of men with nature, with the land of the fathers and the dead."[15]

From the man-woman dialectic the concept of peoplehood and nation arise and from these concepts the Idea of Humanity. How significant is the fundamental relationship and the truth that it embodies can only be realized in the consequences of the relationship. If we learn anything from Hegel it is the realization that the truth of the concept depends upon its particular and singular relationships that form its essential movement. When we move from the abstract nature of the original formulation of the concept we begin to comprehend the multiple existential possibilities that lie within it. Its truth is vast in consequence, but must await continuous realization in the innumerable forms of particularity and individuality in which it enters. The man-woman dialectic that emerges into the idea of fraternity becomes the fundamental norm of social justice, the denial of racism and the realization of the equality of men in rights and duties. The universality of the concept, its dialectical nature, makes it possible to think of mankind as Idea and to act upon this Idea with rational conviction and courage. The love of peoplehood and nation does not exclude the love of humanity. In fact, without the love of nation, there is little possibility to develop a commitment to mankind.

We are forced again and again to face the opposition between the two dialectics. Fessard said that "between the states which rule diverse nations the dialectic of the type of Master-Slave, is in play and wars are ended with the recognition of the character of this dialectic. On the other hand, within every nation, between the State and civil society a dialectic of Man-Woman comes into play."16

The struggle for power that has become, in our generation, religiously ideological and universal gave us the notion of master race and master class. Erasing the dialectic of man-woman, the race and the class return to the abstract character of politics and economics, deify abstractions and use them to sweep away the historical and phenomenological dialectical development that brought civil society into existence with its natural opposition and alternative theories of the good society. In other words, the Master-Slave relationship was raised by both Nazism and Communism which are the paradigms of totalitarianism, to their most abstract reality and introduced into politics and economics pseudo-scientific hypotheses. Refusing to allow the Master-Slave relation to become and remain a philosophical theory which guides, but does not necessarily determine thinking changed its nature and intent. From a speculative theory it became a scientific one. It was given a new genus. The Master-Slave relation is the science of totalitarian society because there it has become ontological truth, the truth of the very being of this society. Where it is an hypothesis, a way of seeing things, it is a relationship that is theoretically accepted, but whose reality belongs to the human dialectic of Man-Woman, to society that develops from law and morality. The attempt to universalize the Master-Slave relationship as *the human* relationship is the highest expression of Paganism in modern human relations. The deification of this dialectic establishes Paganism on an ideological and mythical base. It assumes the scientific validity of an ideological faith whether it is communism or other forms of secular religious fundamentalism. The identification of the natural dialectic with the human is the fatal achievement of Paganism. The will to power lies at the core of totalitarianism. It is its natural law and its comprehension of nature. It divides the world between friend and foe, master and slave. To be consistent it remains in the natural world of contradiction. It destroys every attempt to bring this world into the human dimension of societal values.

There is, however, a third dialectic which Fessard believed makes it possible to view this natural and human dialectic from a higher and more encompassing perspective: the relationship between God and humanity. In terms of this dialectic, Fessard stated that "to have these two opposing attitudes (the natural and the human dialectic) interact and in order that human unity is possible we must suppose that there comes into play a dialectic between Being and Man, analogous to that between Man and Woman. This is the dialectic of *God and Humanity*. This dialectic is present in us and thus, is in temporal events. This dialectic guides them and becomes the principle of a new genesis of humanity, one that is still historical, although it is more than natural, but more properly *supernatural* and truly spiritual."[17]

The love which is at the core of the Man-Woman dialectic establishes the love in and through which man loves God and God loves humanity. This love that flows from God to man and from man to God, however fundamental, is the difference in their natures, nevertheless establishes a relationship or correlation that fulfills the love that is in the family and joins man to woman and woman to man in marriage. This fulfillment man realizes through the course of history as he realizes his human love through the perversities that beset this love in man's egocentricity which returns him to the natural state of mastery and slavery. The return to this state is both internal and external. It is a state in which man experiences depravation and in which he experiences it in the myths and ideologies with which men impregnate nations and groups. The struggle between man's love of God and his devotion to his sensual life is the grand struggle of humanity, the fight for liberation and truth, that endeavor to live the life of spirit, to liberate this life from sensual domination.

The struggle of Israel against pagan sensuality is the widest and most embracing of all dialectic forms. In this dialectic the path is visible that leads from Israel's love dialogue with God to its fruit "born from the Woman who is both Virgin and Mother, *Servant and wife,* symbol of sinful humanity, beloved of God, the Christ who is both Son of God and son of Man."[18]

If we ask about the source of the dialectic we are given a precise answer by Fessard: the dialectic of the Pagan and the Jew. The mystery of the elected people finds its explanation in this dialectic, the source of our comprehension of history and that divine human correlation.

The mystery of Israel is the mystery of Christianity. We see their intimacy and dependence when we refuse to separate these two divine manifestations, when we grasp the continuous revelation of God through his people and his

Church, when we embrace the meaning of God's love in the election of Israel and miracle of the Incarnation. The pagan reaction to this election has been fear and resentment manifested in enmity and brought forth in the realization that in this election the mortal and immortal enemy has appeared. Fessard delineates this reality by showing that "Nazism, by taking as its mortal enemy the Jew, this divine, elected of God, showed not only their hatred of man but entered into a struggle with God who had destined the Jew to be the mortal enemy of every pagan pretension to dominate reality! Similarly, Communism, in its hatred against the 'servile principles' of the Christian who, in reality, is a converted Pagan, focuses upon God who became slave and obedient unto death and destroyed the messianic dreams of the incredulous Jew. Nazi anti-Semitism and Communist anti-Christianity not only reveal the two aspects in which we comprehend the enmity of man to man, but they show that this enmity is rooted in what opposes man to the absolute, to God."19

The depth of Nazi anti-Semitism and Communist anti-Christianity is derivative from the same source: the fear and resentment of the loyalty and devotion of Israel and the Church to the uncompromising monotheism that denied with fierce and unquestionable force the idolatry of Paganism, the deification of every finite reality and affirmed the radical separation between Being and becoming. The uniqueness and incomparable reality of God was the prevalent and demanding force that held sacred this separability. Where it was compromised, where attempts were made to overcome it, where logical schemes were devised to give man the illusion that he had brought the divine and human together, there arose that thundering monotheism with its demand for the sacredness of God's uniqueness and the command to keep apart what belonged to man and what belonged to God. The truth of Israel and Christianity had to be continuously affirmed against the inroads of philosophers, ideologists, myth makers for whom this separation was the challenge to our Promethean needs. In peculiar and refined systems this Promethean urge found more and sophistical ways of attempting to cross the limit of finiteness to the speculative vision of the infinite. Again and again, this attempt had to be declared Pagan and the uniqueness of God's being maintained. Only in the truth of these limits could man preserve freedom, could he liberate himself from his deified ideologies and myths that constantly threatened his moral and political life.

Fessard was convinced that a viable philosophy of history depends upon this Pagan-Jew dialectic because in it natural and supernatural history are related, not only logically, i.e., conceptually, but in commitment and belief.

Fessard believed that theology and philosophy join in the essential endeavor of man to find the meaning of his natural and supernatural destiny. Every philosophical and theological architecture is constructed through belief. The decision not to deny this faith is similarly a decision of faith. In respect of the theology of history Fessard declared that a

> true philosophy or theology of history must make the synthesis between philosophy of essence and existence. This can easily be done if, from the beginning, it is founded upon a consideration of the "historical or existential categories" which Paul used to expose the mystery of Christ. At first, those of pagan and Jew which express the fundamental division of human history in face of divine Revelation and whose dialectic is tied to Christ, the historical person who is situated and dated like every other, making him by this title, according to Hegel, the "hinge of history." This history, instead of being fixed by the reconciliation of being and thought, as imagined by Hegelian idealism or by the suppression of social divisions as Marxist materialism believed, remains open to universal becoming, and at the same time, embraces it because the Christ who is the center of time is also its Alpha and Omega.[20]

Here we have the very important distinction between Fessard and Hegel. Being and thought are reconcilable in the logic of the concept, but what can be reconciled in the concept as divine paradigm is not necessarily reconciled in history. In history there is a sacred separability between human action and divine revelation. The interaction between the two is rooted in faith and not in thought. Thought remains inadequate to the divine; even in its attempt to imitate it, it is utterly and uniquely differentiated from the human. The divine "breaks into" human history to reveal truth in the form of Israel's election and Christ's incarnation. Human history is touched by divine revelation in such a way that its historical development brings forth confrontations in and through which man becomes both moral and political in his need to seek truth and freedom.

Paul also used the existential categories of *slave* and *master* to explain the mystery of Christ. To these he added *woman and man*. Master and Slave gave rise to conflicts which are "the essential motor of social progress, while the other (woman and man), arising from the evolution of nature, benefits from its *élan vital* to project before these conflicts the ideal of love which surmounts them.''21

In the human dialectic of love between man and woman the natural dialectic of master and slave is redeemed. The human dialectic redeems the Master-Slave relation in each of us, its civilizing process is able to reduce the domination of nature's omnipotence over man and finally put aside every philosophy of history that calls forth the process of nature and its necessity as the model for human development. The struggle against the omnipotence of nature is that against the paganism that is in conflict with idealism of the spirit. To the omnipotence of nature belong the utopias and the millenniums that subject the spirit to a deified nature that is disguised ideology or myth. The object of a theology of history, Fessard affirmed, ''cannot be the determination of successive steps toward the future, but more simply and profoundly, the analysis of the historical *being of man* and the discovery of the *dialectic in virtue of which* this being engenders from himself the supernatural life, i.e., Christian becoming.''22

The possibility of the supernatural grounded in the natural is moral, the belief that from nothing something is engendered. This nothing bears within it the divine command, the divine *something* that lies in man and is brought forth in the course of man's struggle for the Idea. This *something* is that divinity that has from the beginning been in the creation as its source and life. It is appearance, is undetermined and momentary, unexpected and unpredictable. It is the negation of all our future attempts to organize and to control the creation in such a way that we eliminate the negation that lies in everything we designate as positive, controllable and determined. In this negation is the freedom and the truth of a mankind that is distinctly and uniquely distinct from the omnipotence of nature.

The human dialectic prepares man for the refusal of the natural and for the affirmation of that profound struggle against the paganism of nature's omnipotence. The dialectic of freedom and truth is that of Pagan and Jew. For the great Neo-Kantian philosopher, Hermann Cohen, the Jew was determined by his profound commitment to Messianism. ''Messianism,'' Cohen stated, ''defies the whole present political actuality of its own as well as of the other peoples. Messianism degrades and despises and destroys the present actuality, in order to put in the place of that sensible actuality a new kind of supersensible actuality, not supernatural, but of the future. This future creates a new earth and a new heaven and consequently, a new actuality. This creation of the future, as a true political actuality, is the greatest achievement of Messianism. And this creation could only be the product of monotheism.''23

These sharp and forceful words characterize the mystery of Israel and its unquestionable faith and loyalty to the future and its Messianic form. Here there is no utopia or millennium, but only the infinite relation between Israel and God, that love dialogue in which Israel asks of God: let me by your beloved. Fessard has drawn us closely to the mystery of Israel because he believed that we are all Semites and that our struggle against philosophical, social and political Paganism is a unique challenge to this Semitic religion. In this challenge philosophy, history, and all other humane studies and activities play an essential role. Paganism is not external to us. We are all existentially pagan. Our struggle is individual and collective. It demands a sense of history. It requires that we understand what it means for us all to be Semites, to grasp the reality of the universal church, the eternity of Israel's election. If they belong together or if they go along parallel paths their truth is in their conflict with Paganism, with the deification of sensuality, with the "omnipotence of nature" and with ideologies and myths that project millennial thinking. The Paganism that engenders the deepest perversity, Fessard knew, was embodied in those philosophers who believe that with their systems are "born the idea of a *rational* genesis of humanity which relates, encompasses and surpasses every previous attempt of incredulity to eliminate religion and, in particular, Christianity and its supersensible genesis."[24]

There is no tragedy in religious commitment, there is no pessimism; there is action that establishes morality and this action is founded in that monotheism that revolutionized the world in which it appeared by destroying its physical and spiritual idols. In this destruction it opened the future to hope. For Fessard, this hope lay in the vision of Paul where Jew and Greek, slave and free man, man and woman would be one in Christ. The creation of the future as a political reality meant that the human world is infinitely correlated to God and that its never-ending effort to deify itself stands before that divine radical negativity that demands that these idols be destroyed. Man faces this negativity in his collective and individual efforts. Man's efforts to comprehend this negation was inseparable from his love of truth and goodness.

Fessard's philosophy and theology of history was profoundly sensitive to the pagan that lived in Jew and Christian and that lives in all of man's relations and actions. His sensitivity to the perversity was developed in the dialectical architecture that formed the intimate relationship between Israel and the Church. There would no longer be that futile polemic and rhetoric between Jew and Christian if we put aside the superiority of one faith over the other. There would be a deeper realization of the meaning of the election of Israel in the Church and of the Church in Israel. "We are all Semites" is a deeply profound sentence. It can be a deeply hollow one if we remain true to the sophism that separates Israel from Church. Paganism in the form of totalitarianism or of terrorism is the enemy of Semitic faith. The power of this faith expressed either by Jew or Christian stems from the unique and incomparable Monotheism that left its signature in creation and has demanded from man a response. Human history is this response.

9

Gaston Fessard and the Problem of Historical Actuality

Gaston Fessard never ceased to think about historical reality as the dimension in which human values, faith in sacred history, found their realm of confrontation and tension. In this confrontation man touched upon the freedom and truth which remained for him enigmatic, but compelling. Thinking about historical reality was never separable from the Jewish Christian dialectic, from Fessard's continuous meditation upon the election of Israel and the meaning for the Christian. Toward the end of his life, Fessard attempted a long and detailed discussion of Raymond Aron's book, Introduction to the Philosophy of History.[1] The book is a major study of the problem of history. Fessard made the book the basis for a detailed and serious discussion of the nature and meaning of history. Man's insistence to preserve his past, to reflect upon its meaning has been a way that has allowed him to preserve his humanity against those ideologies and myths which distort the future by destroying its relation to the past. The unnecessary attempt to obliterate the past remains man's persistent effort to remove this dimension and its values from a society that has made a radical attempt to change and reconstruct its life for the future. The present becomes the tool of the future preparing the way for a forgetfulness that will give the future totalitarian power, filled with the promises of the millennium. Reflection on the past has more than antiquarian power; it reveals a sense of aesthetic, moral and political recollections which tie our spiritual susceptibilities to values which remain to be forever appreciated and desired. The past liberates us from the tyranny of the future as myth. In this liberation we are made aware of our freedom toward the past and our responsibility to the future. In this awareness of time we face the problem of being, our involvement in the political reality and the values that are embodied in it. Reflection on time is reflection on political reality, the confrontation with the structure of being whose meaning we question and in whose question we realize the identity between the self and moral responsibility. We are the moral responsibility we question, we are the values we desire to see in it, and those we want to remove from it. The discovery of the self is in the search for meaning of our moral task which we impose upon being and the self.

We cannot escape the search for meaning. We do not find it given to us and if we do, we put it aside as imposed and detrimental to our freedom. The fight for meaning is the privilege of the thinker. It is the consequence of our decision to think. We are neither forced to seek it nor to be engaged with it. The struggle with meaning begins when we seriously want to think about our history and about the purpose of life. We are serious when it is not only our individual lives that concern us, but also the history of humanity. In our attempt to comprehend this humanity we discover that philosophy is ultimately concerned with assumptions and is not reducible to the definitional method of the sciences. Philosophy is the discourse of reasonable hypotheses. In these philosophy is the discourse of meaning. In this reflection on the theology of history, Henri-Irénée Marrou, observed that what he was attempting to do was not to write the "history of the historians, i.e., history as science defined as the human past measured by the documents which allow us to know it, but the consideration of the problems posed to our consciousness by the truly lived history of mankind, through the totality of its duration, and to which each of us is intimately associated by the historical character of his own existence. In a word, it is the problem of the science of history."[2] In these words lie the major problems of historical thinking because this thinking depends upon the facticity of the person who reflects upon historical philosophy, historical actuality, or the philosophy of history. History yields meaning to the questions that are posed and these questions depend upon the thinking of the philosopher. The philosopher cannot escape the present nor does the present have meaning without the thinker. In other words history yields to us a meaning that is dependent upon the cultivation of our moral and intellectual maturity. Kant remarked that "the fundamental human command is: know yourself . . . in terms of your moral perfection, in relation to your duty. Know your heart, whether it is good or evil, whether the source of your action is pure or impure. Know what can be imputed to you and what belongs to your moral state. . . . Moral self-knowledge which requires one to penetrate into the unfathomable depths and abyss of one's heart, is the beginning of all human wisdom."[3] These words are of crucial importance simply because the comprehension of history depends fundamentally upon the moral attitude of the person who thinks about historical actuality. If it is the same person who thinks about historical actuality and acts from it, then the moral state of the person is the decisive moment in the action and the decision. History is identical with the moral level of the people who think about and who act in it. In history man writes of the struggle which he carries out with himself, his fellowman and nature.

At the end of his book on Raymond Aron and the problem of historical philosophy, Fessard made some pertinent observations about his personal relationship to Aron and the values he attributed to historical problems. Fessard did not form a philosophy of history; he found the structure already formed in Paul's comprehension of the dialectic of Jew and Pagan, in man's struggle to realize the faith that was given to him as he attempted to discover in his experience of non-being the truth that could be awakened in him. From the historical and personal perspective, Fessard sought to comprehend the nature of historical actuality, freedom and truth. With the moral courage that emerged from the faith that is reason and the reason that is faith Fessard indicated that Aron had shown us that "humanity does not need the Jews either to discover political-religious fanaticism, nor to experience in it the inextinguishable thirst for the absolute." Fessard knew that this germ of fanaticism and this thirst for the absolute was in every pagan. "The Christian," Fessard wrote, "is so tied to the Jews, from beginning to the end of history that without them he would neither find the depths in which this germ is embedded nor how inextinguishable is this thirst for the absolute in man."[4] These meditations on Israel's chosenness lay at the core of Fessard's thinking about history. In this chosenness lay the sacred history of Judaism and Christianity as well as the human history of these two faiths. What the mystery embodies is their intimacy and inseparability from which each attempts to tear away, in which each experiences a profound discomfort. The meditation upon the profundities of their oneness, their incredulity and doubts force them to excite within themselves the paganism that never leaves them, but remains their nonbeing. Within this dialectic with its innumerable variations and implications the history of mankind takes on meaning as it moves from human to sacred history, but returns again and again to that deification of finiteness that feeds the paganism that lives in every Jew and Christian. From this dialectic the political and moral questions of historical reality emerge and demand meaning. Man's attraction to the chaotic and catastrophic, his insatiable need for security, and his easily assumed pleasure with mythology and ideology makes our consciousness of this Jew-Pagan dialectic profoundly meaningful. In our need for meaning it provides the perspective from which we comprehend our fear of totalitarianism. From it we know the meaning of our opposition to Nazism and Communism and the penetrating chaos of anarchism and terrorism. In the com-

prehension of history we embrace the meaning of action. In action we comprehend the truth of our being, the freedom which emerges from the confrontation
with evil. The Jew fought Paganism with a fierceness that embodied hatred, and
with the Christianity that grew from it the struggles against new idolatries continue. The Jew represented a new morality, the morality of social consciousness
and conscience and with them he overthrew opposing value systems. He knew
that only in fierce opposition could he maintain the uniqueness of his God, only
in disdain of the Pagan could he worship his God with love.

Fessard's fascination with history and his meditation on Israel's place in sacred history drew him close to the work of Raymond Aron and his studies of
philosophical history. Fessard was willing not only to study the works of Aron
but to see in his writings tendencies toward a recognition of Israel's uniqueness
and his sacred position in history. Fessard was not willing to accept Aron's refusal to comprehend his Jewish destiny, his doubts about the sacred role that the
Jew has in the struggle against the pagan. Often Aron affirmed that he would not
go beyond historical explanations. In relation to the state of Israel he said in his
Memoirs that "nothing in the formation of the State of Israel and in the endurance of the Jewish diaspora defied the ordinary modes of historical explanation." In the same text he posed the question whether his solidarity with Israel is
more intellectual or organic? In reply he said: "Perhaps both at the same time.
In any case, this 'Solidarity' can not be raised to the level of sacred or supernatural history which is for believers and to which I do not belong."[5] Fessard was
dissatisfied with Aron's position. He wanted Aron, who shared many similar
political positions, to come with him to the realm of sacred history where he
could, with faith, grasp a meaning of history that would be "forever denied to
him on the level of human history." This long and arduous dialogue between
Fessard and Aron points to those basic differences that determine the comprehension of history. The word "meaning" can be considered on various levels of
comprehension. Henri-Irénée Marrou reminds us that the "word designates an
image rather than a concept." Certain questions arise from it: "Does history
follow a determined direction (and toward what end)? Has it a significance, a
reason which I can comprehend, a value which can justify so many wasted efforts, sufferings, spilled blood, and so many exploits, so many apparent hinder-
ances?"[6] These questions can be multiplied in all directions. Perhaps man can
find no answers that satisfy all at any particular time but the need to raise such
questions is undeniable and the struggle to live without them. Marrou spoke of
image rather than concept. In other words, the search for meaning belongs to

man's aesthetic as well as moral images. The concept remains theoretical and in it meaning becomes a disembodied intellectual form. Meaning needs representation, the imagery that excites and stimulates the imagination. The image awakens the force of action, it necessitates response, the concrete reply of the senses, the facticity of being and the need "to change and form it anew with new images of beauty and morality." Meaning needs the fierceness of attitude and opposition.

Fessard clearly recognized the power of representation and its inseparability from meaning. In fact his long discussion with Hegel was concerned with the relationship between the concept and the image. In his "Dialogue Théologique avec Hegel" he remarked that in "the course of my dialogue with Hegel I set forth some fundamental criticisms concerning, in particular, his insufficient analyses of historicity and, above all, the domination of the concept."[7] This domination of the concept was for Fessard the weakest aspect of Hegel's system. It ignored the force of the community, of tradition and the necessity of a representation. In other words, history is disembodied in conceptual development. It loses its community with the infinite variability of human imagery which is not formed in concept but lies in the unlimited and undetermined artistry of perception. In the unexpected, unknown and possible dimensions of the perceptual realm of natural and human reality man finds a confrontation with forms which excite his imagination and intellect, but never exhaust their power of affectation. What is formed in the concept remains inadequate to what is imposed upon us by perception. The community of mankind belongs not only to a conceptual history but to the community of imagery, the variety of contingency, in which we embody our sensual and perceptible existence. In this community we discover that history of contingent events which forces us to search again and again for meaning. If representation is separated from conceptualization we are forced to think of two histories. There is a history that is formed and structured through the concept, a history created in the logic of the concept in which representation is only a moment in and through which the concept comes to a realization of itself and its negation. There is also the history of representation, the history of the living community with its traditions, cultural differences and its struggle for the realization of societal life. It is in this community that man's collective efforts find their limitation. It is here that time forces us to realize how deeply we are dependent upon existing reality and how difficult it is to bring about social and political change in a reality whose history has been created through centuries of events and shared cultural values. Man discovers the possibilities of freedom and truth when he seeks to comprehend what it means to speak reasonably, not rationally, about political and historical life. Man attempts to understand the relation of sacred and supersensual history to human events only if he attempts to grasp the relationship between the faith of reason and the faith of revelation. Fessard undertook two major discussions about history: one with Hegel and one with Aron. What emerged from these discussions was a continual exploration of the idea of history. The idea of history could be experienced not only from the contrast between conceptual and representational history, from the opposition between sacred and human history, but also from that crucial opposition between human and natural history. Wherever we turn the struggle for meaning involves that delicate and serious interplay between faith and reason, and between nature and man.

Fessard's studies of Hegel were closely tied to his fundamental work on the *Spiritual Exercises* of Loyola. He remarked that before being influenced by the lectures of A. Kojève (1935-1939) his dialogue with Hegel had been established in a mutual study of the *Spiritual Exercises* "which caused me to criticize Hegelian historicity from the perspective first of form and then of content and finally to rehabilitate the representations of absolute religion against the 'domination of the concept,' at least, to the degree that the concept unilaterally tended to become tyrannical."[8] What was significant for Fessard in his study of Ignatius and Hegel was the dialectical method which he believed revealed the problem of human freedom in its fundamental relationship with the values of human comprehension. With both Ignatius and Hegel man found a way of philosophizing in and through which thinking attempts to analyze the conditions of freedom and discovers the bonds which link the theoretical and the practical in time and space. What was clear to Fessard was the impossibility of such bonds without the relationship between human and sacred history, without that fundamental interaction between the horizontal and vertical dimensions of reality. He refused to believe that one dimension without the other could yield the truth and freedom which belonged to man as bound by his human condition from which he also sought to comprehend the divine intention. Man's destiny lay beyond his human history. Divinity linked him to that force of negation that sought to overcome every attempt of finite history to be deified. The perspective of sacred history, that vertical dimension with its dramatic imagery -- without which thinking remains totally finite -- transformed and transfigured history in such a way as to give it a multidimensional reality. The divine-human imagery represents moral demand and aesthetic affection in consequence of which the political and moral nature of life assumes extreme importance and develops values in opposition to totalitarianism. In it paganism arose to its most radical form of self-deification because what would be considered philosophical and hypothetical as theory became dogmatic and pseudo-scientific as ideology. In fact, the deepest danger of pagan thought is that it needs to fix the limits of thought within the restrictions of fixed independent categories.

Philosophical thinking remains the discourse of categories which is both linear and circular. Fessard observed that "the before and after are only tied from *without* and *arbitrarily*. . . . The *word*, on the contrary, ties them from *within* and *necessarily* because the chain of *des signifiants* -- the sources of meaning -- flow from the past toward the future in natural or cosmic time, before their *reprise* in a reverse order causes meaning to come forth in historical time. From this a relation can be thusly expressed: the sources of meaning are *tempore prius* but *natura posterius*, meanings, on the other hand, are *tempore posterius*, *sed natura prius* -- *natura* signifies here essence or meaning expressed at first, by the speaker, then understood by the hearer."9

The source of meaning is timewise prior revealing the fact that thinking begins in meaning, in that given from which meaning proceeds as meaning in time *posterius*. Meanings are posterior because they follow creation from the source; they are in it potentially and are to be discovered from it. However we employ the terms *prius* and *posterius* we are embodied in relationships which depend upon the use of the terms. Each term gains for itself reality from the other and must be related to the other in thinking. If this method of dialectical thought is accepted it is possible to think history from the perspective of totality. From this perspective we attempt to comprehend that what can be grasped on the level of the *a priori* must again be understood from the perspective of the *a posteriori*. What is clear in this terminology is the fact that whether history is thought of from faith or commitment to its foundation in sacred history or from the analysis of events and causes, we confront the fundamental assumption that the search for meaning is the ultimate activity of those who know that history depends upon the meaning it is given or the meaning that it derives from the sources. This subjectivism involved in given meaning is however, inadequate because the meaning which we give to history lies already in it from the source. History has meaning because it is already meaningful. Its meaning only awaits discovery.

History continually awaits discovery because history is mystery. Mystery is not something that remains in the realm of the unknown and is thus divided from the known. If mystery remained in the unknown it would be the object of man's fancy, the arbitrary play of his imagination. It would have nothing to do with the realization of his being as history. Karl Rahner has stated that "a mystery as something which is absolutely impenetrable is just there, it is a given, it is something that cannot be produced. . . . It is the ungovernable ruling horizon of all understanding that makes all understanding possible while it is constantly present and silent. . . . It is necessarily and essentially a characteristic of God (and from Him also of us)."10

With this description of mystery which is, at first, the realization of the limits of the understanding and the dependence of the self upon the incompleteness of its own mystery we begin to comprehend the meaning of the human experience as historical existence. Whatever man says of himself, whether he identifies himself with rationality or sensuality, he remains mystery. Rationality and sensuality remain indefinable in and for themselves. We use these words and others like them because we become enchanted with the security they offer us, knowing all the time that we live with illusions when we affirm that these terms are anything more than logical possibilities. We could now accept the belief that man "attains the unsurpassable fulfillment of his essence -- toward which he is always striving -- if he prays and believes that somewhere a similar essence has found its *existence* in God in such a way that it has given itself perfectly to mystery and questions the questionless because this *eksistence* was assumed by the Questionless and assumed as His own answer."11

The fraternity of man is founded in the incarnation of this *eksistence*, through the assumption of the Person of the Word of human nature. Man's essence becomes his *obediential potency*. "This potency," Rahner explained, "cannot be a particular capacity in man along with other possibilities but is really identical with the essence of man."12 This fraternity belongs to man's essence, to the mystery which man can only inadequately and arbitrarily grasp because of his unique self-consciousness and the limits of his incomprehensibility. In man's attempt to overcome the mystery of his being, that drama of existence that forces him to flee the disembodiment of his conceptualizations, man returns to those particular representational capacities in and through which he attempts to discover the essence of his being. This confusion between the particularity of capacity and the mystery of being leads either to the tyranny of practice or to that of theory. This was made clear by Fessard when he wrote that "for Hegel human fraternity is founded on 'culture,' the reflection of the reciprocal relations of needs and the work which satisfies them. Its universality remains abstract because it rests only upon the relation of man-nature or is economic and is condemned to 'Cosmopolitanism' if it is opposed to the concrete life of the state."[13] Fessard, like Rahner, had spoken of mystery and with this undefinable reality they understood the impenetrable, the source of all that could be known but is not known because of man's fallibility. They understood this impenetrable reality because they realized how deeply man wanted to surpass mystery with his power of conceptualization, with his attempt to deify his intellect and absorb the Incarnation within the mind's innate ideas. How easily this led to the neverending paganism that was forever being born in man's refusal to accept his finiteness and its limitations. Man is denied the entrance into the Promised Land not because his life is short but because *we are dealing with human life*. Kafka grasped this in his commentary on Moses. The Promised Land is a "lure." There is a vanity in human endeavors for are we not only *dealing with human life?*[14]

Already in 1961 Fessard had remarked about Hegel's fundamental error. He said: "We touch upon the fundamental error of Hegel which was to overestimate the power of language and to believe that the determination of the concept could be expressed in a purely logical discourse which made every image and representation superfluous."[15] Hegel had in the *Encyclopedia* distinguished between the sign and the symbol. The difference was clearly enunciated. "The *sign* is different from the *symbol:* for in the symbol the original characters (in essence and conception) of the visible object are more or less identical with the import which it bears as symbol; whereas in the sign, strictly so-called, the natural attributes of the intuition, and the connotation of which it is a sign have nothing to do with each other. Intelligence therefore gives proof of wider choice and ampler authority in the use of intuition when it treats them as designatory (signification) rather than as symbolical."[16] With the declaration of the victory of the sign over the symbol, and over the world of image and representation we have deprived the natural attributes of intuition of their validity and independence. They are reduced to connotation, to the intelligence and its power of abstraction. The natural world becomes an attribute of thought, manipulated by the mind as if it were its marionettes. In fact, Hegel's reduction of intuition to its connotations and his degradation of the symbol as the means for the representation and image of intuition denies him the possibility to comprehend the reality of community. Community is the consequence of the living historical tradition embodied in its events, historical personabilities and shared values. The historical community is the bearer of truth and freedom. The truth in which it arose remains its truth through time. This is not the conceptual form created non-temporally in thinking. In fact, it is the embodiment of time and space as it carries within it the past to the present and from the present it projects its mystery into the future. The truth from which it emerged and in which it finds its continuity bears witness to the future in which its truth has its continuous and persistent history. The community is the collective symbol of truth; it denies in the individual and in the particular their attempted exaggerations and final deifications. Within the community the individual discovers the dimensions of his thinking which must be realized in the collective and communal history of the tradition. The chaos that followed Hegel's death showed how easily individuality without community returns to the natural condition of conflict for power and legitimacy. In the community of tradition the natures of temporal and spatial existence refuse to yield to the disembodied forms of theoretical speculations. Existence remains infinite in its possibilities and in the community of historical tradition the truths which are born in the continual reflection on the past remain unlimited. These truths live from the original mystery of birth in which the community finds the force of development and the power of its self-revelation. Community is the imperfect unity of body and spirit as man is their unity in an ever more imperfect way. Where either body or spirit is parted from the other and given dominance and perfection, there the original harmony and mystery of the human loses its natural relationship and order, there the spirit is violated for the body and body enslaved by the spirit. Only in the drama of God does He pour forth His essence and remains His essence totally.

From Fessard's perspective "Hegel does not doubt that Absolute Knowledge 'annuls time' and that the dialectic of the *Encyclopedia* gives each man the means of comprehending history and of being reconciled with it in time. In other terms, because of his system Hegel must be not only the 'Christ of the philosophers' but the truth of the historical Christ and the world documented by Christianity for the last nineteen centuries. He must be the veritable Christ of the invisible church where only reason and freedom govern. . . . We know that immediately after Hegel's death there was not only no community, no Hegelian church but the disciples were at once divided between the left and the right precisely by the questions which concerned Christianity: the divinity of Christ, the personality of God, personal immortality, etc. . . ."[17]

Hegel created the invisible church of reason and freedom, the church that emerged from consciousness, negation and the negation of negation. Whether this characterization of Hegel's System is justified is subject to doubt. From

Fessard's view where there is no living church there can be no invisible one. The construct of Hegel's thought remains therefore the most complete expression of the individual mind that had no church to level its individuality before the invisible church. Fessard's esteem for Hegel was so profound that he had no hesitancy to say that "if Aristotle was 'the philosopher' for the Middle Ages and in particular, for St. Thomas, then for our times, Hegel has the right to the same title."[18] While giving Hegel this title Fessard was uneasy with the consequences of Hegel's System and the chaos it fell into after his death. His deepest fears emerged with the realization that with the tyranny of the concept the world of the image and representation was relegated to signs and their natural attributes reduced to intellectual connotations. In other words, the prejudice given to thinking is so deep and overwhelming that the mystery of the body and the senses attached to it is placed in limitation that severely undervalues their power of imagery and creativity. We need only think of the beauty of the human hand and its dexterity. We need only think of Duerer's paintings, of Valéry's essay on the hands, of Bachelard's imagery of fire to realize that the intellectual prejudice of conceptualization harms the close and intimate relationship between mind and body that conceptual philosophy easily tore apart. Philosophy made it possible for a lasting schism to be perpetuated. Its religious background made it possible for philosophy to reduce the primordial truth to speculation theory. Fessard was deeply aware of the dangers of this schism, but he knew from the wisdom of his Church that the historical community of the faith is the continuous revelation of the sacred history of the Mystical Body. The mystery of history belongs to that unceasing interrelationship between the horizontal and vertical dimensions of truth.

This problem of sacred and human history took on various forms in our age with the persistency of millennial schemes and the never ending attempts to discover human 'mediators,' new mythologies and ideologies. Fessard states: "Whatever is the form taken by such a particularity in historical existence: the *Encyclopedia* of Hegelian Absolute Knowledge, the Proletarian party of the unity Man-Nature for atheistic Marxists, the Church for the Christians, it fulfills its mediating role only on the condition of being, on the one hand, open to universal history and enveloping it to the point of making the End already present. On the other hand, it can fulfill its mediating role by penetrating the singularity of the individual to point of directing and orienting, in each *hic et nunc*, his thoughts and his freedom toward the center of time and the Absolute of Meaning which is revealed there."[19]

Three representations emerge from this analysis: Absolute Knowledge, the party of the Proletariat and the Church. The first two are the creations of human intelligence, the third comes forth from the Mystery that ties together the sacred and the human history, but never identifies them leaving the sacred as the Mystery that is unconquered by human thought and which remains bound to both sign and symbol in its expression. Although Fessard enumerated these three forms the fundamental differences between them are clear. We can place Hegel and Marx together, but the mystery of the Church is distinctive and unique because it maintains a radical transcendence.

Fessard characterized the dialectic of singularity, particularity and universality in the following way: "The total unity of the three dimensions of time which includes past, present and future, the circular intelligibility which goes beyond the doubting of the Before and the After and finally universal and singular validity made possible through the means of a particularity. These are the conditions which fulfill the form of the becoming of supernatural history."20 Into this architecture we can place the work of Hegel and Marx. We owe to Hegel the clearest formulations of this structure and it is for this reason that we can assert that with Hegel the contemporary philosopher makes attempts to place the reality of human existence in both time and from the timeless. But whether we say this of Hegel or of Kant, we indicate that philosophy is rooted in assumptions and it is from these that it creates its beginning, its Archê. Fessard knew that when we use this terminology to speak of the Church a radical change of genus occurs because here the terminology always is inadequate and only hesitantly and poorly reveals through both sign and symbol what the sacred attempts to convey. Although Fessard, at times, makes it appear that these various forms employ similar expressions their radical differences must be clarified and emphasized. In conclusion to his important discussion of history in "L'histoire et ses niveaux d'historicité" Fessard observed that his study of history made possible "the synthesis of the three movements of the dialectic of the concept: the movement of the Concept according to Hegel, the movement of faith according to Kierkegaard and the movement of history according to Marx. These movements must be united and not opposed to each other in order to determine the knowledge of supernatural, historical being, or the symbolic comprehension of the human condition, in brief, the intelligence of faith. The intelligence of faith is necessary for all in order that each know it and consent or not to it in order to live and achieve his destiny."21

The "intelligence of faith" lay at the foundation of the thinking of Hegel, Marx and Kierkegaard and it is from the faith expressed either through concept, faith or history that we have arrived at three symbolic images of man's struggle for meaning. Each thinker created the symbolic system grounded in the faith of reason and the reason of faith because each knew that thought is ultimately the creation of imagery in which the thinker attempts to comprehend reality. Thinking is hermeneutic in and through which the comprehension of reality emerges in all its symbolic efficiency. Fessard had made a serious venture into the various forms of meaning that the human dialectic assumed in its struggle for comprehension. He know that these forms were analogous to the divine mystery in which freedom and truth assumed their eternal reality. Man's capacity to grasp hints of this mystery is dependent upon divine grace. Man's assumption that he had discovered them with his intelligence was the constant source of paganism from which he was never free.

At the end of his study of Raymond Aron's historical philosophy Fessard posed a question to him: "To what extent will Aron agree with my analysis of his 'historical philosophy,' the critique which I offered and the interpretation of his dramatic and paradoxical existence which I ventured to defend against the reproach of his old teacher (Brunschvicg)?"[22] How did Fessard understand Aron? He seemed to want to comprehend him more deeply than Aron did himself. The deep roots of Aron's neo-Kantianism, his deeply embedded scepticism and his intimate ties to Max Weber made it possible for him to dedicate the last edition of his *Introduction* to André Malraux and Eric Weil. There is little doubt that Fessard believed that Aron's work was fundamental for an understanding of the problem of history to which he had dedicated long and tedious years of study and writing. Fessard's studies and his contact with Aron go back to the year when he heard Aron defend his thesis in 1938 before such well known scholars as Edmond Vermeil, Léon Brunschwicg, Emile Bréhier, Celestin Bouglé, Paul Fauconnet.[23] Fessard, who was always aware of the significance of political events on the writing and thinking of politically sensitive philosophers, points to the events of the year, the *Anschluss* and the impending German invasion of Czechoslovakia. The tension and confusion caused by these actions remain the important elements in the background of Aron's work. With these in mind Fessard began the Critique of the *Introduction*.

Similar to Max Weber, Aron's scholarly work was tied intimately to his political action. What has become rare is this relationship between writing and action, between thought and practice. Fessard, like Aron, responded to the political events of his time. Why we think of this as rare is because we have become accustomed to the separation of the academic from active political life. Much of the writings of both Fessard and Aron belong to a responsive literature that aimed at clarifying the issue at hand, attempting to clarify its implications and revealing the moral problems that lie within it. In many respects this type of literature demands a sensitivity to values, a serious degree of moderation and that distinct insight into the movement of events which lie within and without what is apparent and immediate. Shortly before his death Aron spoke at the Weizmann Institute in Jerusalem. In reply to the Institute for the doctorate *honoris causa* which it had conferred upon him and other scholars, he stated what he believed to be the responsibility of the intellectual as citizen both for his profession and his public existence. He stated that "personally, I would ask for modesty. However startling are the merits of a writer or a physicist, he does not hold, by this fact alone, an evident superiority when the problems of public affairs and the conduct of external action are put forth. There is no science of war and peace comparable to that of the election, not even at the Weizmann Institute. . . . The last appeal which I address to my colleagues is for moderation. The nobility and fragility of democracy is that it tolerates within itself the positions of its enemies. In criticizing it intellectuals run the risk of weakening their government. This is a risk which democracies do not hesitate to assume betting on the ultimate power of governments of freedom."24

After a long life of political action and thought which brought together journalist and professor, public and academic life, Aron gave us two basic words: modesty and moderation. He knew well that the philosopher loses his calling when "he came to share the fanaticism of skepticism of ideologues, the day that he subscribed to inquisition by theologian-judges. . . . Adviser to the *Prince,* sincerely convinced that a certain regime corresponds to the logic of history, he participated in the struggle and accepted its conditions. But if he turns away from the search for truth or encourages the mindless to believe they hold the ultimate truth, then he abjures his calling."25

The philosopher goes beyond the immediacy of technique. He believes that his calling is the search for values and purpose. He struggles for meaning and the validity of the assumption. The philosopher seeks the limitations of knowledge. He is forced by the power of the Idea to believe in the efficacy of universality. His struggle is always against the Sophism which reduces existence to what is immediately valid and dominant. Whether the philosopher is capable of grasping the good and the true as absolutes is doubtful but at least he knows that

when these Ideas become part of the ideology of the ruling class they are deprived of their universal validity. They no longer exist to measure concrete life
with its limitations and inadequacies. Fessard, who shared Aron's love of freedom and truth, felt a particular sympathy for his historical and political thought.
Few others could approach Aron with the sensitivity and friendship which
Fessard was capable of and which gave him the capacity to appreciate seriously
his thought.

Brunschvicg had remarked, in relation to Aron's *Introduction*, that in
speaking of human existence as dialectical and dramatic Aron had realized a
"unity without drama." Whether this observation is correct depends upon how
it is understood and if it truly applies to Aron's thought. If Brunschvicg read the
Introduction properly is another question, but there is little doubt that the book
does not follow the neo-Kantian emphasis upon mathematics which plagued the
methodology of Hermann Cohen, Brunschvicg and Cassirer. With two words
Fessard attempted to set forth the theme of Aron's work of 1938: truth and freedom. Therefore it was to the last part of his *Introduction* that he gave particular
attention. In this part, "Histoire et verité" the problem of freedom and truth was
carefully delineated and became the source of continuous commentary. The fact
that the world is reasonable and what is unreasonable can be comprehended is
the belief of reason. Aron never relinquished this belief and whether it was
rooted in his neo-Kantianism, his closeness to Heinrich Rickert, or whether it
belonged to that fundamental dialectic of Jew and Pagan which is essential for
the study of history, is better left undecided. Fessard illustrated Aron's position
by quoting his final remarks to the French edition of Weber's two tracts, *The
Scholar and Politics* (1959): The choices which historical men are given . . . are
not demonstrable. The necessity of historical choices, however, do not imply
that thought is subject to essentially irrational decisions and that existence is
achieved in a freedom which would refuse to be submitted to truth."[26]

Aron was deeply Kantian in attitude and he remained committed to the
Kantian belief that man must and should know himself well enough to fulfill
prudently the moral commitment to "know what can be imputed to you and
what belongs to your moral state." This demand to search the self, to comprehend the meaning of moral obligation and to know that there is a universal duty
for all men which denies every action that demeans their dignity or the humanity
in them remained part and parcel of Aron's faith in reason and in his loyalty to
Kant. From this loyalty there emerged his refusal of tragedy no matter how
painfully he judged the destructive capacity of our industrial civilization. "I

continue," he remarked in his *Memoirs,* "to judge as conceivable the happy
end, very much beyond the political horizon, the Idea of Reason in the Kantian
sense."27

It would seem that despite Fessard's attempt to identify Kant with moralism
and Aron's rejection of the attempt to join ethical judgments to the philosophy
of history there is a Kantianism in Aron which is reflected in his sense of critique and limitation and in his refusal to join what can be thought with what can
be known. He remarked that "it is not necessary for the philosopher to grasp
unity, necessity or totality at the level where the scientist vainly seeks them. . . .
Interpretations which eliminate the plurality of the senses or the contingency of
conjunctures are definitely hypothetical and, at bottom useless, since they correspond to the intention of the prophet who announces and accepts fatality."28
Aron, however, was not willing to surrender the claims of transcendence because with them we are able to think the meaning of history even if we cannot
know it. The knowledge of man and history cannot be written by the prophet,
but man can not avoid thinking about the prophetic vision of history. Man needs
to think as well as to know, i.e., he is necessitated to ask the purpose of his
knowledge. Man remains forever tied to the realization which Kant precisely
stated in the *Critique of Judgment.* There he showed that it is within our power
to determine the relationship between what is responsibility and how our actions
are to conform to it. Our confidence and trust in the moral law depends upon us.
The possibility or impossibility of the efficacy of the moral law depends on the
commitment of our faith. Kant remarked: "It is a confidence in the promise of
the moral law. But this promise is not regarded as one involved in the moral law
itself, but rather as one which we import into it, *die ich hineinlege. . . .*"29 Aron
remained firm in his acceptance of responsibility and the need for decision.
Nothing was more fundamental in politics than the force of decision and the
courage to face the unknown consequences.

The question of decision was vital both for Fessard and Aron. Fessard was
quick to point to the significant distinction which Aron made between the
moralist and the ideologist. Aron remarked that "the moralist, although the dis-
cernment of values is human and not divine, hears a word addressed to all. The
command not to kill, to control one's passions, or to obey the categorical imperative, is a command neither for one time nor for one day. Its validity is as wide
as the humanity whose vocation it expresses and whom it reconciles in respect
for itself. On the contrary, the concrete decision . . . obeys no universal law, it
responds to a singular contingency which it does not outlive."30

Choice in history was for Aron the revelation of the self. It went beyond the romanticism of dialogue to the concrete confrontation between man and the event and it demanded of the individual a profound examination of self, of that moral self-knowledge that emerges from the painful examination of the self which Kant required of every morally serious human being. Fessard remarked that although he followed the same path as Aron he would say that "I am persuaded that the unity of his 'dramatic existence' is not to be found in Kant but in the direction which I tried to define as 'historical actuality.' "[31] What we discover in Fessard's attempt to put aside the influence of Kant is his desire to find some place for Hegel in Aron. His position in relation to Hegel is clear: "Hegel was the first to develop a theory of historicity of which we find nothing in Kant even if he posed the premises of this historicity. Today it is clear and recognizable that Hegel's theory is oriented by a catholicizing meaning although more speculative than practical." Fessard added to these reflections the following: "Hegel's profound affinities are much more catholic than those of Kant, although poorly discerned by Hegel himself."[32] Whatever the truth of these manipulations they show precisely the personal implications of historical and philosophical interpretation. Fessard had often declared Hegel the Aristotle of the modern age and dedicated to him important articles and references. To Kant he referred only seldom. The fundamental dualism of knowledge and belief made it impossible for Fessard to comprehend the regulative power of the Idea of Reason, either in their radical or aesthetic formulations. Kant was *the* philosopher of the great neo-Kantian, Hermann Cohen, whose later works were devoted to the philosophy of Judaism and who believed deeply in the significance of the Idea and the Ethics of the Pure Will. This neo-Kantianism which Aron experienced with Léon Brunschvicg never lost its power to stress the importance of responsibility, universality and the faith in reason. neo-Kantianism was ruled by a moral confidence in the realization of the moral law. Judaism has made the singular contribution to Kantianism with its faith in the possibility of moral life. Was the Neo-Kantian Judaism incomprehensible to Fessard or was he sadly unaware of Hermann Cohen?

From this faith there emerged in Aron the most important chapter of his book: *Historical Man: The Decision.* Aron stressed the significance of choice as the path to self-knowledge as well as to historical and political understanding. At the beginning of the chapter he made it clear what he meant by choice. He wrote: "The choice is historical because the values in the name of which we judge the present come from history; they are deposited in us by the objective mind, which we have assimilated in acquiring personal consciousness. And on the other hand, the choice is not an act external to our true being; it is the decisive action by which we commit ourselves and fix the social environment which we recognize as ours. Choice in history merges with a decision about ourselves, since its origin and object are our own lives.''[33] Choice is decisive action because it reveals freedom "as a matter of fact." In this facticity of freedom which is the root conception of all unconditionally-practical laws "man finds the truth of his supersensible reality which makes it impossible for him to be a tool of history or a mere moment in rational progression. In the freedom that is choice man finds his meta-historical purpose: to be within history, determined by it and yet free to comprehend that we are capable of exercising choice with moderation and modesty. Choice remains inseparable from purpose. Man's capacity to comprehend the meaning of purpose reflects his acceptance of his finiteness. Man knows that he must subordinate the immediacies of his personal life to ends; he also knows that the ends which he chooses are determined by his culture, by the commitment he has made to this culture, to the education and development of the moral self which this forces upon him. Kant reminded us that man's "individual happiness on earth, and, we may say, the mere fact that he is the chief instrument for instituting order and harmony in irrational external nature, are ruled out."[34]

Aron was very close to this moral position. He knew that man affirms this position in his power of judgment and in the responsibility that ties him to the reality of choice. "Only in this way," he observed, "does the individual overcome the relativity of history by the absolute of decision, and make the history he bears within, and which becomes his history, truly a part of himself."[35]

Man can never escape what Aron called the "radical questions" which are forced upon him by philosophy. Assuming that these "radical questions" are significant for him or that he is willing to ask them, we face the unconquerable duality between the finiteness of existence with its limitations and dependence on external reality and that freedom which is man's moral responsibility for choice. Man does not hope for reconciliation but he lives with struggle and contradictions in which his action remains in tension with actuality, his individuality with the determinism of history. Man knows that the end of nature is not his individuality but his culture.

Aron spoke of the future as the primary category. This emphasis upon the future as the decisive moment of time was fundamental upon the future as the decisive moment of time was fundamental for Hermann Cohen. It reflected an undiminished optimism in reason and a decided refusal to yield to cults of pessimism and historical determinism. In these Cohen believed the moral life was perverted and man was returned to a fatalism that destroyed the facticity of freedom and responsibility. In this spirit of neo-Kantianism Aron wrote these significant lines: "Historical meaning is often confused with the cult of tradition or the taste for the past. In fact, for the individual as for collectivities, the future is the primary category. The old man with nothing but memories is alien to history as the child absorbed in a present without memory. To know oneself, just as to know the collective development, the decisive act is the one that transcends the real which restores by giving it a continuation and goal that is no longer reality."[36]

This belief in the efficacy of the future is the fundamental commitment to the power of the idea. The future is not formed by the concrete image of a utopia or the expression of a millennium; it is rooted in that power of reason to formulate the Idea of universality as a regulative Idea, to express that faith in reasonableness that is an unending struggle with irrationality and arbitrariness. Reasonableness is also the tolerance of error which again and again returns man back to his finiteness and forces him to recognize the modesty of his achievements and goals. Aron's confidence in the future was tied to his belief in dialogue. He deeply opposed every society that refused confidence in the governed and was constructed on an oligarchy that believed in its own superiority. In an interview Aron remarked that "he had fought for thirty-five years and would continue to fight (against all such oligarchies). The pretensions of a few oligarchs to know the truth and, at the same time, history and the future is untenable."[37]

Confidence in dialogue meant moral refusal of oligarchy. It indicated a respect for the great minds of human history that created the culture which Kant believed was so vital for man's power of choice and judgment. Aron said in the same interview that "he loved dialogue with the great minds and it is a taste which he wanted to cultivate among his students. I find that students need to admire and since they cannot admire their professors . . . they must admire the great minds. The professors must be the interpreters of those minds for the students."[38]

The sensitivity to dialogue and its refusal of totalitarianism in every form constituted the structure of Aron's perspective upon reality. When he used the words modesty and moderation in Jerusalem he indicated an abhorrence of extremes and a confidence in man's rationality and reasonableness. When he spoke of dialogue he pointed to that dependence which man had upon the past but also to his faith in the future. The dialogue which meant persistent and continuous investigation of truth also held at bay the arbitrariness of intellectual oligarchy, the blind commitment to ideology and mythology. Man's limitations, his tendency to err, his need to develop from his error all depended upon the belief we have in man's capacity to go beyond his immediate limitations, to his faith in the future.

Aron commented on Fessard's interpretation of this thought by saying that "Gaston Fessard interprets me in such a way that he makes me essentially a Semite. This is his privilege. I must say that in spite of my great friendship for him I am not convinced of his interpretation."[39] Often Aron repeated a formula which stated that he was French, a Jew by religion who nevertheless was not religious and did not believe in God. How deeply this expressed his fraternity with Israel cannot be gaged. Fessard was convinced that there was a deep feeling of fraternity between Aron and Israel and in this he was correct, but whether this changed his loyalty to France or made it possible for him to believe in the God of Israel or in the chosenness of the people is doubtful. Fraternity had a particular meaning for Fessard and deeply influenced his interpretation of Hegel and his attitude toward Aron. Fraternity was not merely a national loyalty but a religious commitment in and through which God's purpose was shared through community in time. The community of faith participated in both a human and sacred history. It brought collectivity into the world, the divine word as it is revealed through the generations of communal interpretation. This fraternity which the community lived is the source of visible spiritual and historical life; it is a banner against the absoluteness of individuality and the abstractness of universality. In its particular nature it mediates individuality and universality. Fraternity is the living church because it brings to itself the individual with his particular needs and character and the universal with its conceptual power that embraces and embodies them and at the same time sublimates their qualities in fraternity. In fraternity we discover not only an historical belonging to peoplehood but a metaphysical tie and bond to the sources and purposes of history. What is deepest in fraternity is the tradition of interpretation and history which we live as both an individual and member of a collective experience and truth. In fraternity philosophy gains community and tradition.

Fessard wrote some of his most profound pages of philosophical and theological interpretation when he devoted himself to the problem of fraternity.[40] In his article on familial relationships in Hegel's *Philosophy of Right,* Fessard stated that "the historical interpretation of the Reformation and the Lutheran conception of the church are the two profound reasons which explain Hegel's almost complete silence on fraternity. Both, however, depend primarily on the role which he gives to Christianity in universal history and to the role he gives his own philosophy in relation to both Christianity and history."[41] This neglect of fraternity reveals the profound inadequacy of individuality and inordinate stress upon the freedom of the Christian man. The reduction of religion to the individuality of feeling and unconditioned dependence denied it the possibility of being the true and universal expression of the Idea of Humanity, to speak in terms of mankind founded in God. Christianity lost responsibility for our fellowman, for society and for brotherhood. From the collective experience of the Church and the sacred people a fraternity and community developed in whose architecture the Word of God lived a subjective reality which spoke universally, i.e., beyond the subjective truth of the individual and the abstractness of the universal. It spoke from the truth of sacred fraternity in which man discovered the limitation of his feelings and knowledge when measured by the collective experience and truth of community and the fraternity that makes it possible. There is some justification in Marx's characterization of Hegel: "the onanism of Hegel's speculation compared with sexual love."

The realization of the Idea of fraternity was alive in Hegel's realization of a philosophy born in Absolute Knowledge, but its life remained conceptual and abstract. The struggle for its realization belongs to the concept of community, to what Josiah Royce called the "Beloved Community," the "Community of Interpretation" where what is sacred and secular find mutuality and dialogue, where the secular conveys the sacred into history and transforms itself, when in history we recognized the meeting of the sacred and the secular in such a way that neither destroys the validity of the other. This presence of community is the living Church. Community is the opposition to Paganism which is either the revolt of the individual from the universal or the universal from the individual. The purpose of man is not in self-realization but in commitment to community.

With the concepts of Community and Fraternity Fessard achieved the most serious critique of Hegel's thought, but he also attempted to show in Aron's historical philosophy that these two concepts form the basis of his bond to the peoplehood of Israel and conditioned his thought to a degree that went beyond his comprehension. His practice was greater than his thought. Fessard had a deep sensitivity to the reality of these two concepts. He knew how deeply they formed a political perspective but, at the same time, how intimately they were embodied in both a philosophy and theology of history where the representational drama superseded the sterility of conceptualization, where theory and image could not escape from each other because both belonged to the realization of truth. Fraternity embraces body and spirit. it calls forth man as our fellowman. We are made socially and morally responsible for the dignity of life. In our awareness of distress and pain we form community and fraternity. In this community of mutuality and social responsibility fraternity is the immediacy of moral responsibility. Fraternity was not spoken of by Hegel because he relegated to subjectivity the correlation between man and man, and between man and God. What Fessard points to when he speaks of community and fraternity is man's relationship to his fellowman whose dignity is my concern and whose welfare is the concern of the human community. In this community fraternity emerges not only as the Idea of Humanity but as the consciousness of the primordial community of man and God. Where fraternity does not express this divine community, it loses the force of its historical actuality, the meaning of its presence. Fraternity as community is man's struggle for social and political maturity for the realization that culture as community is the purpose of human life and is the ground from which man builds his relation to God. Fraternity precedes individuality. As community it is the basis of thought and action. From fraternity and community man matures into a cultured being, and as this being he comprehends his nature. In this comprehension philosophy is understood as a commentary on tradition, as the return of man to the community of thought from which he emerged and whose truth he grasped the more deeply he moved away from it and looked back upon it. Fessard's belief in the Church as the community and fraternity of God and man made it possible for him to be a philosopher. He lived in and through tradition. He comprehended his being in the universal fraternity of the Church, he knew that where this fratenity is lost or forgotten the philosopher is forced to see in himself the source of meaning and the vehicle of its creation. In this understanding he stands at the abyss of chaos.

Gaston Fessard's Interpretation of Israel in Human and Sacred History

In April of 1985, Milan Kundera, the Czechoslovakian novelist, received the Jerusalem prize for literature. In his acceptance speech he spoke of the greatest discovery of the nineteenth century and of its discoverer, Flaubert. Flaubert had discovered stupidity. Kundera said that the most shocking, the most scandalous thing about Flaubert's vision of stupidity was "that stupidity does not give way to science, technology, modernity, progress; on the contrary, it progresses right along with progress."[1] Stupidity's progress depends upon man's technological and intellectual development. It increases in sophistication and force because it is not simply ignorance that can easily be removed or lessened and which has little power to affect the course of human action. Stupidity has much greater importance for the future of mankind. Ideologies and theories come and go like the fashions of the times, but stupidity is ever-present and has a firm place in man's future. Kundera remarked that "we could imagine the world without the class struggle or without psychoanalysis, but not without the flood of conventional ideas which threaten soon to become a force that will crush all original and individual thought and will smother the very essence of modern European culture."[2] Conventional ideas are forceful. They dominate a manner of thinking that is impenetrable to reason or to what we like to call the reasonable discourse. The conventional idea suffocates, under the pretense of intelligence and meaning, our sense of criticism. The struggle against this insufferable force remains our most painful and dangerous battle. This human enemy has the longest human history and has developed the most serious and effective antibodies to every attempt to penetrate its armory. Its capacity for resistance has grown through the centuries. This problem is acute when we turn to a particular type of conventional idea in the history of religious rhetoric: the conflict between Israel and Christianity. The mountains of rhetorical discourse stagger vision and imagination. When there is an important attempt to defy conventionality and we believe that finally the enemy can be overcome and his armor penetrated, his power is reinforced and we are held in check. It does not happen so quickly or so easily, but there are always hopes and possibilities and they are present in the work of Gaston Fessard, Jesuit priest, philosopher, theologian, publicist and activist. He died in 1918 and left us a literary and moral stature from which emerged a serious attempt to comprehend the relationship between Israel and Christianity. His struggle was against prejudicial and conventional ideas and he understood deeply how they had grown into scholarship, technology and intellectual sophistication.

Conventional ideas in religious conflicts abound. They grow from them and find in their conflicts ways to become overwhelming and grotesque. The problem became acute in our age when we faced Nazi and Communist anti-Semitism. How to explain this phenomenon taxed our imagination and reason. What we did discover was the fact that both Christianity and Judaism had an enemy that was no longer one or the other. It was atheism as racial ideology and as class struggle. In 1900, Fessard had written about anti-Semitism in the Soviet Union. He had, for a long time, known that Nazism and Communism shared a similar heritage and that Judaism was for both the natural danger. At the end of his article "L'antisemitisme en U.R.S.S." Fessard observed:

> It is false to equate the true source of Communist and Nazi anti-Semitism with the Christian anti-semitic millennium as does Jules Isaac's *Genèse de l'antisemitisme* 1956. Such a correlation is, in its simplicity and injustice, more capable of promoting than arresting the "genesis of antisemitism." Preferably we should return to Paul's teaching concerning the opposition of Pagan and Jew and the meaning of this enmity for their final and common salvation. From this perspective it appears that we can speak of a Christian anti-semitism only because there are those who are unfaithful to Paul's teaching and often act like idolotrous pagans and incredulous Jews. There is no anti-Semitism from Christianity. According to Paul the authentic Christian is like Christ, our peace. He believes: "Gentiles and Jews, he has made the two one and in his own body of flesh and blood has broken down the enmity which stood like a dividing wall between them . . . so as to create one of the two a single new humanity in himself. . . . This was his purpose to reconcile the two in a single body to God through the cross on which he killed the enmity."[3] (Ephesians II.14-17)

The struggle between pagan and Jew is fundamental. The history of mankind is written in this struggle. From it Christianity arose as its universal truth. The Church became the eternal and living incarnation of this universality of the truth. To think of a Christianity without Judaism is to imagine a non-entity. The Christianity that is anti-Semitic dissolves itself. Christianity remains the universal faith in the oneness of mankind. This oneness depends upon that dialectic of Jew and Pagan. The Jew, affirming the uniqueness of God, that distinct mono-theism which refuses human activity that pretends to absolute truth, denies the *fact* that only in God is their being. Man would prefer to be like the gods, knowing the difference between good and evil. What would this difference be if, at the same time, he did not know the meaning of life. Man's stupidity grows to grotesque proportions as he seeks to answer all problems.

In significant autobiographical comments Fessard spoke forcefully of the significance of the dialectic, pagan-Jew. What the term, dialectic, means here is the inevitable discourse between two conflicting realities that reveal the nature of a religious history whose form is revealed in the course of this discourse. The Jew and the pagan are both historical and metaphysical forms. Looking back from the perspective of the Church they are not only the preparatory forms of Christianity but they are its living and vital life. Christianity in its universality is this struggle against paganism. Israel is its primordial form and architecture. In Israel it realized God's purpose and living manifestation. Where Christianity is true to its faith, it is true to Israel and its sacred and historical conflict with atheism. Fessard's deepest conviction lay in his refusal to think of Israel apart from Christianity. Unimaginable is the thought that Christianity's mission of salvation could be structured in a form in which paganism and Israel were not the essential elements. In and through history, whether sacred or profane, the fundamental fidelity and community of faith rested in the continuous and eternal dialectic of monotheism and atheism, materialism and revelation.

The autobiographical comments which we referred to expressed Fessard's opposition, in 1940, to both Nazism and Communism as dialectical contradictions. These carried within them totalitarian ideologies and myths and became sophisticated forms of paganism. Their analysis belongs not only to the political, but to metaphysical categories, to primordial oppositions. Fessard, the political thinker, was always the theologian and metaphysician. "Later," he said, "when I took this opposition as the base for an analysis of the mystery of society, I did not feel necessitated to find numerous justifications. The dialectic of Pagan and Jew seemed to me to be a solid foundation. I was surprised to learn how many

Catholics and even theologians were not inclined to give credence to this opposition and to seek in it the solution of their problems.''4 Conventional theology and philosophy would have little tolerance for ideas that made Christianity so deeply dependent upon primordial oppositions which for many would pass away in time and leave Christianity free of Paul's historical understanding of the sacred role of Jew and Greek. The divine tie that brought the historical and social role of Israel into the body politic of the Church would be anathema to those who would prefer to remain blind to the Hebrew Bible and to an understanding of historical actuality. In fact, the deepening comprehension of this categorical opposition made it natural for Christianity to stand together with Israel in continuous opposition to racism, atheism and the mythic dramas of master races and classes. The continuance of this opposition made it impossible to dissolve political and economic problems into utopian visions where conflict would give way to a dreamy peace enforced by the mystic power of supermen and super-classless societies. Fessard knew that the opposition he had comprehended in Paul and had studied in Hegel made him speak of history in such a way that the Abrahamic Covenant, promise and journey was no less sacred than the salvation of Jew and Greek in the one body of the Church. The truth of this salvation was in Abraham's Covenant.

The force of idolatry is similar to that of the violence that lives within reason and is the source of its development and strength. If violence threatens the discourse of reason, then the idols of political and social life threaten that transcendent power which limits this life to imperfection, possibility and chance. In these limitations human life discovers its vanity, humor and seriousness. It knows that when the attempt is made to reduce these qualities to perfections and totalitarian control, this life dies. The idols of perfection, humorless seriousness and self-satisfying theories of historical development reverberate through the paganism that reduces life to what can be conceptually formulated and explained. Fessard had remarked in an interview that ''the pagan who is always living in the atheistic Jew a possibility of the negation of his idols. In fact, the presence of the negating transcendence of idolatry is specifically from the Jew. It is from his elections, his natural vocation and it exists even when he has denied it.''5 The truth of Israel's past in sacred history goes beyond the will or affirmation of the individual, whether he acknowledges the truth of his faith or wants to remain indifferent to it. It is not a question of indifference. The meaning of prophetic Judaism can only enhance the redemptive role of Israel in the scheme of salvation. We are aware that paganism is not obliterated in the Christian, but is his deepest and most painful struggle. In this struggle he bears in himself the truth of eternal Israel and its primordial dialectical opposition to the idols of atheism. In them it has its negative truth.

The conflict and enmity between Jew and Pagan is temporal and non-temporal. There is no temporal solution to this enmity as long as there is human history. Human history is conflict. Those who search for its resolution hope and plan for its destruction. Metaphysical conflict belongs to faith, to the necessary condition of reason, but conflict in its historical form belongs to historical actuality and it is in this actuality that we begin to comprehend metaphysical truth. Knowing that the form that this conflict takes in historical actuality is not predetermined we are, nevertheless, aware that if we are to understand the conflict the metaphysical belief is necessary. The anti-Semitism of Nazism and Communism belongs to the intricate and varied meanings that are embodied in the enmity of Jew and Pagan, in the paganism that refuses its negation and conversion, in the Jew who rejects his Chosenness and becomes indifferent to the monotheism that would set aside his scepticism and indifference. The idolatry that is the cause of man's self-destructiveness and self-adoration reveals more about human nature than much of the psychological jargon that pretends to be scientific. The Christian remains an embodiment of paganism when he fails to comprehend how deeply Jewish is his faith and how essential the Jewishness is for his salvation. It is the truth of the universal church. What Fessard has forced us to see and more deeply to hear, is the fundamental truth that redemption in time belongs to that opposition, which is both "dialectical and historical," between the faith of Abraham and the power of the idols. This opposition we carry within ourselves, there it belongs to our political life and it is reflected in our philosophical presuppositions. The historical forms which we witness in our own times show clearly idolatry in the form of national mythology, racism and in the mythic form of class struggle and classless society. The idolatry bears witness to the primordial dialectic whose truth belongs to metaphysics, to the faith of reason and to that faith in Paul's vision of sacred history.

There is a danger that constantly emerges from the very body of Christendom: the desire to convert the Jews in time. Fessard was deeply disturbed by this tendency to see in time a moment when the Jews would or should be converted. It corresponded to the false utopianism, totalitarianism, and, at the same time, was a distortive reading of sacred history. It failed to comprehend the meaning of the Church in its mission of salvation. Human history is governed both by its own conflictual forms as well as by those of sacred history. Israel

belongs to both histories and from them she assumed a national and a metaphysical role. Her national role has been the preservation of the people which
she is compelled to do politically. For this role she has belonged to secular history and followed its demands for self-preservation. Her role as the sacred partner of a divine covenant gives her a portion in universal history, in the history of
redemption. This history and the dialectic that is forged within it belong to that
divine human correlation which remains hidden and obscure, but demanding
and forceful in faith. At the source of this sacred covenant was the command to
leave the land of the idols to take the divine responsibility for both a sacred and
human destiny. This destiny did not originate with us but came from the realization that human history had been given a purpose. The purpose belonged to the
demands of truth and freedom. The barriers to these lie in idolatry, in its fanaticism and scepticism. Where human life has been embodied within an idol it is
distorted and it becomes destructive. It gives forth as truth what we earlier called
conventional ideas and with these the progress of stupidity, a quality that is peculiarly human, is put forth as a sophisticated advancement.

For Fessard the two great idols of our age are Nazism and Communism.
From the perspective of idolatry he equates the two. However we describe these
two forms of idolatry, and they have been delineated innumerable times, we find
a common feature; a violent opposition to the Jew, a suspicion of his loyalty and
a fear and resentment that secretly his faith in a God makes him unworthy of
national or international loyalty to either nation, race, or ideology. The struggle
against the Jew is that against religious faith, his temporal existence. Destroy
this existence and you have proved your pagan faith. There is that destructive
resentment which comes forth from the temporal existence of Israel. The resentment of the pagan is that where there is religious belief there the clandestine
God gives strength to those who refuse the conventions of the pagan. Human
work transforms reality and there is no dimension of life that cannot be transformed by it. Fessard described this absolute perspective: Would we not find the
end of our evils with a nature that became man, a humanity that became master
of nature and equal to the universe?"6 Class oppression would end, man would
again find his humanity, the proletariat would have made possible that peculiar
awareness of subjection and exploitation which governs the relationships between the exploiters and the exploited. The scandal which is this enslavement
would be overcome in a classless society. With this scheme of history now made
scientific by faith in its speculative philosophical assumptions a party organization developed and the state functioned as the party's instrument for the preser-

vation of this faith. In the party man found the "way" and the purpose of life. Under its rule the new order, the natural order, took the place of the religious. The Christian and the Jew became the dangers to this new idolatry. Fessard asked again and again whether we could understand this form of idolatry without that historic dialectic of Jew and Pagan. What we are sure of is that without his categories we would comprehend differently and perhaps less deeply the pagan quality of life that is alive within us and our ideologies.

The question of why the deep antipathy for the Jew in both Nazism and Communism existed was answered in broad outlines by Fessard in his perceptive article on Soviet anti-Semitism. His words are clear and precise. They reflect years of thought and political activity. We should always remember that Fessard's work, even his voluminous studies of the "Spiritual Exercises" were responses to his time. He was not an ivory tower professor who participated rarely in political events, but his books were responses to the great events of his time. The fortitude and insight they required leaves us with admiration. He was engaged in the truest sense with the issues that most men face from a distance, or in the comfort of a university or in a chair at home. In this sense we understand the depths of friendship that tied him to Raymond Aron and made enemies for him in and outside his church. His clandestine writings during the Vichy period and his unwavering struggle against anti-Semitism did not make him many friends except among those who appreciated his faith and the courage it demanded. When he spoke of Soviet anti-Semitism he remarked that

for a long time I have explained that Communism and Nazism were the products of the decomposition of the liberal world and that these two enemy ideologies were linked by a fraternity not only found in their origin but revealed by their ideal. The one was formed by a people of masters, a race elected by Nature, the other by the proletarian class elected by history, and both by their parallel enmity to Christ's Church. Since the Church arose from Judaism and remains grafted on ancient Israel, it is natural that the positive atheism formulated by Marx as the basis of Communism would engender hatred not only against religious Jews but against all members of ancient Israel, subjects of the same divine election. This hatred could be hidden for a long time. At first it was hidden under the official negation of popular anti-Semitism, which was an inheritance of a "reactionary bourgeois past," and then in support of the struggle against Nazism. Once Nazism was destroyed, this hatred came forth as essentially religious and more profound than neo-paganism because it is derived from an *inverted Judaism,* brought about by *intrinsic perversion* that is proper to communist atheism.[7]

This hidden hatred that Fessard spoke of arose from the conflict between a secular and religious messianism. This secular messianism was as natural to the Jews as the religious. The resentment that was fostered and festered in the Jewish and non-Jewish secular messianism toward the religious was nurtured in the feeling of disloyalty that secularists believed was always part of a Jewish-fostered messianism. Was this secular messianism not really a disguise for the religious prophetism that turned the Jew away from the deification of the natural order, toward one that belonged to a peculiar relationship with his God, his tribal deity, that subordinated every other loyalty? Whether religious or secular the Jew could never satisfy the pagan realism with his loyalty.

The plague of questions that arise when we confront the values and purposes of human existence are unconquerable. If we are willing to ask the questions then we, at least, are aware of how complex and varied are those that force us to retreat from any dogmatic or prepackaged solution. Fessard had the capacity to raise difficult problems because he refused to hide away in the obscurantism of academia and stood like a modern Socrates in the public arena. He spoke of man's immediate problems and the approaches we could take toward understanding them. More serious was his firm belief that these problems, if they could not be resolved, could and should be, at least, comprehended. Comprehension is, however, no excuse for the failure to act. Fessard knew that action was the deepest expression of comprehension. The questions that he asked were expressed in his literary work and these were purposed for his colleagues and the intelligent public. Communication, he knew, is indispensable to serious thought, action indispensable to its comprehension. Both were subject to truth and where this truth was falsified, there Fessard knew it had to be exposed.

In persistent and continuous confrontation with Nazism and Communism, with every form of totalitarianism, Fessard posed a question that leaves us without an answer, but demands a comprehension that is necessarily inadequate to itself. "What is this 'spirit,' " he asked, "that is capable of taking from millions of men their life, 'its personal historical initiative,' and making them believe that through the efficacy of proletarian universality they became the 'creator people of history and humanity?' "[8] The question required some reply and Fessard offered a possibility. The course of human history and its meaning is embodied in conflicts, in the deadly fear of violence and terror that is in the reality of reason and its discourse. This constant confrontation with violence, the violence of the inexplicable, of the explicable in its apparent perfection, is the source of our reasonable defiance and our refusal of its servitude. Fessard refused servitude and he dared to reply to his own question as he replied early to Nazism and to Vichy from 1941 to 1945. He stated:

> To the degree that men allow themselves to be dominated by this "Spirit" which is not only Marxism-Leninism, Nazism or Maoism, but is also the "Spirit" that dwells in each of us and inspires in us the individual or collective desire "to be like God" to that degree it is vain for us to seek to conquer war. Our international institutions and even a world government, as perfect as we can imagine them, could do nothing against the supernatural spirit which is, from the very first, the father of the lie and homicide and will always find the means of causing fraternal struggles.[9]

We have become so secular in our attitudes that we hesitate to speak of sin, of original sin, of those forms that attempt to express man's indomitable inclination and need to transgress and distort, i.e., to sin. We seem to want to remain convinced that good and evil are the consequences of our choices and that our knowledge of them is in freedom. Believing that the knowledge of good and evil is freely determined by us we act as if it is not to be fought for but already within our nature, purview, and action. Fessard was aware that our political and moral action does not belong to knowledge alone, but to the will. In it are the forces of collective violence and terror that can displace reason for its own purposes for the sophisticated use of the lie. The conflict with the sophisticated violence was the new weapon of the idolatry of totalitarianism. Comprehending sin as violence and terror, Fessard deepened his awareness of the Pagan-Jew conflict. In this conflict lay all the other conflicts: master-slave, male-female, and those which are yet nascent and which history will ultimately reveal to us. We have not yet begun to grasp the possibilities of sin. Fundamentally the primordial opposition between our faithfulness to transcendence and our fidelity to materialism reveals the dialectical structure being formed in metaphysics and being realized in history.

Fessard contrasted Communism with Nazism only to show that both sought to resolve the mystery of history in a particular way. Opposed to the ideal society that would evolve when the struggle between man and man, and man and nature was overcome, Nazism affirmed that the "primordial fact of history was not work but struggle and the death struggle. It alone, with its double consequences, the domination of the stronger and the enslavement of the weaker, can bring about the selection of the best and thus achieve 'the will of nature which is given to raising the level of beings.' The role of the stronger is not to surrender domination but to exercise it and to make the weaker serve its ends. . . . The subjection of the weaker to the ends of the stronger and more intelligent is the cause of progress."[10] Fessard's description sought an answer to the question: how do we unmask the secret of human history? For this question the answer lay in the study of totalitarianism, the ideologies and myths it creates to find answers to the meaning of man's history. Totalitarianism lives from answers, it decays in questions. We cannot, however, put aside these ideologies as the fantasies of sick men or the dogmas of party organizations. These ideologies are believed, they enchant and they explain. Men feel secure with them. In their explanations lie their fascination. They belong to the needs that men have for the clear and precise answer and the satisfaction it yields. The appeal to nature, as the model of human action is ever-present. Man's conformity to its laws gives him a sense of its omnipotence because he has accepted the ancient pagan notion of nature: omnipotence. This omnipotence had Esyphian roots and was deeply opposed by Israel's belief in God's uniqueness, His distinct separation from nature as its creator. Nature's omnipotence was prevalent among the pagan peoples with whom Israel had contact and she herself was, often, profoundly attracted to its enchantments, but Israel's history was God's work and incarnated in the Covenant with Him. The return to the belief in nature's omnipotence was modern man's deepest acquiescence to ancient paganism.

Even the *Fuehrerprinzip* which Nazism believed to be the key to the comprehension of history is the consequence of our understanding of nature. "For people who have recognized it and rigorously applied it," Fessard observed,

it assures victory over every historical dialectic and the mastery of the universe. Nature, like the universe is one. . . . The fact that people are unequal and distinct by their innate qualities, some to rule, others to obey, is not only a fact through which science and history impose knowledge, but it is good for humanity which can elevate itself only through the action of the best. Before this elected people of Providence who govern nature, the others can only bend and recognize the right of this providential, prerogative.[11]

History had made a full turn. We are back again to the omnipotence of nature with vengeance and resentment. Vengeance that realizes our resentment against those who had invented a supernatural God, who gave man the freedom to give purpose and meaning to nature and whose freedom, as the *Imago Dei,* gave him the knowledge that he was morally and intellectually not subject to nature, but in relation to her could discover moral life. Man was given the obligation to discover nature's laws, but as their discoverer he was not their subject, but their partner. God is creator, the unique being, whose relationship to his world was through will, command and promise. Man's partnership with nature is through God's command. The world is a variety of possibilities and man had the responsibility for their realization. He is a human creator. He is artist and architect. This creation belongs to a world in change, in becoming, in which no stage of development can be absolutized and no law is immutable. The struggle against Paganism is focused on man's inclination to confuse the relative and the permanent, becoming and being. Man confuses his creative powers with God's. What Fessard recognized in his persistent explorations of Nazism and Communism was this deepening Paganism that infected man's life: its danger lay in its communication, its use of language which hides its intent. The lie becomes the weapon which confuses its enemies. It distorts their balance. Totalitarianism learned how to say one thing and mean another. The ritual of Paganism became attractive in its deception.

Fessard was seriously influenced by Hegel's master-slave dialectic. This is understandable when we realize how deep was his belief in the conflict between Paganism and Monotheism. Metaphysical conflict became meaningful as the primordial condition of social and political life. As the condition of collective life it forms the categories through which we comprehend man's moral and religious purpose. In conflict man's slavery and man's mastery emerge as the two extremes in which the continuing enslavement to idolatry takes on new forms of totemistic rituals and more perplexed structures of taboos. This enslavement incarnates visions of political, social and racial mastery that have tied it deeply to its enslavement to the idols of its rituals, mythologies and ideologies. The slave-master dialectic reduces the conflicting powers to each other, forcing from them new and more forceful dialectical oppositions. The movement of one to the other "represents not only the *first social tie and the origin* of every political

society, but *an essential moment of the genesis* of human reality, i.e., a passage
which is repeated at each moment and at every level of social relationship, from
the least relationship between two individuals to that of world conflicts.''12
However we describe the realms of conflict we find not only confrontation with
the external opposite but the *fact* that the external opposite is also internal. In
other words, what we struggle against is already within us. We can be overcome
not only by what is external, but what is internal. We bear within ourselves what
we want to destroy in the enemy outside of us.

The conflict between Jew and Pagan is meaningful only if we are fully
aware of the fact that the Jew has within him what is already pagan and the pagan the possibility of what is Jewish. The struggle against the Jewishness within
ourselves belongs to our fierce desire to remain within the totemistic architecture we have built to destroy its enemies. Ernst Cassirer remarked, shortly before his death, that Hitler's last address showed a peculiar and distinct attitude.
"He begins to see his defeat," Cassirer observed, "and he feels its consequences. But what does he say at this critical moment? Does he speak of the innumerable evils which his aggression has brought to the German people, to
Europe, to the whole world? . . . His whole attention is still fixed on one point.
He is obsessed and hypnotized by *one* thing alone. He speaks of the Jews. . . .
What worries him is not the future destiny of Germany but the 'triumph' of the
Jews." In conclusion Cassirer added this remark: "If Judaism has contributed to
break the power of the modern political myths, it has done its duty, having once
more fulfilled its historical and religious mission."13 Cassirer's words are clear
and from the perspective of Fessard they speak to that indomitable paganism
which recognized in the Jew the profane action of its ritual, its millennium of
war and its worship of the myth. Here the struggle was no longer perpetual conflict, but death struggle, annihilation and utter ruin. The depth of the antagonism
defies our communication, but demands our remembrance because the antagonism continues with similar and even greater intensity. Cassirer spoke of the religious mission of Judaism, its belief in the ethical ideal, in universalism. Here
he echoed beliefs that he had heard, but never deeply shared, from his old
teacher and friend in Marburg, Hermann Cohen, whose *Religion of Reason out
of the Sources of Judaism* is the most profound attempt to clarify the meaning of
Judaism in the present. Sorrowfully, Fessard never read this text. It would have
confirmed fully the meaning of Judaism's conflict with paganism that Cohen
identified with pessimism, tragedy, fatalism, and sexual manipulation. The Nazi

experience had made Cassirer more receptive to Israel's unique historical role in the history of man's struggle for the Idea of Mankind.

Convinced that Hegel's analysis of the master-slave relationship was fundamental for the perspectives of both Nazism and Communism, Fessard showed that each placed importance on different moments of opposition. He said that both "Communism and Nazism utilize the Hegelian dialectic to explain the development of human reality. The former is centered exclusively on the slave's point of view, the latter on that of the master. From this unilateral position is born their irreconcilable opposition and their contradiction which gnawed at the heart of these two world conceptions. If the faithful of these divinities do not perceive this unilateral position, nor even this immanent contradiction, it is because a word common to both conceals it for them under its extremely complex comprehension. This word is socialism."[14] We are faced with theories that do not only speak of conflict but also of their disappearance. Marx spoke of work but also of revolution, classless society from which freedom can never be born because it destroys conflict. Without entering into the nature of civil society we only want to stress one fundamental point and that is: whether we speak from the point of the slaves or the masters the ending of conflict is also the elimination of freedom and truth. What is unpardonable in any theory or ideology is its attempt to overcome conflict. This overcoming is authentic paganism. In the millennium of either the classless society or of racial purity their totemistic rituals set aside freedom and conflict. Men, as believers, identify their reality with the myths of the state. It was to these myths that the Covenant with God refused to be reconciled. The opposition was violent and terrifying; it revealed the radical contradiction of paganism that lived wherever human society absolutized itself, reduced itself to an element of that society or created a millennium which in time promised the new society, the peace which only the gods of history could impose. Man was reduced to an historical entity, the privacy of life passed away into the grotesque abstraction of historical fate.

Whether we think of master races or classless societies we arrive at the same consequence: totalitarianism. Fessard observed this with clarity "that without the all powerful menacing and exploiting master there is no recognition for the slave, neither of himself nor of the human world. To put it more generally, without the mediation of another self who provides the subject for the appropriation of the object and at the same time, separates him from it there is no recognition of the subject in the object nor of the object in the subject."[15] The drive for recognition is fundamentally the life and death struggle of society and the individual. If we use other denominations such as work we are basically committed to the same struggle. Fessard understood this from Hegel and from his grasp of sacred and profane history. His whole architecture was constructed on that fundamental dialectic of Jew and Pagan in whose structure Christianity and the universality of the Church was given. Conventional ideas, which seem never to be disposable, have always emphasized the Jewish-Christian rivalry, each side attempting to prove the superiority of the one over the other. We need do no more than reflect on the book of Eugène Fleischmann, *Le Christianism 'mis à nu,' La Critique juive du Christianisme* (1970), to recognize the traditional lines of the debate. It was, however, an inadequate one when we think more deeply of Fessard's dialectic. His dialectical understanding embodied the metaphysical form and the categories in and through which the meaning of Israel, Paganism and Christianity are linked to each in that cosmic struggle for salvation. Salvation through Israel is through her conflict with Paganism both within and without her. Salvation through Christianity is the redemption of Israel's incredulity, the conversion of the pagan in her. This does not belong to the millennium of promised utopias but to eternity, to the overcoming of time to the *Kairos*. Fessard's unrelenting battle against the millennium was at its source his profound opposition to the violence and the terror that belong to its rejection of temporal freedom and truth which Fessard knew only lived in the divine-human dialectic.

Words such as Pagan, Jew, Christian, are not simply "historical categories"; they are what Fessard called *existential possibilities,* "which make it possible to define the attitude of each over against the 'totality'; the latter is for each attitude the unity, Man-God, Man-Nature, or *Natura Naturens it Naturata.*"[16] What is significant is the realization that the category bears within it an attitude. The category is not a mere abstraction from which we construct another aspect of a universal system. The category, besides its relationship to other categories, from which it emerged and into which they found a momentary realization, is also an existential attitude. The attitude is lived in conflict and negation, it does not have the preciseness of the category; it is too rich in possibilities and nuance; it remains free of the seeming preciseness and clarity of the categories. The attitude is a lived experience denying sharp limitations and the alleged formal structure of the category. The category makes us aware of what we already know, what is positive; the attitude looks with doubt upon such preciseness, it remains open to the unexpected and the possible. These historical categories, transfigured as attitudes, become the rich *life* of conflict without being molded into definitions and explanations. Paganism, Judaism, and Christianity have been plagued with precise ideas that take from them their life and vitality. They are varied realities that have within them vitalities that persistently defy our clarification.

Fessard had formulated his architecture of Judaism. Since for him the dramatic struggle of history was deeply dependent upon the opposition between Israel and Paganism, his formulation of the opposition is of great importance. He spoke of the intransigence of monotheism, its radical refusal to allow a vision of God that could be expressed in material form. The prohibition against idolatry was uncompromising. Idolatry was created in the hands, figured in the mind or desired in the imagination. The idols moved about in all facets of the human experience. The faith could not be verified in the senses. It set aside sight and enthroned hearing, remembrance, and learning. It knew life in the speaking word, and when and if the speaking word ceased, the faith would die and God recede from the people. Edmond Jabès substantiated this truth: *"La différence entre un être vivant et un mort, c'est que l'un parle et l'autre ne parle plus."*[17] Fessard spoke of Israel's "radical *negativity* which did not oblige the Jew only to an obedient listening but predisposed his intelligence to be even more dependent upon hearing, with a sense of time whose flight is held back only by the memory that is desirous to recall the words that were recorded or understood in Scripture. This forces him to seek truth through critical reflection which through commentaries and subtle discussion move doubtlessly toward objectivity. Such is, if I am not mistaken, the principle reason for the practical reflexivity of the Jew, of his extraordinary capacity for assimilation and adaptation."[18] However weary we may have become of generalizations about national characteristics, what Fessard pointed to was something more serious and fundamental: the nature of the intransigent monotheism, the truth of its moral demand which lies in its purity, its refusal of any contact with sensual reality. Purity is its truth. This can neither be seen, nor can it be heard; it is known. Man's hearing is always fallible but he knows this purity lies in what *should be* heard. This hearing speaks from the utter transcendence of God's untouchability, his pure moral will.

No one caught this untouchability more deeply than the poet Alfred de Vigny in his "Moses":

> Et, debout devant Dieu, Moïse ayant pris place,
> Dans le nuage obscur lui parlait face à face
> Il disait au Seigneur: Ne finirai-je pas?

Où voulez-vous encore que je porte mes pas?
Je vivrai donc toujours puissant et solitaire?
Laissez-moi m'endormir du sommeil de la terre!
Que vous ai-je donc fait pur être votre élu?
Jai conduit votre peuple où vous avez voulu.
Voilà que son pied touche à la terre promise,
De vous à lui qu'un autre accepte l'entremise,
Au coursier d'Israel qu'il attache le frein;
Je lui lègue mon livre et la verge d'airain.19

The images can only be felt; they defy comprehension and explanation. The wonder of this dialogue between Moses and God reflects that powerful loneliness that is demanded of those who are chosen and who bear upon themselves a divine mission. The question that is eternally asked from antiquity to the holocaust is the why of the burden that must be borne with strength and faith. It finds no reasonable answer but is carried along by a profound fidelity that knows that there is truth behind what we experience and believe to be the meaning and purpose of life. Theirs is a tiredness, a desire to sleep the sleep of the earth, to express that painful exhaustion that comes from the fact that one has done all that one can, and has been commanded to do. Moses led the people as God had commanded him. Then the frustration and pain was severe when the final victory and glory had been taken from him. Moses will not see the promised land and there is that hurtful cry that expresses the desperation that came with the loss of hope. The images are painfully beautiful not only because they reveal the anxiety of failure and despair but because of their beauty and sublimity that is in faith and fidelity and which belongs to that clandestine insight that recalls the truth of work and the service to God that it embodies. When Fessard spoke of the existential possibilities of this primordial conflict between Israel and Paganism, it was not always easy to grasp the depths of the conflict and we needed the poet and his images to arouse in us the dramatic power of the contradiction through the ages. Even the holocaust demands its poets and essayists, its transfiguration into literary and poetic form captures our imagination more powerfully than the documentaries and learned treatises. We are beginning with Milan Kundera, Paul Celan, Jean Améry, and George Orwell, to grasp the Paganism of our own age.

Fessard returns again and again to his fundamental belief that the dialectic of Jew-Pagan is the key to contemporary thinking.

Singularly this dialectic explains the *mystery of the Jewish people* placed at the core of all the contradictions of the modern world by a Liberalism which vows to realize its rationalism only from the conflict of master-slave. The mystery of a chosen people who see themselves condemned to extermination by a conception of the world that engenders a chosen race; the mystery of a messianic people who, after having "attained its peak," as Marx said, in the "accomplishment of bourgeois society," in capitalism, sees, on the other hand, atheistic Marxism take up again its impossible dream of temporal messianism. . . .[20]

This dialectic does not only explain what is, but what has yet to be explained. The chosen people is nearly destroyed by the chosen race. Religious messianism envisioned the Tree of Knowledge of Good and Evil again ruled by the Tree of Life and its holiness, but this vision become the dream of a temporal reality in which a classless society will the enforced by organizational and party dominance. The body of symbols which was developed to bring forth the visions of the messianic age yields to political and economic utopias that were guises for totalitarian rule. How deeply the pagan dwelled in the religious, how easily it was transmogrified and became the source of destruction for everything religious and moral. This intimate dialectic reveals how delicately painful is the struggle for religious values in a world that has only just begun to be religious and in evil and goodness has equal shares, where destruction, depravation, sadism, and terror are constituent parts of man's free will and desire, and where our morality is built upon prohibitions and commands that seek to limit the depraved quality of our inclinations. With the visionary comprehension of Fessard we have arrived at the most significant dialectic of historical actuality. No one else has given us such a profound and serious comprehension of the intimate relationship between Israel and Christianity and a deeper grasp of those words of Paul: "There is no such thing as Jew and Greek, slave and freeman, male and female; for you are all one person in Christ Jesus" (Gal. 3, 28-30). From this and similar texts Fessard built his historical categories and existential attitudes. From them the architecture of the Church emerged as the salvation of Jew and Pagan. The sacred history that came forth from Fessard's works makes it possible to comprehend the intimate and necesssary relationship between Israel, Paganism, and Christianity. In this comprehension lies our conquest of atheism.

Our struggle to comprehend historical actuality should never be simply an epistemological problem; the roots go deeply into the human experience. Fessard remarked that there is in each of us not only ''a 'Pagan' and a 'Jew' but also a 'master' and a 'slave,' a 'man' and a 'woman.' We can presume that the interplay of these three oppositions make it possible to show the mediation of Christ and the Church as the place where the double mystery, that each finds in his most secret being, in society and its universal history, is formed and un-formed.''[21] We bear these oppositions within ourselves, these are the architec-ture of society, the nation and of universal history. The Church is the mediation of these oppositions as they reveal the truth of man and society, Jew and Pagan, Christian and atheist. In the Church eternal, the oppositions are redeemed, but the Church is also Christ's body in history and is the reality of these oppositions. In the profane history to which we belong in thinking and acting, there is no re-demption from conflict. There is no Jew who is not a Pagan, no Pagan who is also the possibility of a believer, no Christian who has thrown off his Paganism, no Jew who is not incredulous and willingly puts aside his sacred election for a secular messianism. Wherever we turn, whether we think ontogenetically or phylogenetically, we are revealed in these oppositions. With them we compre-hend societal and international relationships, the demonic nature that over-whelms all mankind whose knowledge of good and evil rests on the recognition that we belong naturally to a humanity that ate of the forbidden fruit and brought the consequences into its body-politic. Instead of the love that ties God eternally to his beloved Israel, the pagan in the Jew and Christian revolts and assumes the role of earthly hero, savior, master or overman. He has struggled to obliterate the divine image, the voice of the divine command; he believes that he is the founder of chosen races and classless societies. He perpetuates that utopian and millennial dream and he weakens and destroys civilization. Fessard knew the demonic depth of these perversions. Sadly, he spoke like Cassandra knowing that mankind naturally destroys the beauty it seeks and fails to recognize. Fessard knew that those who seek the earthly paradise have prepared for man's destruction.

Hermann Cohen spoke of the Jewish martyrs. He understood that the Jew could never be a citizen of the national state where national virtues dominated universal demands. Where national heroes were deified and the manifest destiny of the state became ritualistic forms of behavior the universalism of Israel was threatened. Cohen remarked: ''Messianism breaks the backbone of nationalism, so that the courage of the Jew cannot be degraded to a merely national virtue.

The human courage of the Jew is, as a historical virtue, humanitarian courage, the courage for the truth of the religious ideal of mankind. The mainspring of this courage is that mankind, which had gradually become an ethical idea in accordance with its origin in Messianism, is the highest but inevitable consequence of messianic monotheism.''[22] Fessard would have found little difficulty in comprehending Cohen's view. He knew that Christianity embodied the Abrahamic Covenant and its universal mission; it was this universalism that he saw so fully expressed in Paul. What both these thinkers struggled against were the perversions that were so clearly manifested in fatalism, racism, and pessimism. Fessard, like Cohen, realized that these perversions were deeply embedded in sexual aberrations. Fessard devoted many pages to homosexualism, to the hero-cults that surrounded it, to the asexual ideals, to the deification of the male reality and the rejection of the female quality in the male-female conflict.[23] Where these cultic forms developed, the divine-human relationship with nature was perverted. Its fruitfulness depended upon the denial of an anti-sexualism that refused family life and the values that arose in it. In that life the love of the female civilizes male heroism and creates a mutuality where moderation, prudence and balance reestablish the continuation of the conflict. Cohen had remarked that "the fidelity of love is marriage"[24] and in this fidelity the truthfulness of moral life reveals its foundation. Where the true marriage is disdained, there the love of humanity is an illusion and degenerates into atavism and the sexual perversity that accompanies it. The knowledge that sexual perversity embodied in paganism was a serious threat to Israel was revealed throughout her wanderings among pagan peoples and her contacts with them, with their idolatry and sensualism. The fierce monotheism of Israel had deep sexual roots and consequences: the struggle against the sexual ritualism of idolatry and its aberrations. In Nazism this paganism was revived with fatal consequences for family and societal life.

The fundamental dialectic from which those of master-slave, male-female emerge is that between Jew and Pagan. Fessard was certain that within this latter dialectic we had found the comprehension of human and sacred history. He stated this clearly:

Doubtlessly, the dialectic Master-Slave is capable of universalizing the singular synthesis which is the dialectic Man-woman and, consequently, it is indispensable for the advancement of the historic and natural genesis of humanity. However, it remains powerless to accomplish either without the help of the Pagan-Jew dialectic. It is a further proof of the tie which unites these three dialectics with the three levels of historical reality. This is a sign that the nature or end of temporal and profane society cannot be completely elucidated without reference to the Paulian dialectic.25

The more seriously we read Fessard the more we are aware that these dialectics flow into each other and that they all belong to Fessard's years of devotional study of Loyola's *Spiritual Exercises*.26 In these *Exercises* he found the true dialectic of life. What is significant for us is the deepening exploration of the Pagan-Jew dialectic and its comprehension within Paulian faith. The relationship between Israel and Christianity belongs to this dialectic: to those moments of it that speak of the chosen Jew, the incredulous Jew, idolotrous Pagan, the converted Pagan. However we want to interpret these four moments we know that they are the ones in and through which we can make sense of the history of mankind. We know that only through an understanding of Israel can we begin to make sense of human and sacred history.

The twentieth century gave us, besides Hermann Cohen, great Jewish thinkers and works: Franz Rosenzweig: *The Star of Redemption;* Martin Buber: *I and Thou;* Rav Kook: *Holy Lights,* and numerous works of Hugo Bergmann and Emmanuel Levinas. The vitality of thought concerning the place of Israel in history is of vital importance for the religious tradition. Israel's part in this tradition is primordial. Her truth is her universality. The work of Father Fessard is monumental because of his serious and systemic comprehension of the truth of this tradition, the depths of its life in Israel and the fearsome danger of Paganism that lives in it and outside it. The destiny of Israel and Christianity are one. The reality of Paganism remains perpetually alive in them. Fessard grasped the universality of Israel's faith in the reality of her chosenness and in her incredulity. He found it in the deadly struggle not only with this incredulity, but with the radical nature of its distortive and permeating power. Fessard deeply comprehended Paganism. He made it possible for us to see these perversions on an international level, in the competing totalitarian ideologies, in the violence and terror that emerged from them. He understood the violence in their communication and the courageous struggle that reason and fidelity make for human dignity, truth and freedom.

The validity of Fessard's conception of historical actuality was exemplified in his political attitudes, his opposition to liberation theology, to neutralism and to every continuos attempt to distinguish Communism and Nazism.

We refer to Fessard's sharp and serious critique of Karl Barth's 1948 expression of neutralism between the eastern and western blocs. Fessard's article was published in 1951 and then as an appendix to his book *Paix ou Guerre? Notre Paix*. Neutralism was an impossibility for Fessard and he explained why:

> We believe that his (Barth) conception of Church, even if it is "dialectical," is insufficient, at least, in the sense we give to the world inspired by the teachings of St. Paul. If Barth's conception were more, if it sought to judge from the perspective of the conflict between Jew and Pagan which establishes in the *hic et nun* the End of History it would comprehend that the Church builds and constructs in faith, hope and love when it intervenes in the struggle between East and West and says "no" to atheistic Communism. In this way, the Church in no way contributes to an incitement of conflict between powers, but it fulfills its essential role which is to overturn the wall of enmity and reconcile enemy peoples.[27]

No further commentary, nor remarks are needed to show how Father Gaston Fessard comprehended the world, Christianity and the Church. For him there was no neutralism where truth and freedom were in doubt. His devotion to them forced him to reject those thoughtless conventional ideas that seem forever attached to serious thinking and force it into constant conflict with the ceaseless human propensity to elaborate stupidity with elegant seriousness. The consequence of this seduction is both perversion and destruction.

We began this study of Fessard with some remarks from Kundera and we will end it with an observation of his in a conversation with Philop Roth: "People like to say: Revolution is beautiful, it is only the terror arising from it which is evil. But this is not true. The evil is already present in the beautiful, hell is already contained in the dream of paradise and if we wish to understand the essence of hell we must examine the essence of the paradise from which it originated. It is extremely easy to condemn gulags, but to reject the totalitarian poesy which leads to the gulag by way of paradise is as difficult as ever."[28] If we are serious and do not fear the difficulties that are involved in thinking and doing then the thoughts of Fessard make it possible for us to comprehend, in a profound way, the experiences that reasonable men have with totalitarianism. Fessard has given us not only random insights about the meaning of history but a systematic architecture of thought. His thinking belongs to the major accomplishments of our age. He has written a philosophy of history that embraces the human and the sacred, Israel and the Church, Paganism and the deification of nature. His devotion to truth and freedom made it possible for him to be sensitive to the distortive and pervertive power of the lie in all forms of communication. He fought against the paradises that hid the hell of utopian dreams. He fought for the universality of the Church and the truth of its salvation. He made us comprehend the validity of St. Paul's thought and caused us to hold dear the truth of Israel in human and sacred history.

Discourses of Faith:
Gaston Fessard, Franz Rosenzweig, Hermann Cohen

When Fessard was asked the question: "Would you say that Judaism has a vocation and an undeniable place in the religious destiny of our world today?" Fessard replied: "The presence of the negating transcendence of all idolatry belongs specifically to the Jews. This is their election, their specific vocation, and it will always be, even if they deny it."[1] The struggle against Paganism in the form of Totalitarianism made it possible for Fessard to comprehend the tie between the Jew and the Christian, between the Church and God's chosen people. The question that confronts us is whether it is possible to comprehend the tie without assuming that either Judaism or Christianity has a superiority over the other. There is no doubt that although Fessard loved Israel, he loved his Church more. From the Jewish perspective the same problem arose. When we were not comparing one religion to another and attempting to claim predominance for one over the other, we felt a necessity to hit at a superiority of one over the other. The last significant attempt to comprehend the relationship of these two faiths was the thought of Franz Rosenzweig and his book, *The Star of Redemption*, published in 1921. What would be the purpose of speaking of Rosenzweig, of Hermann Cohen, or Martin Buber, the great figures of contemporary Jewish thought, if we did not believe that a discussion of Judaism without Christianity is senseless and that Christianity without Judaism is hopeless. This is not a *vox clamantis in deserto* but a fundamental conviction that these two faiths proceed from and exist in a single truth. If we become more and more aware of how we have been brought to an understanding of their different ways and how they, nevertheless, belong to each other through their confrontation with paganism, that persistent and unchanging attempt to deify the finite, then we become more conscious of their meaningful and vital dependence.

Fessard, in the depths of his faith, was a political being. His life was a continuous confrontation with political reality. This reality became understandable through the philosophical and theological categories that he developed in order to make it meaningful. He could not conceive of his disengagement from this reality because he believed his values and the faith he had in the Paulian message were constantly being tested and experienced in it. Freedom and truth were for him fundamental values for which the sacrifice of life or the threat of reprisal were of lesser concern. His Christianity, his faith in the truth of his Church, could not be compromised by atheistic ideologies, racism, or the myths of utopias and the fantasies of the millennia speculations. If Christianity bore within it truth, then it was inseparable from the struggle against forces whose clear and precise purposes were to enslave the individual to the deification of state, class and race. In the thought of Franz Rosenzweig (1883-1929) an opposite tendency became very clear: s sharp and contemptuous opposition to the political reality. The faith of Israel is a radical rejection of temporal and spatial reality. Israel lives in cosmic time; it is the eternal expression of the divine calendar. In this life that is revealed by the circularity and repetition of the religious calendar, Israel lives its eternity. The past is the future and its presence is the realization of God's redemption. This is not the same mystery that Fessard was committed to in his faith in Israel's election and her closeness to her God who had chosen her for the purpose of his incarnation and his Church. A radical separateness from the world and its moral, social, and political life would cut Israel from its historical and political destiny; it would give her a peculiar uniqueness that left the profane and the sacred eternally in conflict. We have arrived at a new expression of Manicheanism.

The divisibility between our earthly life and the divine circle of sacred moments in which we live and relive the cosmology of creation, revelation and redemption is so sharp that we feel that movements from one realm to the other defy all comprehension. We would agree with Eugène Fleischmann when at the very beginning of his discussion of Franz Rosenzweig he remarked: "The discussion of the problem Judaism-Christianity is at the true center of Franz Rosenzweig's thought because it was the personal problem which determined his intellectual and spiritual evolution."[2] The problem was intimately related to his inability to decide about his commitment to Judaism and his final and societal commitment to its faith. His dislike of Hegel similarly reflected his rejection of the politics of his teacher, Meinecke, with whom he wrote *Hegel und der Staat*. His feelings changed often toward the venerable philosopher, Hermann Cohen. From his rejection of Hegel he found a new affinity with the late Schelling and, finally, came to believe that Cohen had found his most sincere exponent in Heidegger while Cassirer had become the "schoolmaster" of the Neo-Kantians. From all of these violent springs of thought, feelings, likes and dislikes, there arose a serious but political theology of Judaism with some insightful consideration of Christianity. The Mystery of Israel in the feelings of Rosenzweig would take a radical turn from how it was later understood by Fessard. The radical rejection of political reality remains the most serious problem for anyone who is convinced that this reality is man's ultimate, finite, concern because in it the values and truths which are precious to the human community find the test of their validity. Rosenzweig's dualism reflected that either/or world of the *"enfant terrible"* who delights in radical contrast and builds his architecture with startling dramatic confrontations.

Fessard had always deeply appreciated the work of Hegel although he saw its limitations. His attitude toward Hegel was enunciated by his desire to think with him. This is always the precise value that one philosopher has for another. Hegel understood what it meant to comprehend problems rather than to explain and judge them. Fessard's work traveled in the same direction, but for him comprehension became judgment. Rosenzweig's attitude toward Hegel was dramatically different. Hegel was to be studied in order to be rejected. Fleischmann remarked that Rosenzweig had always considered Hegel as "the principal representative of Paganism, an imaginary enemy which he fought throughout his life without ever conquering him."[3] It is clear that what Rosenzweig wanted to reject he relegated to the profane. The political reality in which man attempted to find the realization of his capacity for civil society and national life was shunted aside as profane. The attempt to understand human history as the power struggle of the nations is debased in favor of man's search for eternity in the realm of the sacred. Man's reason and its expression on all levels of communal life from family to nation is no longer valued as man's highest achievement. If we express this achievement in philosophical terms we would follow Eric Weil and say that reason is the self-discovery of the *"thought* of the negation of all conditions, it is the *thought* of my freedom, the *thought* that I can refuse the given."[4] Human freedom and the dignity that emanates from it is the force that man employs to fight against the monism of totalitarian ideologies. For Fessard, the struggle was for the realization of man's earthly purpose which cannot be devalued and, if it is, the humanization of man is denied.

In his article "Hic et Ubique!" (1917), Rosenzweig had sharply delineated the realm of human history from that of religion. The state existed, according to him, only to suppress human freedom. The breakup of Europe had deprived it of its spiritual values. What was left were empty shells. *"Was bleibt, sind leere Huelsen, der blosse Ismus: Nationalismus ohne Nation, Konfessionalismus ohne Konfession."*5 The denigration of political reality is clear in every reference Rosenzweig makes to it. His decision in Berlin on the Day of Atonement 1913 to remain a Jew was far more than a refusal to convert to Christianity. From this decision a radical re-valuation of life began. It reflected a metamorphosis that implied a literal reading of the word. One world had to be disdained so that another could be exalted. Judaism could arise only if it radically was separated from the world of Hegel, his concept of history and his attempt to comprehend the political. Rosenzweig created the Hegel he needed: a demonic Hegel who, as the last Pagan, comprehended political reality as man's true reality, man's realm of values in and through which he found meaning, as human freedom. Religion remained the realm of refuge.6 It alone was free of history, of the nationalism and war that were the life of the nations. It alone was released from the temporal and found in theogony and cosmic freedom its liberation from history. Rosenzweig saw deeply into the opposition that divided Schelling from Hegel. The Schelling of the *Weltalter* would become his master to overcome Hegel and to construct his poetry of Judaism eternal. In Rosenzweig we begin to see the clear directions from which the architecture of his faith will be formed. Schelling took the place of Hegel; the fervent belief of the convert gave him the courage and commitment to proclaim with fervor Israel's uniqueness and even her superiority to Christianity's religious mission. The poetry of eternity can be lived with greater fervor than the politics of statesmanship which demands and implies prudence, chance, incompleteness and the unexpected. These were qualities required of the political being. Fessard possessed them. Rosenzweig ignored them because he knew he was incapable of expressing them. From his incapacity came the perverse judgment that covered political reality and its specific personality. He could be safe only if these virtues had no role and men would come to the conclusion that Hegel was the philosopher of the perverse and that European civilization could be saved only by "supra-European and supra-human forces."7

These two terms are significant. Rosenzweig's direction was toward the *"uebereuropaeische* and *uebermenschliche* nature of Judaism"; Judaism is the expression of these two qualities and from it will come a new understanding of the relation between pagan, Christian and Jew. What is most significant is the meaning of Israel's chosenness. The thought of Israel's election is at the same time her radical difference from all other people. In this difference Israel be-

comes the stranger in the world. She turns upon herself to find the meaning of
her chosenness and election. Her mediation upon this election become her destiny. Israel's radical difference and separation from the world and the validity of
human events raises the architecture of confrontation between the Star of Redemption and Hegel's cunning of reason, the comprehension of human history.
Fleischmann posed this problem by stating that Rosenzweig's attempt to confront political reality and Judaism has particular meaning. "The problem of the
existence of a Jew in a world divided among nations and which do not recognize
any individual or group which is not defined in this nationalistic spirit is anti-
Semitism. The nationalist world is the source of the particular aggravation of the
'Jewish question' by giving a new and fatal direction to anti-Semitism."[8] In this
radical opposition to nationalism Rosenzweig showed a political acuity which
we would not have expected from him. Nationalism and anti-Semitism had
much in common. Rosenzweig's opposition, however, was not consequential for
an understanding of the political, but was the force that drove him toward a
philosophy of Judaism that went beyond the European and human dimension of
life. The peoples of the world cannot escape their political destinies. They are
embodied in a course of events that are guided by what Meinecke called *die
Idee der Staatsraison*. This interpretation he projected upon Hegel and in opposition to both he turned to eternal Judaism, to the eternity of the Star of Redemption. What we are always confronted with in this sharp opposition and confrontation is their validity. Is the reality of the "reason of state" the essence of
political life? Is nationalism its most deadly condition? Is war a necessity and
can it be comprehended as an abstraction above and beyond the immediacy of
circumstances? Is war always political, can it not be active in multiple other
ways? Are not all the conditions of national and international life the fundamental challenges to the formation of values, hopes and activities in and through
which man becomes man? Whatever be political philosophy, it is not perversity
and it is not radically separable from man's spiritual life.

If Fessard found in his faith the courage to be a political man, Rosenzweig
found in the political man the contradiction from which he needed to flee in order to frame the world of his faith and its calendar. The political world had to be
negated. The religious world could assume its eternal and theogonic reality only
from the ashes of the political world. Man must escape the political if he wants
to find salvation and the truth of his being. The revolt from the political was the
impetus for Rosenzweig's Judaism; in commitment to the political Fessard discovered a Judaism that from the Abrahamic Covenant gave Israel a historical

and temporal, but also divine destiny: the struggle against every deification of finite reality. From this historical responsibility Israel assumed its divine obligation to creation. In it Israel discovered its love relationship to its God. Rosenzweig's personal theology, that firm desire to prove that he was a Jew in the fullest sense of tradition, became the source of deep conviction, sharp confrontation and strongly voiced attitudes toward men and events.[9] The consequence of this revolt from political reality, which is an attitude that afflicts many philosophers, is an irreconcilable dualism that identifies finite existence with unredeemable perversity. This perversity the individual either first discovers within the self or in the external world because of his inability to comprehend the struggle for meaningful existence within a realm of reasonable alternatives. From this failure arises a world divided between profanity and sacredness. If for the moment religion has the honor of being the sacred it does not maintain, indisputably, this peculiar place. Man soon discovers that the "sacred realm" can be acquired for myths and ideologies. Although Rosenzweig hoped to see in Heidegger the legitimate continuation of Cohen's idea of "correlation" and to see in Cassirer only the "schoolmaster" of the Neo-Kantians, we, from the advantage of later history, know that it was Cassirer who realized the deadly danger of ideological dualisms and sacredness given to myth by those who saw little difference between the various forms of religious commitments.[10] The problem was to establish a world of darkness and a world of light and to maintain the sharpness and uncompromising quality of the separation. The realm of the sacred could find peculiar inhabitants.

With Rosenzweig the quality of the personal decision radiated through the architecture of his work. We are not concerned with a theoretical statement about the decision and its significance. We are given the experience as it was lived in the act of conversion and from this act proceeded a life of faith. Fleischmann stated that "the fact that he repurchased his religion through a difficult and agonizing personal decision distinguishes him from the traditional theologians by giving his thought an 'existential' infrastructure. This concrete personal decision, not the abstract principle of decision as in Heidegger, Jaspers and Sartre and its philosophical justification, is the subject of the *Star of Redemption*. For this reason the nature of the personality and 'salvation' of the individual is the key to the understanding of this difficult book."[11]

In the history of thought the opposition between Goethe and Hegel reflected the confrontation that would be perpetuated by Rosenzweig in his life-long rejection of the work of Hegel. Rosenzweig, in a sketch of his *Star of Redemption*,

Urzelle (1917), mentioned that Goethe discovered in himself the first Christian while Hegel found in himself the last of the philosophers. Hegel had realized the *Imanenzgedanke*, the essence of Paganism,[12] Goethe the idea of personality, the freedom that is the *Imago Dei*, the power that keeps man from the quicksand that is the reality of immanence. In other words we can speak of personality as the source of salvation. In a letter to his friend, Eugen Rosenstock-Huessy, Rosenzweig sounded the clarion call of his inner needs: "we do not want to be philosophers. In so far as we philosophize we want to be *human beings*. Consequently, we must give our philosophizing the form of our humanity."[13] This form belongs to "understanding in time." Bound as we are to time we are even more driven by our need to wrest, from this time, eternity. The *salto mortale* of life is this removing of eternity from the facticity of experience. Man needs to link himself to creation, to revelation and redemption. In fact it is that little and highly significant word "and" that is the clue to "The New Thinking." We search for a truth that is not created by thinking, that is timeless and divorced from our need to verify it in our experience. It is a truth we take from its indifference and abstractness. We need a truth that links us through that little word "and" to that rhythm of eternity, to that cosmic time in which we cling to the eternal calendar of faith in which God, man and creation continually discover their relationship and in which one reality cannot speak without the other, without that "first of experience, the experience of the 'and.' "[14] From the beginning of experience to its end this small word embodies a truth which reveals the reality of human experience. In the "and" the relation is formed in and through which the depths of interdependence begin to show that radical belonging which each reality has for the other. But this is more than a theory that yields the abstractness of form. Here we signify the passion of dependence which is at the core of eternal life. Augustine knew how his soul burned for God, Plato knew that philosophy was the awakening of love that drew man from physical to spiritual life and Rosenzweig knew in Berlin on the Day of Atonement how profound was his need to speak to God. He grasped the power of the word, the thought that spoke through the word through the lyrics of the Psalms, in the poetry of Judah Halevi. From the temporal world from which man must escape there looms forth the conscious effort to wrest moments of eternity, to live this eternity and discover its sacred calendar.

From Hegel's *Rechtsphilosophie* the flight to eternity could be eased by Hegel's bitter and constant enemy: the philosopher Schelling. What did Schelling offer Rosenzweig? Fleischmann stated the dependence clearly indicating that Rosenzweig could now develop Judaism and Christianity within the architecture of cosmic time, "a time whose three dimensions, present, past and future, are considered as the principle of the divine creation, a time lived by the religious man independent of vulgar or historical time. With this discovery Rosenzweig conceived all his problems in the light of the philosopher Schelling: mythology and revelation and, from a new perspective, the relations between Judaism and Christianity."[15] What was significant for Rosenzweig was the emphasis upon the Will, upon subjectivity. The problem was to make the finite Will an integral part of the divine Will, to give it participatory power to evoke the divine Will to cooperate with it in the realization of divinity and humanity. Man can live the divine Will because his finite existence is not separated from it. The belonging of the finite to the infinite is not through the concept, through the logic of negation, but through the emerging force of the Will, the essence of Subjectivity, the depth of the personal and individual attempt to discover its primordial relation and belonging to the divine human discourse. "The finite will, finite freedom," Werner Marx observed, "finds its true essence by relinquishing the connotations implied in such subjectivity and becoming an active collaborator in the play of the realization of divine love. Infinite, divine, absolute freedom thus in turn attains its true essence and proves itself to be of such a nature that it limits its absoluteness on its own, i.e., 'contracts itself,' in order to enable finite freedom to come to play as well."[16] What we emphasize is that in opposition to Hegel, Rosenzweig moved radically in the direction of a Judaism deeply rooted in the creation of his Will. This liberated him from Hegel's profound concern with philosophy as the logic of the concept, as the comprehension of reason in time, i.e., in history. We need little insight to realize why Fessard with his moral and political commitment remained close to Hegel, and Rosenzweig needed Schelling to give the chosen people the form of a cosmic community. The disembodied Judaism was left free to dramatize its sacred circularity to unite its will with God's.

The radical change that Rosenzweig effected was his reversal of time. The Jew begins his existence from his belief in redemption. His will to redemption is his will to eternity. The eternal life of the Jew "perpetually anticipates the end and makes it the beginning. In this reversal he denies, as decidedly as possible, time, and places himself outside of it."[17] These words are laden with a fatality. Time is reduced to profane time. The political and moral values that are embodied in it have no validity. The realm of daily human life is reduced to meaninglessness whereas in the sacred the power and awe that flow from the vision of redemption transfigures man and allows him to live in bondage to the Will that is the ground of divine collaboration. Far now from the struggle of the nations, their ideologies and myths is this community that lives its sacred calling to be God's precious people. Now interpreted as isolation and radical separation, Judaism no longer lives in the nations, but above them. The temporal history which men live as citizens of time is reversed in the sacred calendar of Israel where the Messianic Age gives meaning to creation and revelation which the Jew lives in his eternal discourse with the holy cycle of life. Rosenzweig no longer wanted to speak *about* Judaism, there are no polemics with Christianity and Islam or any other faith, no attempt to prove one faith superior to another. Rosenzweig was to speak *from within* the sacred community. He wanted to speak its sacred discourse, its prayers and the language of its holy drama. He spoke the theogonic language of the finite Will participating in its infinite source. In this respect Fessard's conception of Israel's mystery was also spoken of from within the truth of the Church, the mystery of the communion of all those who are saved through His grace. From the eternity of divinity these two faiths are mysteries of communion, but their relation to each other is at the core of their differences of the value they project on each other.

With Schelling as his ally Rosenzweig hoped to overcome the truth of Hegel's system. Fleischmann stated that it was "characteristic of Hegel that history becomes global knowledge. It is the absolute measure of each existent being in time, but since religious man does not exist in time, but against time, he has no need of knowledge in order to have an objective time. For him it is uniquely religious, cosmic time, which counts. Religious time is not personal and subjective because it is the lived experience of a religious community."[18] This reversal of time is so radical that there is no longer any tension between future and past. Israel has achieved a peculiar and unique particularity that is so exclusive that we can speak of Israel's participation and revelation of the life process that is eternally taking place within divinity. Israel lives its eschatological life in the election of the people to the divine *telos*. Ethics becomes submerged in eschatology and loses its vitality as the struggle for societal and national life. The Idea of Humanity is reduced to an intellectual construct whose significance is important only for those who still cling to the values of political and moral life. Rosenzweig knew that from the perspective of the historical and the political, Hegel's attempt to comprehend the nature of a philosophy of philosophy was irrefutable. Man, dwelling in his finiteness, cannot avoid seeking purpose and meaning for his history. The truth of Hegel's comprehension of history is the source of Rosenzweig's attempt to surpass it. Whether or not this surpassing of history belongs to a leap into the life of divinity is disputable. History never eliminates human freedom and never subordinates man's freedom to think and believe; it never surpasses either philosophy or religion. Leaping from the human to the divine, from the temporal to the non-temporal, from history to meta-history leaves man torn between two irreconcilable destinies which do not satisfy the peculiarity of his being. Man is neither one nor the other as man. The either/or man relinquishes his humanity. Man, as an exclusive finite being, loses the truth of his supersensible reality; man, as a moment of divinity, denies his ethical and political responsibility to creative communal life. The question is not one of either/or but of tension, of freedom and the negation that is at its core: the refusal to be absorbed into either world, to be a pawn of their absolute exclusiveness.

In his "Spirit and Epochs of Jewish History" Rosenzweig exclaimed the powerful, painful and shocking words: "We are eternal."[19] For Israel the course of history with the use and fall of nations is of no importance. It's temporal reality has no power over us. We never grew old because we were never young like the other peoples. Their political struggles, their internal histories have nothing to do with a people that lives in and through prayer. The holy community of Israel is redeemed in its monastic isolation dreaming and poeticizing its intimacy with God. Hopefully it prays that the world forget its existence because it has now little to give to a world that it knows is under the domination of history and politics, war and aggression. In his sacred isolation the Jew has remained persistently opposed to war. Fleischmann's observations on this point are pertinent. "Since Jewish life exists in the calm of eternity it has absolutely no relationship with the historical phenomenon of war. Contrary to Christianity that has introduced the ideas of 'Holy Wars,' 'Crusades,' the 'Champions of God,' etc. into universal history, the Jew is the only person who does not deal seriously with the fact of war and thus is the sole pacifist."[20] Israel lives the "Kingdom of Heaven." In this kingdom war is no longer present. The violence that afflicts man's national and international life finds the repudiation in Israel's sacred community. Israel lives humanity by placing before it the embodiment of eternal peace. It speaks out against the rule of nations; it is the sacred voice raised against Hegel's philosophy of law. The philosophical need to comprehend man's political and moral reality is superseded by man's ceaseless longing to find eternity.[21] Wherever we follow Rosenzweig's thought we discover that it transcends reason and comprehension. A way of life has been transfigured by a faith and a sacred history in which the discourse of reason has become the discourse of redemption. It is a clear defiance and confrontation with every thinking perspective that attempts to comprehend finite reality and give it significance. Whether the Judaism that Rosenzweig imagines is valid is of no importance because it is a faith that embodies eternally what the world cannot comprehend because it is its radical other. Franz Rosenzweig poetically created his Judaism from his personal experiences and his realization that Hegel was the philosopher of a world he could not live. The consequences of the radical separation of Israel's non-temporality from temporal reality leaves the world in its perversity condemned to a circularity that perpetuates the state and its search for power and survival. Whether this separability does violence to political reality was of little concern to Rosenzweig. He needed a dualism to validate his conception of Judaism and he forged it through a dogmatic misconception of Hegel. From another point of view, that of Hermann Cohen, Judaism emerged with a deeper relationship to the world. In fact, Cohen believed that the ethical dimension spoke the word of God. Rosenzweig's relation with Cohen was uncertain. Cohen's systematic approach to philosophy was unpalatable to Rosenzweig. If we think of the activity and work of Fessard we might imagine that he would have found Rosenzweig's attempt to elucidate Israel's mystery attractive as a divine aesthetics, but he would have found in Cohen's courageous and serious refutation of myth, ideology, racism, pessimism, the true expression of Israel's confrontation with paganism: the veritable struggle of all ages.

What we seek to understand in Cohen is how Judaism becomes part of the world, how it injects its faith in God's uniqueness into a world of becoming and attempts to condition man's finiteness in such a way that God's uniqueness is neither compromised nor weakened. The uncompromising oneness of God makes it impossible to conceive of the deification of the finite. Thus historical world stands before the judgment of God's commandment, the moral law, the Idea of Humanity. The commandment denies human action and thought and the possibility of becoming absolute, but, at the same time, it gives it the possibility to become moral. Man's relation to God and to his fellowman has not yet begun to be moral and religious. In fact, if we accept that the Idea of mankind has only just begun to impregnate world history, then we can understand our efforts as the moral task of our collective life. This collective life must grow to the task, but the task only remains infinite in its obligation and demand. Man and mankind's striving for the Idea is its eternal history. There can be only approximation and anticipation in moral action. In fact, moral and religious life belong to the realities of approximation and anticipation, to those infinitesimally small changes which bear within themselves vast consequential effects. This struggle for the realization of the Idea became for Cohen the profound confrontation with the idolatry of finiteness. The "should be" remained the fundamental command to the "is" and denied it the right to assume for itself absolute reality. Its reality belongs to the future, to the *yet to be,* to the moral idea which commands man in freedom and love.

Cohen's later philosophy belonged to two books: *Der Begriff der Religion im System der Philosophie* (1915), and, *Religion der Vernunft aus den Quellen des Judentums* (1919). Both books were published when Cohen had already left Marburg in 1912 and resided in Berlin. There he died in 1918. Both books attempt to find the uniqueness of Judaism in relation to philosophy conceived systematically as logic, ethics and aesthetics. The discovery of man as fellowman was a central problem in ethics as well as in religion. In the discovery of man as fellowman we find our relationship to God. The problem is both abstract and concrete but in it we comprehend the meaning of Judaism as a faith in which reason plays a vital and central role. Reason cannot be put aside by faith unless we return again to a dualism which radicalizes the difference between the sensible and the supersensible. With the reason that controls ethics and with faith in the goodness of God's creation, Cohen moved to a characterization of man's relationship to man and God. He stated that the "correlation of man and God cannot be actualized if the correlation of man and man is not first included. The correlation of man and God is in the first place that of man, as fellowman, to God. . . . Since the share of religion in reason consists in its share in morality, if ethics is impossible religion also becomes untenable for then the correlation disintegrates: man then is no longer fellowman, the link in the correlation with God. . . ."[22] These remarks by Cohen set forth a path that is fundamental for his conception of Judaism as the embodiment of ethics but at the same time standing before its God and experiencing in Him, through covenant, His commandment. They experience their election, their historical purpose in the world, the hope for messianic redemption, but, above all, their struggle against the "idols" of paganism. The "idols" are physical and spiritual, i.e., wherever man's search for reality is deified, then Israel is threatened and the ethical relationship between man and man is blunted and destroyed. Man denies the humanity of man and the concept of man as fellowman. In this loss he turns away from God, whose spirit is in every man, from man as fellowman. Man is returned to a form of instrumentality, to a technical status in which fellowship has little meaning.

In correlation man, however, discovers the infinity of the moral task and the infinity of the future where this task is never completed.

What we realize in this discovery of man as fellowman is that this act does not depend upon our subjective feeling or decision but upon a *fact:* God's creation of man. This is a *fact* of reason from which we can comprehend the nature of responsibility and commitment. Through this *fact* we are committed to the universality of reason and not simply to the arbitrariness of the personal will. The moral history of man begins with this *fact.* The struggle of man to rise to a comprehension of this *fact* depends upon his moral education. The moral education of mankind depends upon the concept of the fellowman. At the very core of monotheism lies this belief in God's creation of man. It stands before man as a Commandment that demands of him a moral attitude and respect which he knows he is incapable of bringing forth from himself. Religion demands of him the commitment of his will. Different from morality which is always a theoretical or customary problem, religion can speak directly to his faith and can speak categorically. Monotheistic religion speaks against polytheism, against idolatry and against the identity of Being and becoming. In speaking about correlation between man and man religion speaks for social justice and political freedom. The respect for the dignity and humanity of man becomes the demand of a serious political and legal philosophy. It is idolatrous to deify a man or a class, to create heroes, worship myths and become enslaved to fatalistic doctrines of life and history. Cohen remarked that "out of the unique God, the creator of man, originated also the stranger as fellowman."[23] In our respect toward the stranger we force apart the chains of atavism, we open our perspectives to the being of our fellowman and not necessarily to our neighbor. When we go beyond our neighbor to the stranger we begin to comprehend what it means to realize the Idea of Humanity. The love which we must arouse in ourselves toward the Idea cracks the insulating walls of our societal isolation and forces us to the universality which belongs to the Idea. Cohen often remarked how dearly he loved "the Idea." He believed that his faith in Israel opened to man the Idea, because for him Israel's election was a universal mission for the realization of the Idea of a moral law.

The social justice embodied in the moral law is clarified when we know that "the 'next man' (*Nebenmensch*), becomes unavoidably the 'opposing man' (*Gegenmensch*), for the social differentiation does not appear to be organized according to rank and order of coexistence, but according to subordination and subjugation. It is in opposition to this that the problem of the fellowman has to arise.''[24] The question of subordination and subjugation reflects the master-slave relationship, the division of rich and poor that evolves from it. From the consequences of this natural subordination arises the problem of the fellowman. The natural relationship has to be overcome, although it is never eliminated. The belief that there is a correlation between God and man and man and God makes it necessary to think in terms of political and social reality. The correlation that Cohen developed in his book on the concept of religion in the system of philosophy became the fundamental concept of his religion of reason. In correlation the theoretical and practical consideration of man's social politics became intimately related. The fellowman that is born in man's relation to man is primordially created in God's relation to man. What remains unknown in man's relation to God is not unknown in man's relation to man. There the respect that is owed to the spirit that lives in every man and gives him the dignity of his being is not dependent upon the arbitrariness of our will, but is commanded by our moral reason, by the divine presence whose immediacy is moral command. The very presence of God is synonymous with the universality of the moral command. The fellowman is the creation of God's will. His presence in man removes all arbitrariness from our relation to our fellowman. In God's presence the fellowman *is*. In it is the demand that we create a political reality that makes it possible for every man to realize the divine spirit that dwells within him. The wellbeing or suffering of our fellow being is the source of our concern and responsibility. We are not indifferent to what happens about us, to the misfortune to which man succumbs. Man's misfortune is the revelation of his finiteness and dependence.

Cohen, who could never separate religion from ethics, although he knew that the faith that they required was different but complementary, allowed ethics to speak religiously and religion to speak ethically. His Judaism belonged to the education of humanity and its intimate connection with the universality of reason. It spoke of Ideas and Ideals to a mankind that had only just begun to be ethical and religious, whose struggle with Ideas was only touched by the beginning of spirituality. Man's spirituality is not only related to his intellectual development, but also to his moral development. In this development the problem of human suffering is fundamental. Cohen's remarks were deeply characteristic of his devotion to ethical life. He wrote: ''The metaphysics of suffering, which considers suffering as the fate of mankind or even more ambiguously, as the fate of all living creatures, does not belong to an earnest religion; its earnestness has nothing to do with the play of poetry and art. Suffering only reaches ethical precision as social suffering. Whoever explains *poverty* as the suffering of mankind, creates ethics, or if not philosophical ethics, yet still religion with its share of reason. Only the religion of reason is moral religion, and only moral religion is truthful and true religion.''[25]

We are far from Franz Rosenzweig but close to Gaston Fessard. Cohen, who believed in an earnest religion, in a precious and close relationship between God's Word and man's action, between God's moral reality and man's moral law, would have found it strange to have reduced Israel to the timelessness of the social community. Cohen could not develop a personal theology because he never ceased loving the Idea. His thought and action stood before the law of command and the social suffering of mankind became the source of the socialism with which he identified his responsibility to mankind. "Moral religion" meant religion in the service of suffering mankind, a religion that had its eschatology in world peace and justice but whose historical reality was only hinted at by the level of man's moral development. "Moral religion" was social politics, the rule of law, the dignity of man, but its development only put further stress upon the individual who took his moral task seriously and did not fear its infinite approximation to the Ideal. Clearly and distinctly Cohen could say that man's correlation with God "is built only upon the basis of this social relationship."[26]

We have so easily thought of man's relation to God in personal terms that we quickly forgot that the relationship is also social. Beyond our personal needs and sufferings is our fellowman, our society, our nation and the world. We wonder at the life of the religious man who has given so much of his faith and courage for the values that belong to social politics. Fessard's struggle against Hitlerism and Marxism belonged to that firm and resolute faith in man's freedom and in truth of God's creation, revelation and redemption. Cohen belonged to that generation of men for whom reason remained the universal command and whose personal decisions flowed from that universality. In his further remarks on suffering, Cohen said that "it fills the entire human consciousness and helps to determine all its other proceedings and activities. Therefore, its objectivation should not be permitted to be erased: the suffering of poverty must always remain the problem: the religious problem, but not the metaphysical one."[27] Suffering is not a metaphysical problem because it must not cover man with a fatalism that determines the nature of man and transforms this nature into a law. The omnipotence of such fatalism and such a law would degrade the ethical responsibility of man. Fatalism would reduce human action to a predetermined consequence and would remove man's decision from the realm of responsibility and give it over to that of necessity. Suffering is a religious and moral problem because man believes his will to be free and that God's Will is not necessarily opposed to his. Man's freedom reduces good and evil to human decision and effort. They are not the architecture of man's moral life; they are the possibilities of his moral dignity or degradation. Man knows that suffering is physical and spiritual pain. In the smallest social and personal way man can struggle against pain. His attempt to alleviate pain is his religious and moral obligation. If moral, it is personal, if religious, the personal proceeds from God's command.

Pain is political and affects man spiritually and physically. The struggle against totalitarianism is against the pain that is brought to mankind through the loss of freedom and truth. When the social fabric of society suffers, mankind suffers with it. Where social suffering is the reality there the social consciousness of every human being is pained. Cohen remarked: "*Only social suffering is spiritual suffering.* All the complexity of consciousness, including knowledge is effected by it and brought to take part in it. This is the profound meaning of social suffering: that the entire consciousness of culture is implicated in it."[28] Nothing seemed to have affected Cohen more deeply than man's moral and religious growth which he associated with infinite development. Nothing touched his faith more seriously than the fact that social suffering was at the base of true moral religion. The religious act was intimately bound to our consciousness of social and individual pain, to the action that followed from this consciousness and the awareness that our action was both personal and social. The social consciousness of suffering lay at the very core of the religious unity of mankind. The fight against pain was our homage to God and our fellowman. We fight to alleviate the suffering and pain that fills His world. Where and when men suffer we are forced to fight against it, because God created man and he created in us the spirit of holiness, the awareness of moral responsibility. Cohen beautifully stated this truth: "For even if I had no heart in my body, my education alone would have brought me to the insight that the great majority of men cannot be isolated from me, and that I myself am nothing if I do not make myself a part of them . . . a relationship arises that means more than merely coordination or even subordination, but which produces a community. And the community produces the fellowman."[29] In community we find our fellowman because here we overcome the natural condition of the slave-master relation. This overcoming means that social consciousness has become moral awareness and this awareness is the beginning of our desire and responsibility to alleviate the suffering and pain that is prevalent where man's natural condition of subordination and subjugation remains. Cohen knew the scars and pain that permeated a society that remained plagued with racism, atavism and mythical nationalism. Against these he raised the commands of universal reason, the Idea of Mankind and the Moral Law. He remained faithful to his mentor, F. A. Lange, and his philosophical heritage that brought him into intimate contact with the overwhelming influence of Plato and Kant, Schiller and Goethe, Mozart and Rembrandt. This tradition of universality created for Cohen a spiritual community, but this community was not enough; he needed a moral and religious community in and through which he could comprehend man's correlation with man and the responsibilities which flowed from it.

Cohen knew that religion belonged more to man's responsibility toward his fellowman, to the discovery of the significance of that concept, than it did to man's relation to God. He knew that suffering is social suffering and that "an individual ground for suffering has to be eliminated" because he believed that it could only hinder our obligation to community. This obligation transcends our subjective decision and feeling. Again and again Cohen indicated the need to think and act from universality, from the abstractness of the Idea, from God as Idea, and from the realization that the individual act must be rooted in the universal as the sensible is rooted in the supersensible. Cohen referred repeatedly to the fact that relgion discovers the fellowman in social suffering, that individual suffering is truly "the social state of distress of the human race." Man's response to suffering must also be social. Not individual pity which reduces pity to arbitrariness, but pity in response to the social problem of suffering. Here pity becomes the moral reaction not simply of the individual, but of the feeling in which the individual assumes universal responsibility. Pity raises the individual to universality because it mediates between the personal feelings of the individual and the universal quality of the moral nature of mankind. "Pity," Cohen would say, "is the messenger of the will, therefore of the thing-in-itself. And this thing-in-itself means the identity of all that appears as man."[30] For Cohen the force of Judaism was its profound comprehension of human relations. Religion, and in particular Judaism, heightens our awareness of the striving for holiness that man accepts when he declares God to be holy. In the infinity of this striving for holiness, for correlation to God, in the intimate relationship between holiness and moral action, in "eternal moral becoming" which is man's earthly destiny, man discovered what it means to speak of the holy spirit within him and his responsibility to it. To these fundamental problems of moral becoming and the holiness of the spirit man finds his way through his religious commitment. From Cohen's perspective, Israel embodied the way which found correlation to God. This is Israel's chosen and purported role in God's scheme of history.

When Cohen turned to historical examples concerning the reality of pity and the fellowman, he observed that Socrates had "no sense for the problem of poverty . . . Socrates' teaching is preserved through his assertion of the preeminence of the intellect. This assertion is his contribution to ethics. Virtue is knowledge. But the poor man too can have knowledge. Can he actually? Socrates does not ask this question."[31] The prophet has another problem; he needs to know how the fellowman emerges from pity for the poor man. Cohen's insistence that in pity we discover the fellowman means that pity has become the ethical factor in the education of man from his natural condition of slave-master to the human and moral condition in which man becomes fellowman. We can ask if man is man before he becomes fellowman, before he becomes aware of his responsibility to the poor man, before social injustice becomes a factor of his moral consciousness? The movement of natural man to moral man is the infinite task of ethics, but it is also the task of religion which affirms the belief that God's spirit dwells in every man. Man's consciousness of human suffering and poverty must be able to to awaken in man the feeling of pity. The problem of human suffering does not belong to mythologies which explain this suffering as the consequence of historical necessity or the tragic interplay of fatalistic forces. In Israel, Cohen said, there was an absence of tragedy. "Suffering," he remarked, "is to be resolved in reality and not merely in the illusory feeling of the spectator. The prophet becomes the practical moralist, the politician and jurist, because he intends to end the suffering of the poor."[32] The problem of suffering, Cohen rightly stated, belongs to reality, to man's discovery of pity for his fellowman and for mankind. The resolutions of problems of social injustice demand both economic and moral insight. When the moral insight is lacking, where we find that the moral consciousness remains undeveloped and ignored, we know that the economic or political solutions are inadequate. They arise from abstract social theories, philosophies of history, myths of master races or destinies of social classes. The mediating power of pity as the motor power of social and moral consciousness elevates man to fellowman, to the moral being in whom the Idea of Humanity begins to have significance both for the intellect and the will. Cohen's Judaism was the realization of the *Kingdom of God* on earth. For him this meant the realization of the unity of mankind, of God's goodness and holiness. His goodness is man's forgiveness from sin, his holiness is his incomparable uniqueness. Mankind belongs to the future; it has no past nor present. In the future, when God's name shall be one, mankind will assume its unity, its form shall be one. Judaism was for Cohen this belief in the future oneness of mankind that was deeply dependent on the realization of God's unique oneness.

These two concepts of Judaism give some understanding of how Judaism has been conceived by its recent philosophers. Fessard's conception of the Pagan-Jew dialectic gave Israel the vital role in God's plan for redemption. It was a role that assumed the universality of the Church as the full realization of Israel's place in human and divine history. The struggle against Paganism was also fundamental for both Rosenzweig and Cohen. In Rosenzweig, Paganism was identified with Hegelian philosophy, with nationalism and the reason of state. Cohen fought Paganism in racism, atavism and fatalism. He struggled against the past and the present for a new vision of the future, for a universality that belonged to the unity of mankind and unity of the divine name. Fessard came to the profound realization that between Judaism and Christianity there could no longer be divisions and useless polemics advocating the superiority of the one over the other. The struggle for freedom and truth forced these two faiths that had the same divine source to express the truth of their unity. Their common struggle against the Paganism that remained in them and which belonged to a world that sought its own deification, its compromises with demonic forces, continuously denied the truth of man's freedom. If we remain with some comprehension of Fessard's philosophical and theological commitment, we then know that the faiths of Judaism and Christianity have a common purpose. We have just begun to fight the physical and spiritual Paganism that affects us individually and perverts us as mankind. The struggle belongs to both faiths. Neither is possible without the other. The truth of the universal Church is Israel's election. The truth of Israel is in her inseparability from the Church's struggle against Paganism. How we form our idea of Israel or Christianity makes it impossible for us to avoid the power of Paganism. If we have only just begun to be religious as Cohen knew, it is because we have only now begun the struggle against the perversity in and outside of us. We know that Israel belongs to sacred history. We know that the Church is an integral part of this same sacred history. Where one is endangered, the other is threatened. The sacred fellowship and community is the true realization of their divine purpose. Fessard has made the reality of this community and purpose meaningful. We must meditate upon it.

12

Shame, Repentance, Ressentiment: The Foundations of Morality

Hermann Cohen spoke persistently of the refusal of monotheism to compromise with pagan imagery. "It is significant," he remarked, "that the scorn of the prophets and the psalms for pagan images is expressed through the idea that the idol worshiper will be ashamed. One misrepresents the though by translating it: 'They shall be confounded.' The Hebrew word means the inner shame that overcomes a man. The shame is the symptom of truthfulness that will arise in the pagan worshiper."[1] The word shame, inner shame, is intimately connected with truthfulness, with a love of God free from eroticism, a purity of longing which "is never beset by an enticement that would mar its chastity and invalidate its innocence."[2] Shame emerges in compromise with truthfulness, with the truth upon which it is based, upon God who is the source of truth. Truthfulness belongs to man; it necessitates his humility before God and the moderation which is fundamental to his relationship with his fellowman. In moderation man finds what is deeply human in his attitude toward knowledge, morality and beauty. Moderation becomes the highest expression of man's humanity, a feeling of limitation but also of dignity and distinctness. In moderation man finds the path to what is comprehensible in his attitudes and actions. Moderation is the foundation of the moral and political order.

Shame and idolatry belong to each other in such a way that when shame arises in the idolator, image worship declines. Cohen knew that the test of a civilization depended upon the shame which was evoked toward both the makers and worshipers of idolatry. He quoted with profound sincerity of belief the psalmist: "Ashamed be all they that serve graven images that boast of idols" (Ps. 97:7). "They that make them [images] are like unto them; yea everyone that trusteth in them."[3] Where shame is comprehended as the foundation of man's relation to truthfulness and truth we are at the beginnings of a morality that understands man and his relation to truthfulness as the primordial structure, as the Archê, of moral life. In this structure shame comes forth as the realization of truthfulness. In shame man grasps the meaning of truthfulness and he knows the perversity that belongs to the images and myths of idolatry. In them the truth of God is reduced to image and myth. In this reduction truth is no longer transcendent. In its immanence it established that identification between nature and truth, the pantheism in which the radical otherness of God's uniqueness is eradicated. Man now believes that it is possible to affirm the identity between being and thinking. From this identification philosophy emerges into a new form of idolatry.

The struggle of Jew and Idolator became a symbolic and sign language in Fessard's attempt to form the natural and historical categories of a philosophy and theology of history. The conflicts of master-slave, male-female and Jew-Pagan are structured through the use of categories to comprehend the relationship between secular and divine history. The comprehension goes beyond history into the realm of values and it is in this realm that we discover the significance of shame, repentance and ressentiment as the primordial conditions of a human morality that determines not only man's relation to his fellowman, but also his relation to God. Within the structure of human relationships the three forms of dialectical oppositions reveal the various categories which determine human values. The category can be explained from an Aristotelian, Kantian and Hegelian perspective. From Aristotle's perspective these oppositions are the predicates which determine every historical subject. The predication of these historical and natural categories give rise to a meaning of history which makes it possible to comprehend these oppositions as *a priori*. If they are assumed to be *a priori* then they are attitudes whose categorical forms permit us to subsume the course of history within their conceptual forms. "It is for this reason that the author [Fessard] believes that through a more and more condensed analysis he reveals, in every problem derived from history -- the objection of conscience, Christian neutralism or Communist-Catholic dialogue -- the dialectic interplay of Pagan and Jew which is the source and unity of the other two."[4] In the Hegelian sense Pagan and Jew "designate the conditions of the identity of knowledge and the object of knowledge; only the unity of being and thought of the I and God to which the categories lead remain always conditioned by Christian faith, hope and charity and not by Hegelian *Vernunft*."[5] However we consider the categories they are the constituent possibilities of an intelligible grasp of history. These particular oppositions and thus these categorical forms depend upon the faith and commitment we have to values which we believe are fundamental to a comprehension of history and to the meaning of our civilization. The

categorical forms which develop from our attitudes toward values, toward freedom and truth determine the nature and quality of the rational discourse and
community we develop and to which we give our loyalty. These categories are
subject to discourse, i.e., to expansion and reformulation, in essence they deny
absolute value. There is no absolute category which is not in itself determined
through discourse. The categories are subject to persistent mediation and inspi-
ration. They remain bound to our faith in transcendence whose uniqueness denies all identification between knowledge and the object of knowledge.

From this comprehension of the categorical forms of Fessard's thought and
of the unique value which he gave to the Pagan-Jew oppositions, we now seek to
know the significance of this opposition from the perspective of human values.
The oppositions have significance only if they embody conflicting and contradictory value systems. Cohen had spoken of the shame that accompanies idolatry because he believed that truthfulness was the fundament of human values.
Truthfulness is the unceasing search for truth which man knows is always accompanied by ignorance and error. Truthfulness, therefore, demands the right of
repentance. In repentance and confession Cohen had seen "the first step toward
action, which in turn proceeds in two steps: in the casting away and in the new
creation."[6] For Cohen the "new heart" and the "new spirit" remained man's
eternal ethical task. Like Maimonides before him, Cohen knew that the "new
heart" and "new spirit" made the I the infinite task. The I must be able to ask
for repentance because, as Maimonides observed,

> if the individual believed that this fracture (the expression of an opin-
> ion or moral quality that is not preferable in truth) can never be reme-
> died, he would persist in his error and sometimes perhaps disobey even
> more because of the fact that no stratagems remain at his disposal. If,
> however, he believes in repentance, he can correct himself and return to
> a better and more perfect state than the one he was in before he
> sinned.[7]

As we move from the dialectical plane of Pagan and Jew to the values that are
embodied in this infinite conflict, we grasp the great conflict of values that are
embodied in this primordial opposition and we see that in the work of Hermann
Cohen the struggle is again resumed with a powerful thrust that went lost not
only in post war Germany, but in Western thought. Man sought out his misery
and chaos and made them the object of his reflections. We read the works of

Musil, Karl Kraus, Broch, Kafka and we found ourselves in a world where human qualities have become chaotic and perverse. Little interest could be developed for Cohenian values where slowly, but surely, the mysteries of Heideggerian philosophy turned the fascination of men away from the political and the ethical realities of life, toward those more arcane searchings into the fragments of pre-Socratic philosophy to hear the voice of those sources which we would later understand as the "true" tradition of philosophy.

Fessard recognized that the conflict of Pagan and Jew was the primordial struggle between that infinite ethical task laid before man by his own conscious awareness and the infinite solution which in God was man's most powerful challenge. Man's task is infinite, the future draws within itself the past and the present. Cohen remarked with profound insight that "all existence sinks into insignificance in the presence of the point of view of this idea [of future], and man's existence is preserved and elevated into this being of the future. Thus, the thought of *history* comes into being for human life and the life of the people."8 The struggle of Jew and Pagan is infinite. The divine task is given with an infinite solution. At this point the Jew moves in his peculiar arena for his struggle with the Pagan, while Christianity takes the Jew into itself and gives itself a similar struggle, played with different symbols and stage settings.

Fessard saw within the struggle of Jew-Pagan man's consciousness of sin, the inclination to worship at the altar of idolatry, but also the shame which comes forth in man when he sees the perversity of his nature, the corruption that overtakes his fellowman. He knows the shame that pains him in the sight of man's intolerance, the fantasies of atavism and the morbid pessimism that conditions his attitude toward life. He feels shame when human life is reduced to fate, when individual freedom is dominated by cyclical theories of history in which human action becomes meaningless and wasteful. In shame before the various forces of idolatry man preserves the dignity of his humanity and the sense of human goodness. Where we are left with the nobility of our individual and independent efforts, there we preserve that joy and cheerfulness toward life which makes us know that it has purpose and is worth living. In shame before the idols we find the goodness of human life.

Fessard was rightly convinced that shame, *vergüenza, pudeur,* was the necessary and sufficient foundation of moral life. This recognition he found in his beloved Ignatius and confirmed in the philosopher Max Scheler. Fessard in his continuous commentary to the *Exercises* of Loyola related to them every philosophical position which he discovered in philosophy from Maine de Biran to

Hegel and Blondel. In particular, Fessard was deeply attached to a philosophy that probed deeply for the truth, and in its moral courage symbolized that beauty that is inseparable from morality. He spoke of these philosophical characteristics at the end of his book on Maine de Biran:

> Also for the philosopher the model is the saint whose life is both rigor-
> ous truth and harmonious beauty. Like the saint who is never disturbed
> in his inclination toward the good through the recurrence of continued
> sacrifice, the philosopher does not have deeper confidence in the true
> because of the perpetual denial of doubt. If the thought of the latter
> only develops through antinomies, the will of the other is conquered
> only through temptations. Fundamentally, the same ideal of Sovereign
> Freedom fascinates them creating here and there the eternal conflict
> between what is and what must be.[9]

Where the ideal remains truth and freedom and where morality conditions attitudes toward knowledge and beauty, there the condition of shame dominates and controls our feeling toward every compromise with this ideal. Shame is the history of mankind when this ideal loses its significance and nobility. The man of shame walks among his fellowman when they no longer live with truth and freedom.

Exploring the emotional reaction which we call shame, Fessard observed that this emotive reality "characterizes humanity, at its highest, in its historical existence and refers in the more immediate way, peculiarly, to such existence. Neither the pure spirit, angel or god, nor the simple animal, beast or child experiences such a feeling."[10] What we discover with this unique feeling is the depth of an effect that awakens us to that inner space which we characterize as the dwelling of the moral sense. This is not something we create through habit but a *given,* a *fact* which we discover, explore and examine. It is the source of that peculiar truthfulness that is bound to what we know, enhances human dignity and revolts at its distortion and perversion. The shame which emerges from perversion reveals the indelible sense of humanity which is natural to us as beings, not only endowed with reason, but with the moral sense. We approach with a sense of terror that paganism which destroys this sense. We comprehend paganism on various levels in political or religious oppression, in tyrannies and despotisms. We now begin to grasp it in even more sophisticated psychological forms where man himself is changed morally by the apparatus of the state and where the sense of shame has been relegated to a primitive form of human existence.[11]

Faced with new and radical forms of paganism which make the old idolatry seem mild, we realize how deeply the sense of shame and the repentance which belongs to it remain the fundament of the human condition that is still anchored to the moral, to conscience and to a fearsome opposition to sin. We know that this human condition can be radically changed, that the "inner space" which we believe harbors the moral sentiment can be snuffed out and reduced to a relic. We fight with greater anxiety for that moral consciousness which we realize is the precious gift easily eliminated by the new totalitarianisms. Fessard reminded us that "the importance of such an awareness is not momentary. In fact, it is because the feeling of shame shows man the cleavage between the essence of *his nature* and *his historical existence* in which it [historical existence] is not what it should be since man can envision the proclamation of laws attempting to re-establish the harmony, or at least prevent the disequilibrium and the fostering of the most distressing consequences."[12] Where shame and repentance play the fundamental role in the awareness of our moral responsibility, there man's commitment to freedom and truth remains possible. Where man believes that this commitment is not only an individual and personal one, but the foundation of the human community, there again man has forged barriers against the tides of paganism which reduce him to moral indifference and thus, to bestiality. What Fessard has designated as the conflict of Jew and Pagan has become the struggle for man's moral autonomy, the independence which must be allotted to every individual who knows that his moral self is found in his responsibility to his fellowman.

In this responsibility man finds that his autonomy is truly a heteronomy, that the possibility of divine love emerges from his love of his fellowman in and from whose life there comes forth man's realization of his theocentricity. This theocentricism is immanent in man's relationship to man, in the preciousness of life and in his commitment to its dignity. The theocentricism is man's action, in his active and courageous commitment to freedom and truth. The realization that the natural and supernatural orders belong to each through action is a truth which we comprehend more precisely when we come to terms with the fact that our moral speculations have political consequence, and we are required to struggle with and for them in the individual and communal realm. We are reminded of the decisive words of Maurice Blondel: "What one cannot know nor, above all, understand distinctly, one can always do and practice: that is the use, the eminent reason of action. . . . Its meditation is permanent: it is a perpetual means of internal conversion."[13]

The great value of Fessard's discussion comes from the knowledge that his theoretical formulations belong to political events and his speculations bore that peculiar responsibility which is accompanied by a loyalty to freedom and, in essence, was "a loyalty to loyalty" that defied indifference to public action. This Roycean notion had deep ramifications in Fessard's thought because his discussions carried with them the undeniable obligation of community responsibility.

In the first lines of his study of shame and the feeling of shame, Max Scheler stated "that the *peculiar place and position of man in the hierarchy of world essences,* his position between the divinity and animality, came forth in no other feeling so clearly, sharply and immediately as in the feeling of *shame.*"[14] If we accept this assumption and we affirm that shame is the "root and germ of all morality," *Wurzel und Keimpunkt aller Moral,* then our problem is not only to understand it as a moral *fact,* but to grasp its place within the dialectic of Jew and Pagan. If shame establishes the sense of humanity between individuals, if it is rooted in the depths of sexuality, touching the most sensitive nature of human intercourse, it also reveals the distortion and perversions which inhabit the same intercourse. In shame we discover love, in shame we find moral consciousness, in shame the individual is aware of a dignity that emerges from the limitations placed upon his emotion and sentiment.

Fessard remarked that according to Scheler, shame, *pudeur,* related to the sexual instinct in two ways. Negatively, shame, inhibited and refrained the the libidinal drives. Positively, it brought forth sexual sympathy. "Indeed," Fessard said, "from the fact that shame prohibits tendencies to self satisfaction it concentrates energy within the individual and in this way 'elevates and preserves the unity of life' against the fickleness and irresoluteness of sensuality which 'tends to crush it into a powder of sensations.'"[15] In the struggle against sensuality shame holds man from the immediacy of gratification, it draws him from the present to the future. Man is confronted with the fear and anxiety that the present can be its unchanged human condition and from this condition man is given his nature, the prison from which there is no escape, a fate which even the gods cannot reverse. Into this present man walks with a fearfulness which not only permeates his being but determines its limitations. Shame before the idolatry of the present is man's deepest moral outcry, the call of a love that knows that there is a future which forces open the fateful nature of the present and reduces it to a moment in the elevation of spiritual life over the idolatry which embodies the identification of man and destiny.

Against this idolatry whose consequence is a radical metamorphosis of human nature, Cohen spoke the words of prophetic faith. "Messianism," he said, "degrades and despises and destroys the present actuality, in order to put in the place of this sensible actuality a new kind of supersensible actuality, not supernatural, but of the future. The future creates a new earth and a new heaven and consequently, a new actuality."16 Shame before the gods of the present, before the arbitrariness and indifference of our moral and societal life, makes it possible to comprehend human nature in its inadequacy and incompleteness. In these conditions we discover the need to believe in the future, to hope that we hear within ourselves that moral conscience which will allow us to continue the struggle against that sensuality which drives us toward bestiality.

Shame gives man his distant place in the universe. In shame "spirit and flesh, temporality and eternity, essence and existence allude to each other in a striking and mysterious manner." Scheler continues these remarks, showing how

> man deeply feels and knows himself as a "budge," as a "transition" between two orders of being and essence in which he finds himself rooted and can sacrifice, not even for a second, one or the other and yet call himself a "man." No being who lives beyond this budge and transition can possess this feeling: No God and no animal is able to be ashamed. But man must, and not from this or that "reason" -- but as this transition itself be conceived as continuous movement. Man is ashamed in himself and "before" the God in him.17

With these thoughts Scheler awakens us to that painful, but unavoidable conflict between spirit and flesh, between the demands of sensuality and the expression of reason, between our imprisonment in temporality and our search for eternity, our capacity to oppose the future to the present. In this struggle between the spirit and the flesh shame is essential because where it is the primordial feeling of consciousness and conscience, there the conflict remains and man does not find himself the easy prey of the flesh. Man knows that he is more animal than spirit, that its lower forms of life are more powerful than the higher, that the return to animality is more nature than the work and activity of the spirit. The spirit is the exception, the rare creation which defies the flesh and hopes that the creations will not, in the end, again be reduced to the voluptuous powers of the flesh, to the forces of existence and temporality. Fessard realized that in the struggle of Jew and Pagan all the forces of the flesh and its sexual powers reduced man to his earthly reality with an unconquerable power. The adventure into spirit made it possible for man to comprehend shame before that divinity that lay within him and liberated him from the flesh in those rare and distinctive moments of life. In history man discovered not only this vast and inescapable battle, but he found it on every level of life: male-female, master-slave.

With a distinct clarity, Scheler remarked that this "feeling of shame doubtlessly possesses a very internal cohesion measured with *Individualization* of living unities."[18] This would indicate that the realization of the self depends forcefully upon this primal feeling of shame. Where this measure of individuality is hampered or restricted is where it is reduced to the amorphous collective, where it is uprooted or eliminated by the state or where in myth, ideology and irrationality it is relegated to the meaningless and undesirable. In idolatry man surrenders critical judgment to emotional tyranny. The shame that accompanies the loss of human dignity, the dignity which constitutes our individuality, is lost. Shame is the primal feeling which conditions and affects the humanity of our being, it emerges, unknown to ourselves, wherever and whenever this dignity is threatened, violated or debased before human action that ignores, denies and mocks the humanity of our being.

Cohen had repeated often that "poverty becomes the main representative of human misfortune." In relation to poverty Cohen spoke of suffering but rejected its metaphysical implication because it belonged to poetry and art. "Suffering," he said, "only reaches ethical precision as social suffering. Whoever explains poverty as the suffering of mankind, he creates ethics, if not philosophical ethics, yet still religion with its share of reason."[19] What we have arrived at is an interpretation of life in which poverty is more significant than death. Far more profound than Scheler is Cohen's consciousness of poverty as human suffering, because here shame before the suffering, poverty and needs of our fellowman is the realization of the self as task, the task that burdens us with the moral demand to see in our fellowman, however despicable, a hint of God's image. In our fellowman we find our moral obligation, and only in the obligation do we comprehend the shame that accompanies our inadequacy and equivocation. With our fellowman as moral responsibility, shame emerges as the feeling that fulfills the demands of our moral being. In poverty we take shame in our abundance; in suffering, shame in our superiority, our condition. The well-being of my fellowman can never be a matter of indifference to me. If it were I could not feel shame at my indifference or insufficiency. When it becomes possible to brood upon death, then it is possible to ignore human woe, but where the problem of death is relegated to those who find entertainment in pondering its existential reality, there we have shunted aside the social and moral earnestness of human life, there human sickness yields with disdain, to the metaphysical speculations of the "infinite judgment."

Suffering and shame belong together. They bring together the character of the human condition. They awaken the feelings that pervade every human condition and make us aware that it can be changed because man himself can change. We speak of suffering not only as an emotive condition but as the "reality of consciousness, it fills the entire human consciousness and helps to determine all its other proceedings and activities. Therefore its objectivization should not be permitted to be erased, the suffering of poverty must always remain the problem: the religious problem, but not the metaphysical one."[20] If the problem was metaphysical there could be no feeling of shame before man's inadequacy and moral indifference. As the ingredients of human consciousness suffering remains the unconquerable problem of man's struggle to bring spirit from flesh, with the pain that accompanies the moral awareness of the waywardness of his actions and commitment. Where this problem exists man remains morally whole because he is active. In shame before suffering man preserves his moral dignity. He affirms the humanity in himself.

Shame belongs to the moral order. The discussion of shame goes beyond its phenomenological reality which is only preparatory for its ethical significance. When Cohen spoke of shame and idolatry he understood its reality in man's struggle against idolatry throughout the ages, he grasped the nature of the historical conflict which the moral spirit has waged against the realm of the flesh for generations. He knew that ideas and speculative formulations mean little without action. He believed with a depth of commitment that "action establishes the realm of morality." Fessard moved in this direction from the time of his studies of Blondel and Maine de Biran and his life is a monument to that necessity between thought and action. If in Heidegger the political was eliminated by indifference and indiscretion, in Fessard it reappeared with an earnestness that could not be achieved by those whose thoughts and actions bear witness to a union that has taught man to value right and freedom, to think and assume responsibility for thought. Fessard knew that shame extends gradually to all fields of human relations founded upon this interrelationship -- that between man and woman being the source of that between man and man and man and nature -- to all "morals" which come forth from social as well as individual ethics. As this morality develops and is refined its influence is diffused into every relationship with the other person even if, assuming its *psychic* and *spiritual* aspect having always more importance than its simply *corporeal* and *sexual* side, it finally expands in the form of modesty, "tact" and "discretion" in every human relationship.[21]

Fessard indicated that he had grasped shame as belonging to the ethical problem which means that it had become a political force. Political behavior whether it comes forth in the reduction of all conflicts to that of friend and foe, or whether the role of national interest remains dominant is constantly faced with Max Weber's distinction between the ethics of intention and that of responsibility. Action and thought which emphasizes one or the other to the destruction of the civic order leads ultimately to the debasement of moral life and the domination of resentment. In the debasement man loses his humanity; he has surrendered his freedom and his right to pursue the truth to a new order in which the "new man" is born, for shame is no longer a reality.

Scheler reminded us of a profound truth in relation to shame: "People who rarely feel shamed and are embarrassed are mostly of a cold and empty nature and we should be certain that children who show no embarrassment and who are easily enticed to show off their abilities, e.g. to recite a poem, are cold characters."[22] The lack of shame and modesty should be carefully noticed. We wonder whether the self-dominance of our nature has so completely conquered our inadequacies that shame is no longer a possibility. We also wonder if this self-dominance leaves too little room for compassion or for the waywardness of human nature that faced with human debasement and triviality, we no longer have the capacity to rise against it and fight for those values which have always given man a sense of his human dignity and his eternal moral task. In fact we agree with Scheler when he speaks of *Schamgefühl* and *Gesundheit* as that harmonious tie between spirit and flesh. In this possibility of harmony shame appears as "beautiful" as the promise of beauty. "Its manner of promising," Scheler said, "is beautiful because it is an unwished for promise and it unintentionally points to its hidden existence through the hiding of the beautiful. Also the good which can hide as spiritual shame becomes beautiful through the form of immediacy in which it comes to reality.''[23] Shame points to a goodness and beauty through the feeling it expresses about the relationship between the spirit and the body, but this goodness and beauty is not purposed by shame, it is formed within it, in its expression and the distinctiveness of its feeling. In this distinctiveness it mediates between divinity and animality and gives man his unique place in the hierarchy of being. In this meditation shame finds its peculiar and distinct character, its goodness and beauty. But this is not enough, its aesthetic nature remains an empty configuration and its goodness a formal manifestation. What is lacking here is its significance in moral action. This lack is pointed to by Cohen and Fessard. For them the moral and social dimensions characterize what is essentially important about the phenomenon of shame.

Scheler pointed to another dimension of shame which must be considered: *Schamreue* or the relationship between shame and repentance. In 1921 appeared *Vom ewigen im Menschen, On the Eternal in Man*, with the significant essay ''Repentance and Rebirth.'' Eight years earlier Scheler had made clear the role of shame as the foundation of ethical life and had explored this phenomenon in the varied aspects of its reality from sexual life, to love, beauty and goodness. Hermann Cohen had expanded its reality into the struggle between paganism and the ethical messianism which he believed was immanent in the message of Israel to mankind. Fessard reinterpreted this struggle to embody the dialectical conflicts of male-female, slave-master and ultimately and a more embracing one, that between Jew and Pagan. In this latter conflict Christianity came forth as its universal expression, called upon to reveal to mankind the meaning of the dialectic between Jew and Pagan, the problems which are brought forth in it and the deeper burdens that weigh upon the universal church in its catholicity to bear these burdens with dignity, strength and courage.

But, at every stage, man comprehends his inadequacy and seeks to renew his strength. He seeks repentance for his insufficiencies in a universal struggle with an ever increasing, more subtle and more devastating evil. This evil in its totalitarian form has reached such dimensions of psychological sophistication that Lucifer now learns from man. In fact, man in his sophistication can set him aside and see in his work the play of a child. In the relationship between repentance and shame, *Schamreue*, man seeks renewal, the need for strength to reorder the past in terms of the future, to seek new paths to face evil, to find in his weaknesses the power of commitment and loyalty. Scheler observed that ''we are not the disposers merely of our future; there is also no part of our past life which . . . might not still be genuinely altered in its *meaning* and *worth*, through entering our life's total significance as a constituent of the self-revision which is always possible."[24] What is significant in Scheler's remarks is their clear defiance of fate, their firm and undeniable acceptance of human freedom to deal with every aspect of human life. In his refusal to affirm economic, social or political determinism Scheler gives to man freedom, both a peculiar nobility and a painful awareness of its limitations. In this recognition of dignity and limitation man discovers in repentance a way to envision new means and unchartered possibilities in the painfulness of his moral and intellectual shortcomings.

Repentance bears within it the notion of return. There is in it the reality of restoration. From the point of view of return and restoration, repentance carries not only a message for the individual but is a political and social force. Nations can be restored, they can overcome the evils that they have harbored within them, they can reestablish social justice and international peace. Things do not change simply because men want them to; they are restored and developed anew because there has been a radical change in feeling. In this sense the confrontation with evil, with sin, is the beginning of change. In fact, without the confrontation with evil there can be no discussion of practical ethics.

Cohen had remarked that the prophets had become politicians "and with regard to international relations the prophet turns his thoughts to history, he becomes the originator of *world history*."[25] This insight into the origin of a world history is fundamental for our understanding of the conflict between Jew and Pagan. History begins with the vision of the future because it is with the future that we ask about the meaning of the past and the present. History begins with the search for an answer to a basic question which proceeds from a human need: man needs to know if his activities have any meaning. If the prophet becomes the politician it is because he knows that man must have faith in his capacity to change events, that he is not a creature of fate nor the consequence of a myth. History has significance because man can change his conditions. He believes that there is a purpose for him and his activities that goes beyond a forceful slavery to historical, natural and supernatural determinisms. History is no longer directed to origins. This history "is the history that narrates the past of its nation. A history of mankind," Cohen reminded us, "is within this horizon impossible. Mankind did not live in any past and did not become alive in the present; only the future can bring about its bright and beautiful form. This form is an idea, not a shadowy image of the beyond."[26] With these profound words Cohen laid the foundation for an interpretation of repentance that not only included the individual but embraced world history. From this idea of world history and the dominance of the future over the past and present Fessard attempted to give the struggle of Jew and Pagan universal meaning and make it bear a message to mankind which spoke the truth of the church universal.

Repentance, Scheler believed, had a significant place in historical reality because he affirmed "historical reality is incomplete and, so to speak, redeemable."[27] With this observation Scheler established man's unique place in the universe. Man is the being who struggles against the fixity of the past and present, against the fate which determines his flesh, reduces his spiritual life to the powers that control his sensual reality. In repentance the spirit is given the opportunity and hope to force animality, with all its unconquerable forces, to allow the spirit to affirm its opposition even though its ability to ward off the natural superiority of sensuality is never contested. Wherever the spirit maintains its force there we discover the human miracle. In relation to history Scheler observed that "history comprehended frees us from the power of the history we live. Likewise the *knowledge* of history (as distinct from that saga of humans and intellectual adventures which 'tradition' hallows) is first and foremost a liberator from historical determinism. . . . Repenting is equivalent to reappraising part of one's past life and shaping for it mint-new worth and significance."[28]

With a striking observation Scheler had given repentance a distinct and unique place in man's moral life. In fact, repentance becomes a "moral rejuvenation," that peculiar activity in which we discover our freedom to be more than the object of history, to be its subject. We see in knowledge man's unique weapon to oppose and control every force that attempts to reduce him to the arbitrariness of the will. Weakened often in the struggle against the flesh the spirit wants to tranquilly surrender, but aware that surrender is the death of human dignity the spirit has in repentance a source of new power. In repentance it cries out against its inadequacy, the insufficiency of its forces when compared to the senses and the immediacy of their pleasures, but the cries of despair can be redeemed. The spirit must affirm its own rejuvenation, its belief in its efficacy and its loyalty to man's humanity. Repentance is the most significant power of the self. If the self had no such power how would it combat the forces of sensuality, prevent them from giving final form to our animality. With repentance the self again is established in its freedom. It is able again "to begin with a spontaneous virginal beginning a new course springing from the center of the personality which, by virtue of the act of repentance, is no longer in bonds."[29] We wonder about this estimation of repentance, this purification and illumination of the self which it causes and we ask about its social and political consequences.

From Scheler's perspective repentance goes beyond conduct to Being, "the more it grasps the *root* of guilt and the more also it makes the transition from shame over a particular deed to that completeness of 'hearty contrition' out of which an endwelling force of regeneration builds up a 'new heart' and a 'new man.'"[30] Repentance is a sanctification of the self, it bears within the power to create the "true I." This is man's freedom from the determination that perpetually seeks to entrap him. This sanctification of the self is the pure Idealism of the I that assumes the regenerative word powers to belong to the I. These powers give it the capacity to transcend itself, to separate the I from Being, to maintain a radical division between thinking and Being.

In this separation the I becomes for itself an infinite task and in an analogous way it attaches infinity to God. The approach to God is an infinite process and obligation, but it is in this infinity that man discovers his moral responsibility. Philosophy is aware that a "man's thought that not only proves but even constructs God can only be true if it is not *God* who exists for them, it is at the same time, false."[31] Knowing that human thought does not posit God's existence does not deprive that thought of analogies or metaphors in and through which it attempts to transcend itself. If the God is radically separated from the thought of God we are then faced with a "double truth" whose reality makes revelation contradictory to reason which assumes that it is its task to clarify a revelation whose *logos* defies reason and mocks its relevancy. In this separation God as the foundation of ethical truth is destroyed and if we accept Scheler's thought "that repentance is the mighty power of self-regeneration of the moral world, whose decay it is constantly working to avert," then we must assume that this repentance is also commanded in the Idea of God. If we affirm that the Idea of God is the most significant moral power in the world then we can also affirm Scheler's further statement that "not utopianisms but Repentance is the most *revolutionary* force in the moral world."[32] But is this valid for the God who transcends the Idea?

If we assume the truth of Scheler's statement about repentance then we know what it means to speak of the dialectic of Jew and Pagan. In this dialectic two radically opposed moral systems face each other throughout history. Man moves from one to the other. No man is free of the slave morality that is embedded in paganism, that fixed and unchanging imprisonment in the ideological dictums of human thoughts that have assumed apodictic certainty. Whatever be the changing idols of this total thought the same danger and perversion emerges from it: the deification of finite reality and the growth of ressentiment which

Scheler at one moment defines in these terms: There is "organic mendacity whenever a man's mind admits only those impressions which serve his interest or his instinctual attitude."[33]

If we followed Scheler we would believe that only the "change of heart" can alter the debased human situation, but it is difficult to reconcile the faith in repentance with the undeniable realization that there is a mendacity which no longer needs to be. The lie has become the truth. Repentance is possible with the moral dimension of human life, but when that dimension has been subverted and the lie and the truth interchanged then repentance has no meaning. Like shame it vanishes from the feelings and convictions which govern life. Falsifications become truthful, the genuine is reduced to the distorted while honesty and dishonesty are identical. Where this transvaluation of values the "new man" is born, his nature radically changed. When religion spoke of the "new man" it envisioned a rebirth of justice, courage and truthfulness but the "new man" of totalitarianism is born of this transvaluation of values.

This "new man" is the man of ressentiment who "cannot justify or even understand his own existence and sense of life in terms of positive values such as power, health, beauty, freedom and independence. Weakness, fear, anxiety and a slavish disposition prevent him from relating to them. Therefore he comes to feel that 'all this is vain anyway' and that salvation be in the opposite phenomena: poverty, suffering, illness and death."[34] With this sense of vanity the man of ressentiment seeks his revenge, but this revenge relieves his "inner torment" because he has created for himself a reversal of values and with this reversal he inflicts those who remain with a sense of beauty, freedom and truthfulness. With this power of infection the man of ressentiment "now feels 'good,' 'pure' and 'human.'" He has now accomplished a perversion of values, a reinterpretation of history, a distortion of tradition. He has created the "new man" who now accepts the "falsification of the value tablets" and for whom the behavior of the "Tarantulas" is accepted and admired. We are far from the idols of past history. We have reached new levels of psychological, political and social paganism and when we speak of the conflict with the Jew we are in need of a deeper comprehension of these positive values that are so easily perverted by those who hold them and who, nevertheless, can distort them.

If "thirst for revenge is the most important source of ressentiment" then the struggle of master and slave can become the continuing source in and through which the morality of the slave infects those who rule in such a way that the thirst for revenge distorts both their misery and whatever goodness lies in those who remain sympathetic to their suffering. In the moral distortion that is created through ressentiment, the falsification of values which becomes the new truth, there emerges the desire to venture into the depths of *Schadenfreude*, those perverted and malicious pleasures, which open to us the imagery and fantasy worlds of evil. Ressentiment is not *Schadenfreude*. It is the sublimation of these fantasies. In the sublimation the ressentiment increases enormously; in the failure of actual realization its intensity is magnified and it is in the magnification that we discover the devilish dangers of resentment. From this power of ressentiment we turn toward repentance and ask whether it and shame can touch the man of ressentiment or whether this man has placed himself beyond the force of repentance.

In repentance, Scheler had remarked, "we might create the idea of God." "Repentance begins with an indictment! But before *whom* do we indict ourselves? Is it not then in the nature of an indictment that there should be a person who receives it and before whom the charge is laid?"[35] We comprehend these observations, but we ask how does the man of ressentiment, the one who has fallen out of the moral problem, the man whose nature has been radically changed -- and today we are well informed of these possibilities -- find the least meaning in repentance? While the moral fabric remains alive repentance remains the hope. The question which constantly came forth from the discussion of repentance was enunciated by Scheler: "What kind of a world must it be, and how created, in which such a thing (guilt-repentance) should be necessary and possible?"[36] The question hangs over us like an eternal inquiry from which we continuously seek in faith and knowledge, *in lumine Dei*, a path to that divine love which responds to the depths of our repentance. "Man," Scheler remarked, "comes finally to the knowledge that he has received strength for that consummation as a taker of God's love and mercy."[37] The strength which man receives in repentance, in his capacity to love God makes it possible for him to comprehend and feel the power of restoration and return which it bears within it. Outside of its power lives the man for whom repentance does not exist, who lives from the imagery of social injustice, from the difference in education, power and property. The observation of the more fortunate releases in him the potent imagination of ressentiment, whose envy and jealousy awaken his impotency and makes him more eager to worship the idolatry of social mythologies and ideologies. The struggle against paganism must be fought in part against the realities of the man of ressentiment. He is man's great enemy.

We are faced with the drama of dialectical oppositions which Fessard constructed with care and profundity, but we are also confronted with a dualism which divides mankind so deeply between those who remain loyal to the tradition of values which arose in our faiths and in classical antiquity, and the reality of the "new man" created by communist totalitarianism and its reversal in anarchism. There are conflicts which belong to value systems that stimulate and increase the significance of the value systems, and then there are conflicts from which no reconciliation is possible. How we deal with this contradiction must depend upon moderation, strength and the refusal to be duped. Fessard made us aware of the dimensions of the conflicts which determined human history from the time of the opposition between monotheism and polytheism, from the confrontation between the Jew and the Pagan.

Fessard comprehended this from the dialectical perspective of St. Paul. He affirmed again and again that this perspective was valid for universal history. He knew that "the enmity of the two peoples reveals the truth of human nature which is always divided between the need to incarnate the absolute in the finite - - the need which makes the idolatrous pagan -- and the demand which is essential to reason, i.e., to transcend the given. It is this demand which makes the *Jew* incredulous and *rejected*, at the same time appears the truth of mediation which at every moment, can enter into this radical division and heal it."[38] What is fundamental to Fessard's thought is the realization that Jew and Pagan remain together in every man who comprehends the depth of the struggle between these two groups of values. However deeply we attempt to grasp the meaning of the Jew, the Christ, the Church from the values that are embodied in shame and repentance, and however seriously we understand their values as fundamental to man's good, to his persistent search for the truth, we are confronted with an opposing and contradictory value system which seeks its destruction in its attempt to create a "new man" from the force and imagination of the man of ressentiment. How does this man speak. Nietzsche captured his words well: "What justice means to us is precisely that the world be filled with the storms of our revenge. . . . We shall wreak vengeance and abuse us all those whose equals we are not. . . . And will to equality shall henceforth be the name for virtue, and against all that has power we want to raise our clamor."[39] With these words our modern paganism comes forth and we ask again and again about the force of our confrontation. The question belongs not only to ourselves but to our civilization. In it lies the crisis of values, the profundity of our moral battle, and the propinquity of our destruction.

The work of Fessard is significant because he is the philosopher with who a continuous dialogue is possible. The architecture of his thought encompasses man's most vital struggle which in Paganism reaches its most threatening challenge to freedom and truth. Fessard forces us to remove the shroud of virtue that hides the most devastating tyrannies. From the faith that encompasses his work there emerges that fine sensibility that uncovers the "will to power," "the frenzy of revenge" that is in those whose shallow universalism and humanism hides the tyrannical ambition for political power and social control. We read Fessard to rediscover the values of our religious traditions and to comprehend how deeply they are entwined with idolatry, how infinitely long is our struggle against the idols and how dependent we are upon that eternal dialectic of Jew and Pagan. We know that this dialectic embraces our political and social reality and that where we lose sight of its demand we have also lost sight of our religious and moral task. Hermann Cohen called it the infinite task of monotheism to maintain a radical separation between man and nature, Being and Should Be. Fessard turned us toward political philosophy because he know that only within its dimension does man comprehend his moral responsibility and it is in this responsibility that he finds his humanity in his comprehension of the man of ressentiment. If we accept Fichte's assumption that the philosophy we choose depends upon the man we are, we can then broaden this assumption and say that the quality of a civilization's survival depends upon the values it is willing to confront and overcome. In this willingness lies its self understanding and from it its growth and significance.

Notes

INTRODUCTION

1. Eric Weil, "L'intérêt qui l'on prend pour l'histoire" (1935), in *Essais et conferences* (Paris, 1970), I, 221.

2. Ibid., 228.

3. Ibid., 229-30.

CHAPTER 1
The Meaning of History:
Wilhelm von Humboldt and Immanuel Kant

1. George F. Kennan, *The Decline of Bismarck's European Order* (Princeton, 1979), 3-4.

2. See the fundamental and groundbreaking study of Eric Weil, *Problèmes kantiens* (Paris, 1970). "The political ceases, with Kant, to be a preoccupation for philosophers; it, like history, becomes a philosophical problem, action within and upon the totality of thought" (pp. 140-41).

3. Wilhelm von Humboldt, "On the Historian's Task," in *The Theory and Practice of History,* ed. Georg G. Iggers and Konrad von Molthe (Indianapolis, 1973). See the convenient three-volume edition of Humboldt's work, W. von Humboldt, *Studienausgabe* (Fischer Taschenbuch Verlag, 1971), in particular, 2:289-304.

4. *Theory and Practice,* 8.

5. "Auf diese Assimilation der forschenden Kraft und des zu erforschenden Gegenstandes kommt allein alles an" (*Studienausgabe,* 2:291).

6. *Theory and Practice,* 9-10.

7. It is important to quote Aristotle in full: "Hence, while the equitable is just, and is superior to one sort of justice, it is not superior to absolute justice, but only to the error due to its absolute statement. This is the essential nature of the equitable: it is a rectification of law where law is defective because of its generality. In fact this is the reason why things are not all determined by law: it is because there are some cases for which it is impossible to lay down a law so that a special ordinance becomes necessary. For what is indefinite can only be measured by an indefinite standard." *Ethics,* 1138a 6-7 (Loeb Classical Library, 1975). See H. G. Gadamer's significant article "Sur la possibilité d'une éthique philosophique," in *Archives de Philosophie,* July-Aug. 1971.

8. *Theory and Practice*, 10.

9. Gadamer, "Le faisable n'est pas seulement ce qui est bien (recht) mais aussi ce qui est utile, ordonné à une bien et, dans cette mesure, 'droit' (richtig)" (p. 404).

10. *Ethics*, 1005b 6.

11. *Theory and Practice*, 14.

12. Ibid., 15-16.

13. Ibid., 16.

14. F. Meinecke, *Cosmopolitanism and the National State* (Princeton, 1970). Meinecke quotes from a memorandum of Dec. 1813 -- "Nations like individuals have tendencies that politics cannot alter" -- to prove that von Humboldt had a sense for the peculiar nature of the state and granted it its right. Meinecke states: "Our purpose was only to understand how it was that Von Humboldt, unswayed by the universalistic idealism of his contemporaries, could grant the national state its original claims and develop a more realistic position in this question than Stein could" (pp. 140-41).

15. *Theory and Practice*, 17-18.

16. Ibid., 18. See Kant, "Idea for a Universal History with a Cosmopolitan Purpose," Ninth Proposition: "A philosophical attempt to work out a universal history of the world in accordance with a plan of nature aimed at a perfect civil union of mankind, must be regarded as possible and even as capable of furthering the purpose of nature."

17. *The Limits of State Action*, ed. J. W. Burrow (Cambridge, 1969), 19.

18. Ibid., 32.

19. Ibid., 33.

20. *Theory and Practice*, 23.

21. *The Limits of State Action*, 77.

22. Three recent books on Kant's philosophy of history can be consulted with profit: Yermiahu Yovel, *Kant and the Philosophy of History* (Princeton, 1980); Michel Despland, *Kant on History and Religion* (McGill-Queen's University Press, 1973); William A. Galston, *Kant and the Problem of History* (Chicago, 1975). Fundamental is: Kurt Borries, *Kant als Politiker* (Scienta Verlag Aalen, 1973).

23. "On the Common Saying: This May be True in Theory, But It Does Not Apply in Practice," in *Kant's Political Writings*, ed. H. Reiss (Cambridge, 1970), 89.

24. Emil Lask, *Gesammelte Schriften* (Tübingen, 1924): "Wenn mir die ertötete Sinnlichkeit erkennbar wäre, dann hätte Kant recht! Und wenn es auch transcendentale 'Logik' gibt, dann ist schon mit diesem Dogma gebrochen. Es gibt bei Kant auch eine Kritik der praktischen Vernunft und eine Metaphysik der Sitten. Was Kant da treibt, ist doch nicht sittlichen Verhalten, sondern theoretische Betrachtung. Und worüber wird Klarheit gesucht? Uber die Majestät des Sittengesetzes, die Würde des Menschen . . ." (3:250-51).

25. *Problèmes kantiens*, 161.

26. Kant, *Religion within the Limits of Reason Alone*, ed. T. M. Greene and H. H. Hudson (New York, 1960), 27.

27. Kurt Borries concludes his study with the remark: "Denn das höchste Gut besteht nicht in friedlich sicherewn Besitz und seligem Genuss, sondern ist pflichtbe-

wusste Tun und Streben. . . . Kant begnügt sich mit der uralten faustischen Weisheit: wer immer strebend sich bemüht, den können wir erlösen" (pp. 233-34).

28. Weil: "Ce n'est pas pour dévaluer l'homme, c'est pour lui donner sa chance d'humanization que Kant parle du mal radical." We should note that Weil more than any other contemporary philosopher has grasped the importance of the *Religion* for an understanding of Kant's concept of history and its intimate relationship to morality. Kurt Borries in his fundamental book fails to deal with the *Religion,* and the distinguished contemporary German philosopher Manfred Riedel, in his *I. Kant: Schriften zur Geschichtsphilosophie,* makes the same omission.

29. *Religion,* 120-21.

30. Ibid., 34.

31. Kant, *Critique of Judgment,* trans. J. C. Meredith (Oxford, 1969), no. 91, 144-45.

32. *Religion,* 19n.

33 Hermann Lübbe, "Philosophiegeschichte als Philosophie," in *Einsichten: Gerhard Krueger zum 60. Geburtstag* (Frankfurt am Main, 1962), 223. "Die Vernunft erscheint als das Produkt ihrer eigenen Genesis und die Philosophie in ihrer Geschichte ist der Ort dieser Genesis."

34. Kant, "An Answer to the Question: What Is Enlightenment?" (1784), in *Kant's Political Writings,* 54.

35. *Problèmes kantiens,* 174.

36. *Metaphysics of Morals, Doctrine of Virtue,* trans. Mary J. Gregor (New York, 1964), no. 29, 120.

37. *The Conflict of Faculties, The Conflict of the Philosophy Faculty with the Faculty of Law,* in *Kant's Political Writings,* 188. A complete translation is now available by M. J. Gregor (New York, 1979).

CHAPTER 2
Hume and Kant:
The Nature of the Historical Object

1. Fritz Medicus, "On the Objectivity of Historical Knowledge," in *Philosophy and History: Essays Presented to Ernst Cassirer,* ed. R. Klibansky and H. J. Paton (New York, 1963), p. 149.

2. Eric Weil, *Problèmes Kantiens* (Paris, 1970), p. 97. "Nous nous égarerions si nous confondions cette idée, principe de compréhension, avec un concept moyen ou condition d'explication. Nous sommes maîtres et sources du sens *parce que* nous ne sommes pas maîtres des faits: si nous les dominions, nous serions Dieu et n'aurions aucun sens à découvrir ou à réaliser."

3. David Hume, "That Politics May Be Reduced to a Science," in *Essays Moral, Political and Literary* (Oxford Univ. Press, 1963), p. 14.

4. "On the Independency of Parliament," in *Essays,* pp. 40-41.

5. See the general discussion of philosophical history in Duncan Forbes, *Hume's Philosophical Politics* (Cambridge, 1978).

6. Hume, *An Enquiry Concerning the Principles of Morals* (1751), in *Hume's Moral and Political Philosophy* (New York, 1948), p. 175.

7. Ibid.

8. Ibid., p. 177.

9. *The History of England,* in *David Hume: Philosophical Historian,* ed. Norton and Popkin (Indianapolis, 1965), p. 143.

10. Ibid.

11. Hume, *Of the Standard of Taste and Other Essays,* ed. J. W. Lenz (Indianapolis, 1963), p. 49.

12. Ibid., p. 50.

13. Ibid.

14. Ibid., p. 51.

15. Ibid., p. 52.

16. Ibid., pp. 52-53.

17. *Enquiry Concerning the Principles of Morals,* "Conclusion," p. 257.

18. *The History of England,* pp. 372, 376.

19. "Of Refinement in the Arts," p. 55.

20. "Of the Standard of Taste," p. 6. The text is vital: "Among a thousand different opinions which different men may entertain of the same subject, there is one, and but one, that is just and true; and the only difficulty is to fix and ascertain it. On the contrary, a thousand different sentiments, excited by the same object, are all right; because no sentiment represents what is really in the object."

21. "Of Refinement in the Arts," p. 57.

22. *Enquiry Concerning the Principles of Morals,* "Conclusion," pp. 253-54.

23. *The History of England,* p. 373.

24. Kant, "First Introduction to the Critique of Judgment," trans. J. Haden (Indianapolis, 1965), p. 28.

25. *Enquiry Concerning the Principles of Morals,* p. 176.

26. Kant, *Critique of Judgment,* trans. J. C. Meredith (Oxford, 1969), no. 9.

27. Ibid., no. 1.

28. Aristotle, *The "Art" of Rhetoric,* trans. J. H. Freese (London: Loeb Classical Library, 1967), 1356a 7-8.

29. *Critique of Judgment,* no. 10.

30. Ibid., no. 11.

31. Ibid., no. 17.

32. Ibid., no. 19.

33. Ibid., no. 22.

34. "Of the Standard of Taste," p. 6.

35. *Critique of Judgment,* no. 22.

CHAPTER 3
Leopold von Ranke:
Unknown Follower of Kant

1. Eric Weil, *Philosophie politique* (Paris, 1971), 127.

2. Ibid.

3. Kennan, 422

4. Friedrich Meinecke, *Historism* (London, 1972), and *Cosmopolitanism and the National State* (Princeton, 1970); Leonard Krieger, *Ranke: The Meaning of History* (Chicago, 1977); G. G. Iggers and K. von Moltke, *The Theory and Practice of History* (Indianapolis, 1973); G. G. Iggers, *New Directions in European Historiography* (Middletown, 1975); T. H. von Laue, *Leopold Ranke: The Formative Years* (Princeton, 1950); Leopold von Ranke, *Aus Werk und Nachlass,* Tagebücher, Vol. I (Munich, 1964).

5. Tagebücher, 159, 154, 155, 159, 144.

6. Idid., 168. See also "Die Form wird durch Übung vollständig erlangt, und aller wahrer Unterricht soll seiner Bestimmung nach mehr auf diese als auf dem stoff gehn." Ibid.

7. Iggers and von Moltke, 53.

8. "On the Relations of History and Philosophy" (a manuscript of the 1830s), in Iggers and von Moltke, 30.

9. Ibid.

10. "The Role of the Particular and the General in the Study of Universal History" (a manuscript of the 1860s), ibid., 59.

11. Ibid., 55.

12. Tagebücher, 160. "Der wahre Staat des reinen Begriff ist in der Religion. Da ist die ewige Weltordnung. Da ist der ewige König; mit dem ein Jeder in unmittelbar Bezug steht."

13. "A Dialogue on Politics" (1836), in Iggers and von Moltke, 115.

14. Ibid., 118-19.

15. "The Great Powers" (1833), in von Laue, 217.

16. Ibid.

17. Ibid., 218.

18. Ibid.

19. "Preface to the First Edition of Histories of Latin and Germanic Nations" (1824), in Iggers and von Moltke, 138.

20. Ibid., 145.

21. "Preface to History of France" (1852), ibid., 150.

22. "Preface to History of England" (1859), ibid., 152.

23. Ibid., 156.

24. "Preface to Universal History" (1880), ibid., 163.

25. It is significant to note the remarks of the great historian Johann Gustav Droysen, *Principles of History* (New York, 1967). "Human existence is Mind under the ban of finitude, spiritual and sensuous at once and in an inseparable manner, a contrast which is reconciled every moment in order to its renewal, renewed in order to its recon-

ciliation. Our being, so long as it is in itself, healthy and awake, can at no moment be merely sensuous or merely spiritual'' (pp. 91-92).

26. ''Wenn ich nun das Einzelne fasse und verstehe, und es kommt mir aus dem Leben desselben das Ganzen zu Gedanken und Gemüte: o dass die Entwickelung dieses Leben so klar würde, wie es selbst gewesen ist, -- dass mich Dein Geist besuchte, Siebzigjähriger, -- dass sich auf dem festen Boden des Historischen das Ideale wahrfaft erhübe: aus dem Gestalten, die da gegeben sind, was nicht gegeben ist, herausspringe! -- Dass uns Blut zu Gold werde!'' Tagebücher, 174.

27. See this profound and inexplicably neglected article, ''What Is a Breakthrough in History?'' Daedalus, Spring 1975.

28. Kant is a follower of Hobbes: ''Hobbes' statement, status hominum naturales est bellum omnium in omnes is correct except that it should read, est status belli, etc. For even if one does not concede that actual hostilities are continually in progress between men who do not stand under external and public laws, yet the state (status iuridicus) is the same . . . a state in which each wants to be the judge of what shall be his rights against others, but for which rights he has no security against others, and gives no security: each has only his private strength . . . for this state is a continual infringement when the rights of all others through man's arrogant insistence on being the judge in his own affairs and giving other men no security in their affairs save his own arbitrary will.'' Religion, 89n.

29. Ibid., 92.

30. Ibid.

31. Ibid.

32. ''On the Failure of All Attempted Philosophical Theodicies'' (1791), in Michel Despland, Kant on History, 293. I owe my attention to Job to my colleague Livio Sichirollo of the University of Milan.

33. Critique of Judgment, no. 91.

34. Ibid.

35. In the ''Progress of Metaphysics'' Kant states the problem of freedom: ''. . . aber nicht nach dem, was es seiner Natur nach ist, sondern nach demjenigen, was es im Ansehung des Thuns und Lassens für praktische Prinzipien begründet, zum Gegenstand ist.'' G.S., 20:293.

36. Progress: ''sondern was wer, bloss dadurch, dass wir es in ihn legen, uns verständlich machen können, der also eigentlich zwar kein Bestandteil der Erkenntnis des Gegenstandes, aber doch ein von der Vernunft gebenes Mittel oder Erkenntnisgrund ist ... und dies ist der Begriff von einer Zweckmässigkeit der Natur'' (p. 293).

37. Critique of Pure Reason, trans. N. K. Smith (New York, 1950), B 867.

38. Critique of Judgment, no. 91.

39. Ibid., n. 1.

40. Ibid., no. 91.

41. Ibid.

42. Problèmes kantiens, 104.

43. Ibid., 106.

44. Ibid.

45. Critique of Pure Reason, B 884.

46. *Kant's Political Writings,* 181.

47. Ibid.

48. Ibid., 185.

49. Ibid., 189.

50. Goethe, *Faust,* trans. C. F. MacIntyre (New York, 1957), 5.

51. Ranke's "Confessions" (1880), cited in Krieger, *Ranke,* 142.

CHAPTER 4
Herder and Kant:
Nature or Freedom

1. Kant, "On the Common Saying: This May Be True in Theory, But It Does Not Apply in Practice," in *Kant's Political Writings,* 89.

2. For a profound discussion of these points see Eric Weil, *Hegel et l'état* (Paris, 1970), 41-42.

3. Ibid., 33.

4. Herder, *Yet Another Philosophy of History for the Enlightenment of Mankind* (1774), *Essay on the Origin of Language* (1772), *Ideas for a Philosophy of the History of Mankind* (1784-91), in F. M. Barnard, *Herder on Social and Political Culture* (Cambridge, 1969); *Herder's Social and Political Thought: From Enlightenment to Nationalism* (Oxford, 1965); Isaiah Berlin, *Vico and Herder* (London, 1976); F. Meinecke, *Historism;* J. G. Herder, *Reflections on the Philosophy of the History of Mankind* (Chicago, 1968).

5. *Vico and Herder,* 145.

6. *Yet Another Philosophy of History,* trans. in *Herder on Social and Political Culture,* 184.

7. Barnard, *Herder's Social and Political Thought,* 61-62. In 1792-93 Herder wrote his *The Spirit of Hebrew Poetry* (2 vols.).

8. *Yet Another Philosophy of History,* 185.

9. Ibid., 187.

10. Ibid., 188.

11. Ibid., 195.

12. Ibid.

13. Ibid., 202.

14. Ibid., 209.

15. *The Origin of Language* (1772), in *Herder on Social and Political Culture,* 173.

16. *Philosophy of History,* 215.

17. Ibid., 217.

18. Ibid.

19. Ibid., 223.

20. Ibid.

21. *Reflections,* 84-85.

22. Ibid., 86.

23. Ibid., 89.

24. Ibid., 99.

25. Ibid., 101.

26. Ibid., 107.

27. Ibid., 112.

28. Ibid., 116-17.

29. "Review of Herder's Ideas for a Philosophy of the History of Mankind," in *On History*, 38.

30. Ibid., 37.

31. In 1785 Kant wrote a second review, extending to Book X his discussion of Herder's *Ideen*, which when completed had 20 books.

32. Ibid., 48.

33. Eric Weil has clearly and firmly enunciated this point of view in his Kant book: "Man deals with the thing-in-itself not with phenomena; because the essential is not knowledge but action, i.e., decision toward action. Decision is of a completely different order than knowledge; it deals with things-in-themselves, it is the act of a thing-in-itself." *Problèmes kantiens*, 37.

34. Canon, B 829.

35. "Natural Dialectic of Human Reason," B 697.

36. Ibid., B 704.

37. Ibid., B 705.

38. Ibid., B 708.

39. Ibid., B 722.

40. Ibid.

41. "History of Pure Reason," B 884.

42. *Critique of Judgment*, #83.

43. Eric Weil addressed this problem in his last publication, "La 'Philosophie du droit' et la philosophie de l'histoire hegelienne," in *Hegel et la philosophie du droit* (Paris, 1979), 26: "The philosophy of history responds to man's question about the possibility of philosophy; it shows how freedom, the essence of man's humanity, at first acting imperceptibly and secretly not only its nature but even of its presence, comes to grasp and think itself in them not by projecting itself into an inaccessible and inefficacious transcendence, but by transforming the given world so that freedom and reason act there together, freedom no longer obliged to be a negative force, negating the world as it is, but is recognized within the world, in the institutions and constitution of the state."

44. *Metaphysical Elements of Justice*, Conclusion: Perpetual Peace.

45. Weil, "What Is a Breakthrough in History?" 35-36.

46. *Vico and Herder*, 206.

47. See E. Weil, *Problèmes kantiens*, 140. See also M. Riedel, "Historizismus und Kritizismus Kants Streit mit G. Forster und J. G. Herder," in *Studien zum achtzehnten Jahrhundert*, Vol. 2/3.

CHAPTER 5
Hermann Cohen and Kant

1. "What Is Orientation in Thinking," in *Critique of Practical Reason and Other Writings in Moral Philosophy,* trans. and ed. L. W. Beck (Chicago, 1950), 305n.

2. "Conjectural Beginning of Human History," in *On History,* ed. L. W. Beck, 51. Cohen, in his *Kants Begründung der Ethik* (Berlin, 1910), 520, finds the awareness of a sense of decency to be the preparation for reason, the turn to the future, in which the present is openness to purpose.

3. *Metaphysics of Morals, Introduction to the Doctrine of Virtue,* 37.

4. See chap. XXI of *The Religion of Reason.*

5. *Metaphysics of Morals,* no. 18.

6. Ibid.

7. Kant maintained: "By the fact that I fulfill a duty of love to someone I obligate the other as well: I make him indebted to me. But in fulfilling a duty of respect I obligate only myself, contain myself within certain limits in order to detract nothing from the worth that the other, as a man, is entitled to posit in himself." *Metaphysics of Morals,* no. 25.

8. Kant had referred to the lie in a similar way: "The greatest violation of man's duty to himself merely as a moral being (to humanity in his own person) is the contrary of truthfulness, the lie." *Metaphysics of Morals,* no. 9.

9. *Critique of Judgment,* trans. Bernard (New York, 1951), 155.

10. *Groundwork of the Metaphysics of Morals,* trans. H. J. Paton (New York, 1956), 101. "A rational being must always regard himself as making laws in a kingdom of ends which is possible through the freedom of the will. . . . The position of the latter he can maintain, not in virtue of the maxim of his will alone, but only if he is a completely independent being, without needs and with an unlimited power adequate to his will."

11. *Critique of Practical Reason,* trans. Beck, 245.

12. *Religion of Reason,* 71-78. "Denn diese Schöpfung bedeutet jetzt vielmehr das Sein Gottes, welches das Sein des Unsprungs ist" (p. 75).

13. *Religion,* 136.

14. Ibid., 157n. "For in whatever manner a being has been made known to him by another and described as God, yea, even if such a being had appeared to him (if this is possible) he must first of all compare this representation with his ideal in order to judge whether he is entitled to regard it and to honor it as a divinity."

15. *Critique of Judgment,* ed. Bernard, 72.

16. "Idea for a Universal History," 2nd thesis, in *History,* 13.

CHAPTER 6
Eric Weil:
History as the Reality of Reason

1. Eric Weil, *Philosphie politique*, 11.
2. Ibid., 257n.
3. Ibid., 256.
4. Ibid., 253.
5. Ibid.
6. Ibid., 233.
7. Ibid., 232-33.
8. Ibid., 243.
9. Ibid., 61.
10. Ibid., 243.
11. Ibid., 245-46.
12. Ibid., 247n.
13. Ibid., 255.
14. Ibid., 248.
15. G. W. Hegel, *Philosophy of the Mind,* Part III of *Encyclopaedia of the Philosophical Sciences* (1830) (Oxford: Oxford University Press, 1973), 1973), 552.
16. Eric Weil, *Philosophie politique,* 250.
17. Ibid., 252-53.
18. G. W. Hegel, *Encyclopaedia,* #462, addition.
19. G. W. Hegel, *Philosophy of Right,* trans. T. M. Knox (Oxford: Oxford University Press, 1949), #187.
20. Ibid., #31.
21. Eric Weil, "La dialectique objective," in *Les Etudes philosophiques,* July-Sept. 1970, 345.
22. Valéry, "Politics of the Mind" (1932), in *The Outlook for Intelligence* (New York, 1967). See E. Weil's important discussion of the category of "Oevre" in *Logique de la philosophie.*
23. Eric Weil, *Philosophie politique,* 11.
24. Ibid., 254.
25. See Weil, *Logique de la philosophie,* category of "action."
26. Weil, *Philosophie politique,* 257.
27. Ibid., 260.
28. Ibid.
29. Ibid., 261.
30. Ibid., 257.

CHAPTER 7
The Philosopher and the Theologian:
The Friendship of Raymond Aron and Gaston Fessard

1. *De l'Actualité Historique* were essays published in 1960 in two volumes. Aron's lecture is in *Raymond Aron, Histoire et Politique* (Paris: Julliard, 1983).

2. "Gaston Fessard Devant *l'Actualité Historique*," 520.

3. Gaston Fessard, *La Dialectique des Exercices Spirituels* (Paris: Aubier, 1950), Vol. I, 17.

4. Ibid., 50.

5. Ibid., 69.

6. Ibid.

7. Gaston Fessard, *Église de France prends garde de perdre la Foi!* (Paris: Julliard, 1979), "Annexe," 292-93.

8. "Gaston Fessard Devant *l'Actualité Historique*," 521.

9. Ibid., 522.

10. Ibid., 523.

11. Ibid., 524.

12. Ibid., 525.

13. Ibid., 526.

14. Quoted in the book review of *Le Monde*, May 24-85, p. 16.

15. Gaston Fessard, *De l'actualité Historique* (Desclée de Brouwer, 1960), Vol. I, 232.

16. Gaston Fessard Devant, 527.

17. Ibid., 527. See also, *De l'Actualité Historique*, Vol. I, 136.

18. *La Dialectique des Exercices Spirituels*, 51.

19. *France prends gard de perdre la Foi!* (Paris: Julliard, 1979), 250-51.

20. Raymond Aron, *Le Spectateur Engagé* (Paris: Julliard, 1981), 244.

21. Now published in *Le Philosophie historique de Raymond Aron* (Paris: Julliard, 1980), 390-404.

22. *Philosophie historique*, 397.

23. *Mémoires* (Paris: Julliard, 1983), 524.

24. Ibid., 525.

25. Ibid., 526.

26. *La Philosophie historique*, 177.

27. See pp. 276-277 for Fessard's analyses.

28. Ibid., 276.

29. Ibid., 276-77.

30. Ibid., 277.

31. Nicolas Baverez, "Raymond Aron et le Père Gaston Fessard," in *Histoire et Politique*, 199.

32. "Gaston Fessard Devant *l'Actualité*," 529.

CHAPTER 8
The Dialectical Forms of Human History

1. Gaston Fessard, *La Dialectique des Exercices spirituels de Saint Ignace de Loyola* (Paris: Aubier, 1956), 50.

2. Fessard, *Chretiens Marxistes et théologie de la liberation* (Paris: Lethielleux, 1978), 310.

3. Gaston Fessard, *De l'Actualité Historique,* Vol. I (Paris: Desclée de Brouwer, 1960), 200.

4. *Ibid.,* 141.

5. Ibid., 147.

6. Ibid., 149.

7. Milan Kundera, *The Book of Laughter and Forgetting* (New York: Penguin Books, 1981), 157.

8. Gaston Fessard, *De l'Actualité Historique,* 103.

9. *Karl Marx, Frederick Engels' Collected Works,* Vol. III (New York: International Publishers, 1975), 295.

10. Gaston Fessard, *De l'Actualité Historique,* 166.

11. Ibid., 167.

12. Franz Kafka, *Letter to His Father* (New York: Schocken Books, 1966), 87.

13. Gaston Fessard, *De l'Actualité Historique,* 170.

14. Ibid., 170.

15. Ibid., 171.

16. Ibid., 172.

17. Ibid., 173.

18. Ibid., 174.

19. Gaston Fessard, "Avant Propos" to the *De l'Actualité Historique,* 39-40.

20. Gaston Fessard, "Théologie et histoire" in *De l'Actualité Historique,* 118.

21. Ibid., 119.

22. Ibid., 112.

23. Hermann Cohen, *Religion of Reason out of the Sources of Judaism,* trans. S. Kaplan (New York: Frederick Ungar, 1972), 291.

24. Gaston Fessard, *De l'Actualité Historique,* 202.

CHAPTER 9
Gaston Fessard and the Problem of Historical Actuality

1. Raymond Aron, *Introduction à la philosophie de l'histoire* (Paris: Gallimard, 1981). This book was originally published in 1938.

2. Henri-Irénée Marrou, *Thèologie de l'histoire* (Paris: Editions du Seuil, 1968), 15.

3. Immanuel Kant, *Metaphysics of Morals: The Doctrine of Virtue,* trans. Mary J. Gregor (New York: Harper Torchbooks, 1964), 441.

4. Gaston Fessard, *La philosophie historique de Raymond Aron* (Paris: Julliard, 1980), 373.

5. Raymond Aron, *Mémoires, 50 ans de refléxion politique* (Paris: Julliard, 1983), 525-26. There are several references to Fessard. See pp. 522-25.

6. Henri-Irénée Marrou, *Théologie de l'histoire*, 15.

7. Gaston Fessard, "Dialogue Théologique avec Hegel," in *Stuttgarter Hegel Tage, 1970* (Bonn: Bouvier, 1974), 248.

8. Ibid., 231.

9. Ibid., 236-37.

10. Karl Rahner, *Spiritual Exercises* (London: Sheed and Ward, 1980), 101. This book is Rahner's commentary on the *Spiritual Exercises*.

11. Ibid., 103.

12. Ibid., 102.

13. Gaston Fessard, "Dialogue Théologique avec Hegel," 240.

14. See the chapter on "Kafka" in Georges Bataille, *Literature and Evil* (New York: Urizen Books, 1973), 128.

15. Gaston Fessard, "Attitude Ambivalent de Hegel en face de l'Histoire," in *Archives de Philosophie*, April-June 1961, p. 240.

16. *Hegel's Philosophy of Mind*, III, Encyclopedia (1830), trans. A. V. Miller (Oxford: Oxford University Press, 1923), #458.

17. Gaston Fessard, "Attitude Ambivalent de Hegel en face de l'histoire," 226.

18. Gaston Fessard, "Dialogue Théologique avec Hegel," 248.

19. Gaston Fessard, "Savoir de l'historicité surnaturelle," in *Sciences Ecclésiastiques* (Oct.-Dec., 1966), Vol. XVIII, 355.

20. Ibid., 355.

21. Gaston Fessard, "Savoir de l'historicité surnaturelle," in *Sciences Ecclésiastiques*, 357.

22. Gaston Fessard, *La philosophie historique de Raymond Aron* (Paris: Julliard, 1980), 373.

23. See *ibid.*, "Introduction, Une Soutenance de Thèse."

24. Raymond Aron, "Les Intellectuels et la politique," *Commentaire*, Summer 1983, pp. 262-63.

25. Raymond Aron, "The Social Responsibility of the Philosopher," from *Dimension de la conscience historique* (Paris: Librairie Plon, 1960), now in *Politics and History: Selected Essays by Raymond Aron* (New York: Free Press, 1978), 259.

26. Gaston Fessard, *La Philosophie historique de Raymond Aron*, 137-38.

27. Raymond Aron, *Mémoires*, 741.

28. Raymond Aron, *Introduction to the Philosophy of History*, trans. G. I. Irwin (Boston: Beacon Press, 1961), 287.

29. Immanuel Kant, *Critique of Judgment*, trans. I. G. Meredith (London: Oxford University Press, 1969), #91, p. 146n.

30. Raymond Aron, *Introduction to the Philosophy of History*, 333.

31. Gaston Fessard, *La philosophie historique de Raymond Aron*, 165.

32. Ibid., 166 and *n.*2. See Fessard's reference to the book of J. L. Bruch, *La philosophie réligieuse de Kant* (1968) and his quote: Hegel's system has "a catholic vision of the history of the church through its insertion into a philosophy of the history of religion which makes of it a theology of history" (p. 242).

33. Raymond Aron, *Introduction to the Philosophy of History*, 3329.

34. Immanuel Kant, *Critique of Judgment*, #83.

35. Raymond Aron, *Introduction to the Philosophy of History*, 334.

36. Ibid., 342.

37. Raymond Aron, *Le Spectateur Engagé Entrétiens avec Jean-Louis Missika et Dominique Wolter* (Paris: Julliard, 1981), 301.

38. Ibid., 302.

39. Ibid., 244.

40. "Les Relations Familiales dans la philosophie du droit de Hegel," in *Hegel-Jahrbuch*, ed. W. R. Beyer, 1967, 63.

41. Ibid.

CHAPTER 10
Gaston Fessard's Interpretation of Israel in Human and Sacred History

1. Milan Kundera. Complete text distributed by Israel Information Office, New York.

2. Ibid.

3. "L'Antisémistian en URSS," in *Etudes*, Sept. 1960. The Bible text is from the translation of *New English Bible* (Cambridge University Press, 1972). All biblical quotations are from this edition.

4. Gaston Fessard, *De l'Actualité Historique*, Vol. I (Paris: Desclée de Brouwer, 1960), "Avant Propos," 38.

5. *La philosophie historique de Raymond Aron*, Appendix III, "Le mystère d'Israel" (Paris: Julliard, 1980), 391.

6. "Esquisse du mystère de la société et de l'histoire," in *De l'Actualité historique*, Vol. I, 132.

7. "L'antisémitisme en URSS," 18.

8. *La Violence, Recherches et Débats* (Paris: Desclée et Brouwer, 1967), 146. This is a volume of discussions centered upon a single theme. Fessard participated in discussions on "Vaincre la guerre."

9. Ibid., 147.

10. *De l'actualité historique*, 137.

11. Ibid., 140.

12. Ibid., 148-49.

13. "Judaism and the Modern Political Myths" (1944). The opening and closing paragraphs are reprinted in *Symbol, Myth, and Culture*, ed. D. P. Verene (New Haven: Yale University Press, 1979), 240-41.

14. *De l'actualité historique*, 151.

15. Ibid., 156-57.

16. *La philosophie historique de Raymond Aron*, 368n.

17. *El, ou le Dernier Livre* (Paris: Gallimard, 1973), 15.

18. *La philosophie historique*, 276-77.

19. *Poésies complètes* (Paris: Garnier Frères, 1962), 8.

20. *De l'actualité historique*, 175.

21. Ibid., 179.

22. Hermann Cohen, *Religion of Reason out of the Sources of Judaism*, trans. S. Kaplan (New York: F. Ungar Pub. Co., 1972), 439.

23. *De l'actualité historique*, 190-94.

24. *Ethik des reinen Willens* (1907) (Hildesheim: Georg Olms, 1981), 583. See also p. 629 for the notion of sexual perversity.

25. *De l'Actualité historique*, 233. Fessard, at times, spoke of a natural male-female, superman-master-slave, and historical-Jew-Pagan level of reality. These levels, however, could be comprehended within the fundamental dialectic of Jew and Pagan.

26. *La Dialectique des Exercices Spirituels de Saint Ignace de Loyola*, 3 vol. (Paris: Aubier, 1956, 1966, 1984).

27. "Le neutralisme chrétien de Karl Barth" (appendix), in *Paix ou Guerre? Notre Paix* (Paris: Monde Nouveau, 1951), 104.

28. Milan Kundera, *The Book of Laughter and Forgetting*. "Afterword: A Talk with the Author," by Philip Roth (New York: Penguin Books, 1981), 234.

CHAPTER 11
Discourses of Faith:
Gaston Fessard, Franz Rosenzweig, Hermann Cohen

1. Gaston Fessard, "Le mystére d'Israel" (1973), Appendix III, in *Le philosophie historique de Raymond Aron* (Paris: Julliard, 1980), 390-97.

2. Eugène Fleischmann, *Le Christianisme 'Mis à Nu'* (Paris: Plan, 1970), 182.

3. Ibid., 183.

4. Eric Weil, *Hegel et l'état* (Paris: Vrin, 1950), 33.

5. Franz Rosenzweig, "Hic et Ubique!" in *Kleinere Schriften* (Berlin: Schocken Verlag, 1937), 474.

6. Franz Rosenzweig, "Aller Geist war 'Volksgeist,' das Volk zum Haus des Geistes schlechtsweg, das Volk, genauer die Voelker. Nur eine Art von Geist sicherte sich negen den Voelkern noch eine Behausung, der seinem Sesen nach nun einmal nebenvoelkische Geist der Religion." Ibid., 472.

7. Rosenzweig could easily say: "Ich habe die Hegelsche Philosophie schon fuer schaedlich gehalten, als ich den Hegel enfing zu schreiben. Meine Ansicht ist kurz gesagt die, von vielen anderen ja geteilte, dass die europaeische Kultur heute zusammenstuerzen droht und dass sie nur gerettet werden kann, wenn die Hilfe kommt von den uebereuropaeischen, uebermenschlichen Maechten." Ibid.

8. Eugène Fleischmann, *Le Christianisme 'Mis à Nu*, 186.

9. See in particular Rosenzweig's earlier attitude toward Hermann Cohen in the letter to Hans ehrenburg, 9-19-1917, in Franz Rosenzweig, *Briefe* (Berlin: Schocken Verlag, 1935), 228-233. His attitude is negatively critical and, at times, borders on the impolite. His attack is leveled against Cohen's *Deutschtum und Judentum*. After Cohen's death in 1918, he discovered through a careful reading of his *Religion der Vernunft* a work which he now claimed to be superior to both Hegel and Schelling. An odd turn of events.

10. See "Vertauschte Fronten" (1929), in *Kleinere Schriften,* 356.

11. Eugène Fleischmann, *Le Christianisme 'Mis à nu,'* 196.

12. Franz Rosenzweig, "Urzelle des Stern der Erloesung," in *Kleinere Schriften,* 370. Der Imanenzgedanke-und was ist das Heidentum sonst!

13. Franz Rosenzweig, *Briefe,* 718. "Wir wollen nicht Philosophen sein, indem wir philsophieren, sondern Menschen und deshalb muessen wir unser Philosophieren in die Form unserer Menschlichkeit bringen."

14. Franz Rosenzweig, "Das Neue Denken," in *Kleinere Schriften,* 395.

15. Eugène Fleischmann, *Le Christianisme 'Mis à nu,'* 200-01.

16. Werner Marx, *The Philosophy of F. W. J. Schelling* (Bloomington, Ind.: Indiana University Press, 1984), 82.

17. Franz Rosenzweig, "Sein ewiges Leben naemlich nimmt staendig das Ende vorweg und macht es zum Anfang. In dieser Umkehrung verleugnet es die Zeit so entschieden wie nur moeglich und stellt sich aus ihr heraus." *Stern der Erloesung* (Heidelberg: Verlag Lambert Schneider, 1954), Bk. III, 205.

18. Eugène Fleischmann, *Le Christianisme 'Mis à nu,'* 203.

19. Franz Rosenzweig, "Geist und Epochen der juedischen Geschichte" (1919), in *Kleinere Schriften,* 23-24.

20. Eugène Fleischmann, *Le Christianisme 'Mis à nu,'* 209. In the *Stern* Rosenzweig remarked: "Ja der Jude ist eigentlich der einzige Mensch in der christlichen Welt, der den Krieg nicht ernst nehmen kann, und so ist er der einzige echte 'Pazifist.' " Vol. III, 90.

21. Franz Rosenzweig, *Stern der Erloesung,* III, 94-95. "Epochs are the hours of universal history, and only the state introduces them through it martial spell which makes the sun of time stand still until on any given day 'the people shall have prevailed over its enemies.' Then there is no universal history without the state. Only the state drops into the current of time those reflections of true eternity which, as epochs, form the building blocks of universal history." Trans. W. W. Hallo, *The Star of Redemption* (New York: Holt Rinehart and Winston, 1971), 334.

22. Hermann Cohen, *Religion of Reason out of the Sources of Judaism,* trans. S. Kaplan (New York: Frederick Ungar, 1972), 114.

23. Ibid., 124.

24. Ibid., 128.

25. Ibid., 135.

26. Ibid.

27. Ibid., 136.

28. Ibid.

29. Ibid., 137.

30. Ibid.

31. Ibid., 143.

32. Ibid.

CHAPTER 12
Shame, Repentance, Ressentiment:
The Foundations of Morality

1. *Religion of Reason out of the Sources of Judaism,* trans. S. Kaplan (New York: Frederick Ungar, 1972), 419

2. Ibid.

3. Ibid., 57.

4. Nguyen-Hong-Giao, *Le Verbe dans l'Histoire* (Paris: Beauchesne, 1974), 305. This book is a valuable survey of the various perspectives of Fessard's thought. Our analysis of the categorical uses of these oppositional terms follow that of Nguyen-Hong-Giao.

5. Ibid.

6. *Religion of Reason,* 203.

7. *The Guide to the Perplexed,* trans. Shlomo Pines (Chicago: University of Chicago Press, 1974), III, 56.

8. *Religion of Reason,* 249.

9. *La Méthode de Réflexion chez Maine de Biran* (Paris: Bloud et Gay, 1938), cited in *La Verbe dans l'histoire,* 71.

10. *La Dialectique des Exercises spirituels de Saint Ignace de Loyola* (Paris: Aubier, 1966), II, 128.

11. See Michel Heller, *La Machine et les rouages* (Paris: Calmann-Levy, 1985). See the review of Alain Besançson, "Lire Michel Heller," in *Commentaire,* Autumn, 1985. "Il s'agit de montrer à quelle profondeur agit le communisme dans son projet fondamental de changer l'homme."

12. *La Dialectique des Exercices spirituels,* 129.

13. *L'Action* (1893) (Paris: Presses Universitaires de France, 1950), 408. Cited from Louis Dupré, *A Dubious Heritage: Studies in the Philosophy of Religion after Kant* (New York: Paulist Press, 1977), 106.

14. "Uber Scham und Schamgefühl," in *Schriften aus dem Nachlass* (Bern: Francke Verlag, 1957), 67. This work appeared in 1913.

15. *La Dialectique des exercices,* 131.

16. *Religion of Reason,* 291.

17. "Uber Scham und Schamgefühl," 69.

18. Ibid., "einen sehr inniger zusammenhang mit dem Masse der Individualisierung lebendiger Einheiten."

19. *Religion of Reason,* 135.

20. Ibid., 136.

21. *La Dialectique des exercices,* 130.

22. "Uber Scham und Schamgefühl," 132.

23. Ibid., 101.

24. "Repentance and Rebirth," in *On the Eternal in Man* (Hamden, Conn.: Archon Books, 1972), 40.

25. *Religion of Reason,* 246.

26. Ibid., 250.

27. "Repentance and Rebirth," 41.

28. Ibid., 41-42.

29. Ibid., 42.

30. Ibid., 48.

31. "Absolutsphäre und Realsetzung der Gottesidee," in M. Scheler, *Schriften aus dem Nachlass,* I, 183. This remark was made in criticism of Hermann Cohen's *Ethik des reinen Willens.*

32. "Repentance and Rebirth," 56.

33. *Ressentiment* (New York: Free Press of Glencoe, 1961), 77-78. See the German text, "Das Ressentiment im Aufbau der Moralen," in *Vom Umsturz der Werte* (Bern: Francke-Verlag, 1955). The text dates from 1912.

34. Ibid., 76.

35. "Repentance and Rebirth," 61.

36. Ibid., 62.

37. Ibid., 65.

38. "Dialectique du Paien et du Juif," in *De L'Actualité historique* (Paris: Descleé de Brouwer, 1959), 107.

39. *Thus Spoke Zarathustra,* Second Part, trans. W. Kaufmann (New York: Viking, 1968), 212.

William Kluback

Paul Valéry
Philosophical Reflections

American University Studies: Series V (Philosophy). Vol. 22
ISBN 0-8204-0386-5   177 pages   hardback US $ 30.50*

*Recommended price – alterations reserved

Where the philosopher has feared to tread, in a realm that has been declared not only non-philosophical, but anti-philosophical, this study attempts quietly to illuminate Paul Valéry's reflections on literature, painting, sculpture and poetry. Professor Kluback ventures into this world of aesthetic insights which has often seemed reserved only for the artist, and off limits to the philosopher, whose explorations tend increasingly to be confined to the technicalities of logic and dialectic.

Contents: Philosopher meets poet – The creative force of chance – The beauty of our mortality.

PETER LANG PUBLISHING, INC.
62 West 45th Street
USA — New York, NY 10036

Francis Schwanauer

PHILOSOPHICAL FACT AND PARADOX

American University Studies: Series V (Philosophy). Vol. 32
ISBN 0-8204-0429-2   274 pages   hardback US $ 37.50*

*Recommended price – alterations reserved

Philosophical Fact and Paradox represents an attempt to show that reality is not disclosed by way of talking about facts but rather by allowing facts to do the talking. This correlates the rules of syntax (and logic) with the law of causality and turns decision procedures into an aesthetical mathematics of change.

Contents: Based on the premise that the law of causality is a fact(-ory) of facts which represent units of pleasure or pain in terms of knowledge or consciousness.

PETER LANG PUBLISHING, INC.
62 West 45th Street
USA – New York, NY 10036